GRAPHIS DESIGN ANNUAL. 87/88

GRAPHIS DESIGN ANNUAL 87/88

THE INTERNATIONAL ANNUAL ON DESIGN AND ILLUSTRATION

DAS INTERNATIONALE JAHRBUCH ÜBER DESIGN UND ILLUSTRATION

LE RÉPERTOIRE INTERNATIONAL DE DESIGN ET ILLUSTRATION

EDITED BY/HERAUSGEGEBEN VON/RÉALISÉ PAR

B. MARTIN PEDERSEN

EDITOR AND ART DIRECTOR: B. MARTIN PEDERSEN

ASSISTANT EDITORS: HEINKE JENSSEN, JOAN LÜSSI

PROJECT MANAGER: ROMY HERZOG

DESIGNERS: MARINO BIANCHERA, MARTIN BYLAND

PHOTOGRAPHERS: ULRICH KEMMNER, WALTER ZUBER

GRAPHIS PRESS CORP., ZURICH (SWITZERLAND)

GRAPHIS U.S. INC., NEW YORK, N.Y. (USA)

GRAPHIS PUBLICATIONS

GRAPHIS, International bi-monthly journal of graphic art and photography
GRAPHIS DESIGN ANNUAL, The international annual on design and illustration
PHOTOGRAPHIS, The international annual on photography
GRAPHIS POSTERS, The international annual of poster art
GRAPHIS PACKAGING VOL. 4, An international survey of packaging design
GRAPHIS DIAGRAMS VOL. 2, The graphic visualization of abstract, technical and statistical facts and functions
GRAPHIS COVERS, An anthology of all GRAPHIS covers with artists' short biographies and indexes of all GRAPHIS issues
GRAPHIS ANNUAL REPORTS, An international compilation of the best designed annual reports
ARCHIGRAPHIA, Architectural and environmental graphics
FILM + TV GRAPHICS 2, An international survey of the art of film animation

GRAPHIS-PUBLIKATIONEN

GRAPHIS, Die internationale Zweimonatszeitschrift für Graphik und Photographie
GRAPHIS DESIGN ANNUAL, Das internationale Jahrbuch über Design und Illustration
PHOTOGRAPHIS, Das internationale Jahrbuch der Photographie
GRAPHIS POSTERS, Das internationale Jahrbuch der Plakatkunst
GRAPHIS PACKUNGEN BAND 4, Internationaler Überblick der Packungsgestaltung
GRAPHIS DIAGRAMS BAND 2, Die graphische Darstellung abstrakter, technischer und statistischer Daten und Fakten
GRAPHIS COVERS, Eine Sammlung aller GRAPHIS-Umschläge mit Informationen über die Künstler und
    Inhaltsübersichten aller Ausgaben der Zeitschrift GRAPHIS
GRAPHIS ANNUAL REPORTS, Ein internationaler Überblick der Gestaltung von Jahresberichten
ARCHIGRAPHIA, Architektur- und Umweltgraphik
FILM + TV GRAPHICS 2, Ein internationaler Überblick über die Kunst des Animationsfilms

PUBLICATIONS GRAPHIS

GRAPHIS, La revue bimestrielle internationale d'arts graphiques et de la photographie
GRAPHIS ANNUAL, Le répertoire international de la communication visuelle
PHOTOGRAPHIS, Le répertoire international de la photographie
GRAPHIS POSTERS, Le répertoire international de l'art de l'affiche
GRAPHIS EMBALLAGES VOL. 4, Répertoire international des formes de l'emballage
GRAPHIS DIAGRAMS VOL. 2, La représentation graphique de faits et donnés abstraits, techniques et statistiques
GRAPHIS COVERS, Recueil de toutes les couvertures de GRAPHIS avec des notices biographiques des artistes
    et le sommaire de tous les numéros du magazine GRAPHIS.
GRAPHIS ANNUAL REPORTS, Panorama international du design de rapports annuels d'entreprises
ARCHIGRAPHIA, La création graphique appliquée à l'architecture et à l'environnement
FILM + TV GRAPHICS 2, Un panorama international de l'art du film d'animation

PUBLICATION No. 186 (ISBN 3-85709-187-8)
© Copyright under Universal Copyright Convention
Copyright 1987 by Graphis Press Corp., 107 Dufourstrasse, 8008 Zurich, Switzerland/
Graphis U.S. Inc., 141 Lexington Avenue, New York, N.Y. 10016, USA
No part of this book may be reproduced in any form without written permission of the publisher
Printed in Japan by Dai Nippon
Typeset in Switzerland by Setzerei Heller, Zurich
Typefaces: Garamond ITC Light Condensed, Futura Extra Bold

ABBREVIATIONS

Australia .... AUS

Austria .... AUT

Belgium .... BEL

Brazil .... BRA

Canada .... CAN

Denmark .... DEN

Finland .... FIN

France .... FRA

Germany (West) .... GER

Great Britain .... GBR

Hungary .... HUN

Iran .... IRN

Ireland .... IRL

Italy .... ITA

Japan .... JPN

Netherlands .... NLD

Spain .... SPA

Sweden .... SWE

Switzerland .... SWI

USA .... USA

ABKÜRZUNGEN

Australien .... AUS

Belgien .... BEL

Brasilien .... BRA

Dänemark .... DEN

Deutschland (BRD) .... GER

Finnland .... FIN

Frankreich .... FRA

Grossbritannien .... GBR

Iran .... IRN

Irland .... IRL

Italien .... ITA

Japan .... JPN

Kanada .... CAN

Niederlande .... NLD

Österreich .... AUT

Schweden .... SWE

Schweiz .... SWI

Spanien .... SPA

Ungarn .... HUN

USA .... USA

ABRÉVIATIONS

Allemagne occidentale .... GER

Australie .... AUS

Autriche .... AUT

Belgique .... BEL

Brésil .... BRA

Canada .... CAN

Danemark .... DEN

Espagne .... SPA

Etats-Unis .... USA

Finlande .... FIN

France .... FRA

Grande-Bretagne .... GBR

Hongrie .... HUN

Iran .... IRN

Irlande .... IRL

Italie .... ITA

Japon .... JPN

Pays-Bas .... NLD

Suède .... SWE

Suisse .... SWI

REMARKS

■ Our sincere thanks are extended to all contributors throughout the world who have made it possible for us to publish a broad international spectrum of outstanding work.

■ Entry instructions may be requested at: Graphis Press Corp., Dufourstrasse 107, 8008 Zurich, Switzerland

ANMERKUNGEN

■ Unser herzlicher Dank gilt Einsendern aus aller Welt, die es uns möglich gemacht haben, ein breites, internationales Spektrum der besten Arbeiten zu veröffentlichen.

■ Teilnahmebedingungen: Graphis Verlag AG, Dufourstrasse 107, 8008 Zurich, Schweiz

AVERTISSEMENT

■ Nos sincères remerciements vont à tous les collaborateurs du monde entier, qui nous ont permis de publier un vaste panorama international des meilleurs travaux.

■ Demande de participation: Editions Graphis SA, Dufourstrasse 107, 8008 Zurich, Suisse

Who does what? Where and how? How much and why? Better or worse? Are we going uphill or downhill? These are the kind of thoughts that ran through my head when Marty asked me to write this introduction.

You ask yourself these questions, and many more every day, before, during and after the job. The curse of the designer is: you feel as good (or as bad) as the last project or meeting. And why? Simply because you hope that with each new problem you'll come up with the ideal solution! That is, after all, our duty: to solve the problem optimally and to present it aesthetically perfect. But then come the demands; the various stages, the étapes - just like in a Tour de France. Concepts and thoughts should correspond, harmonize, the text should be short and snappy - and yet casual! Visually everything must be in unison, new and attractive, and don't forget some sprinkling of pepper. Then come the client's wishes which are sometimes in opposition to the designer's aspirations: you must be able to come to an agreement too, see that you are both pushing in the same direction. Now and again you get a client who'd be prepared personally to risk a thing or two and attempt something new, but his/her firm is so conservative that the solution would be regarded as counter-productive - or questionable to say the least.

What to do? Where is the middle of the road: that fine line between all these justifiable requirements? To find the optimal solution amidst all these stipulations is the challenge of the designer. And - paradoxically as it may sound to the uninitiated - there lies the joy of our work! To search, to experiment, to weigh, to reject, and, if necessary, to start again from scratch and to know before you are finished: it'll be OK - it'll be good - becauce all these aspects have been checked, watched, considered, and the solution has really been figured out! Then the finale: the finished product . . . Great! And then comes that brooding thought - next time it's got to be better. Those three aesthetic mistakes surely should have been spotted! You're a bit disappointed . . . but not exactly discontent . . . and from time to time you even know: it's super, it's a hit!

That's what this yearbook is all about - about the hits of 1986!

How did these hits materialize? Who's behind them, and, above all, what's new this year? And now we are getting to the heart of the matter. Graphic design has always been a mirror of our times - a freeze-frame of our attitudes. Already we've reached an aspect that is not particularly positive: today in general, everything looks the same - worldwide. The great mass of design work is not so great . . ., and the top performances of Australia resemble those from Europe, USA or Hongkong. Admittedly, they're all first-class solutions, but is that enough? One thing is sure though - if they've been honestly worked out, they do have a certain character and will therefore survive - meaning they'll still be considered brilliant a few years hence. If the designer succumbs to the trend of the moment (as only too many do, because it's obviously easier), then tomorrow nobody's going to be interested in his designs. By the way - just a personal remark here: What I again like so much about Europe (after nine years back here) is the fact that far less heed is paid to trends here! Let's be grateful too that they bring less influence to bear. You're less apt to do trendy design than translating a clear idea into a message which hopefully still incorporates some aspect of century old culture in an avant-garde way.

That's why we do go and look at medieval cities in Italy! That's why we take old masters as examples that make ourselves feel so inadequate... The old masters had a different conception of quality - and naturally, of time. We all sense this when we look at such a masterpiece: the longer you look, the closer you observe, detail after detail - the richer, the deeper, the more substantial becomes the work. No matter whether it be a picture, a façade or a simple tool. To search and produce today quality is the challenge of present-day designers - in spite of lack of time or financial restrictions.

These kinds of masterpieces are what this book is all about - the 1987/88 yearbook of top solutions.

What are the prerequisites for visual communications that hit the bull's eye and generate

YOU CAN AFTER COMPLETITION OF
A JOB, READ THE CLIENT'S STANDPOINT
·IN THE RESULT
OF THE GRAPHIC WORK.

excitement, that make it in this annual? On the part of the designer it is certainly a pinch of talent next to intelligence and tolerance. On the part of the client it is trust, intelligence and tolerance. The most important of all though is that there is mutual respect. And there lies the key to the secret. Only if you trust and understand each other, can you be frank enough and come to the core of the problem. That is a further fascination of our scope of work. And, you can after the completion of a job, read the client's standpoint in the result of the graphic work. For example – *Esprit* – the corporate image, the products, the designs, and the management must logically be a perfect whole, homogeneous! Why? Because obviously everybody at *Esprit* must get a great

kick out of his/her work – and for that reason is this company (and a few others) in every respect successful. Total communication – a sign of today! Perhaps today the Best of the Best for some, and a beginning (since the sky's the limit) for others... The current possibilities are enormous. Obviously you need vision, strength and staying power, a readiness to face risk, and the conviction that you can also do it differently. There is a great difference between imitating and keeping in trend – to finding new solutions. To feel the *Zeitgeist* in order to translate it verbally and visually, to the astonishment and to the pleasure of the general public. Being sensitive to feeling, to their concerns, and incorporate all this into a design solution, that's what

makes life more interesting and hopefully richer. *It is exactly this difference that this yearbook is all about!*

Now I have had my say! Please leaf through and enjoy...

Fritz Gottschalk is graphic designer, art director and design consultant. He heads Gottschalk+Ash Int'l Design Consultants in Zürich. As well as in Zürich, this company has branches in Montréal, Toronto and Milan. The scope of Gottschalk+Ash Int'l encompasses all fields of graphic art, including architecture and signage, the design of annual reports, exhibition design and corporate identity programs.
Fritz Gottschalk was born in Zürich in 1937 and studied in Zürich and Basle. In 1963 he went to Montréal to Paul Arthur & Associates. Here he was primarily engaged in the preparations for Expo '67.
In 1966 he founded, together with Stuart Ash, the company Gottschalk+Ash Int'l, in Montréal. He returned to Switzerland in 1978 and since then has headed the Zürich branch supported by 5 employees. Fritz Gottschalk has dual nationality – Swiss and Canadian.

Wer, was? Wo, wie? Wieviel, warum? Besser oder schlechter? Geht's bergab oder geht's bergauf? – Das sind alles so Gedanken, die mir durch den Kopf gingen, als mich Marty bat, dieses Vorwort zu schreiben.

Diese Fragen und viele mehr beschäftigen einen ja jeden Tag, vor, während und nach der Arbeit. Das Los des Gestalters ist: man fühlt sich so gut (oder schlecht) wie die letzte Arbeit oder Sitzung. Und warum eigentlich? Ganz einfach, weil man bei jedem neuen Problem hofft, die Ideal-Lösung ästhetisch perfekt zu präsentieren! Da kommen dann die Bedingungen, verschiedene Etappen, wie bei einer Tour de France. Das Konzept, der Gedanke müssen stimmen, das Verbale sollte spezifisch, knapp und doch locker sein, optisch muss alles aus einem Guss, neu und attraktiv sein, der Pfeffer darf nicht fehlen, dann kommen die Kundenwünsche vs die Aspirationen des Gestalters! Verstehen muss man sich auch noch! Und am gleichen Strick ziehen! Hie und da hat man einen Kunden, der gewillt wäre, persönlich etwas zu riskieren und etwas Neues zu wagen, aber – seine Firma ist so konservativ, dass die Lösung ganz bestimmt als kontraproduktiv oder fragwürdig angesehen würde. Was tun? Wo ist der Mittelweg, diese feine Linie zwischen all diesen mit Recht gestellten Bedingungen? Unter all diesen Stipulationen die optimale Lösung zu finden, das ist die Herausforderung an den Gestalter, und so paradox es für den nicht Eingeweihten tönen mag, das

ist die Freude unserer Arbeit. Zu suchen, zu probieren, abzuwägen, zu verwerfen, wenn nötig neu zu beginnen und vor der Fertigstellung zu wissen: es wird gut – es wird gut, weil all diese Aspekte gecheckt und beachtet wurden und die Lösung erarbeitet worden ist. Dann das Finale: das fertige Produkt! Toll! Und schon kommt der Gedanke – das nächste Mal muss es besser werden. Drei kleine ästhetische Fehler hätte man sehen müssen! Man ist etwas enttäuscht... aber nicht gerade unzufrieden... und hie und da weiss man sogar: das ist aber super, ein Hit! *Darum geht es eigentlich in diesem Jahrbuch, um die Hits des Jahres 1986!*

Wie entstehen diese Hits? Wer steckt dahinter und vor allem was ist dieses Jahr neu? Und jetzt kommen wir zu des Pudels Kern. Die Grafik war immer ein Spiegel unserer Zeit, ein Freeze-Frame unserer geistigen Haltung. Schon sind wir bei einem Aspekt, der nicht besonders positiv ist: generell sieht heute alles etwa gleich aus – weltweit. Die Masse der gestalterischen Arbeit ist schlecht, und die Top-Leistungen aus Australien gleichen denen aus Europa, USA oder Hongkong. Zugegeben, es sind alles erstklassige Lösungen, aber genügt das? Eines ist sicher, wenn sie ehrlich erarbeitet werden, haben sie einen gewissen Charakter und werden demzufolge «überstehen», also auch noch in einigen Jahren gut dastehen! Sollte der Designer (wie nur allzuviele, weil es natürlich viel leichter ist) dem momentanen Trend verfallen sein, so wird

die Sache morgen schon niemanden mehr interessieren. Übrigens, noch eine persönliche Anmerkung, wenn Sie gestatten: was mir nach 9 Jahren in Europa wieder so gut gefällt, ist die Tatsache, dass Trends hier viel schwächer beachtet werden. Auch Gott sei Dank viel weniger Einfluss haben. Man ist weniger darauf bedacht, etwas im Trend zu machen, als eine Idee klar umzusetzen, zu erarbeiten.

Warum schauen wir uns mittelalterliche Städte an in Italien? Nehmen die alten Meister als Vorbilder und fühlen uns so klein? Weil diese Leute eine andere Vorstellung hatten von Qualität und natürlich auch Zeit. Das alles spürt man doch beim Betrachten eines solchen Gegenstandes: je länger man hinsieht und Detail für Detail anschaut, desto reicher, richtiger, substantieller wird die Sache, gleich ob es sich um ein Bild, eine Fassade oder um einen Gebrauchsgegenstand handelt. Diese Qualität trotz Zeit- und Gelddruck herauszuarbeiten, ist die Herausforderung an den heutigen Gestalter. *Um diese Arbeiten geht es eigentlich in diesem Buch, dem Jahrbuch der zeitgemässen Lösungen des Jahres 1986.*

Was ist die Voraussetzung für visuelle Kommunikation, die ins Schwarze trifft und Lösungen hervorbringt, die es ins Jahrbuch schaffen? Seitens des Gestalters sicher eine Prise Talent, nebst Intelligenz und Toleranz. Seitens des Kunden Vertrauen, Intelligenz und Toleranz. Das allerwichtigste aber ist, dass man sich gegensei-

TROTZ ZEIT- UND GELDDRUCK QUALITÄT HERAUSZUARBEITEN, IST DIE HERAUSFORDERUNG AN DEN HEUTIGEN GESTALTER.

tig mag. Dort liegt der Schlüssel zum Geheimnis. Nur wenn man sich als Mensch versteht, kann man offen sein und im Klartext miteinander über Probleme so sprechen, dass die Möglichkeit entsteht, etwas Spezielles zu entwickeln. Das ist eine weitere Faszination unseres Arbeitsgebietes: man kann selbst nach getaner Arbeit die Haltung eines Kunden am Resultat der graphischen Arbeit ablesen. Beispiel *Esprit*: die Produkte, das Erscheinungsbild, die Designs und das Management müssen logischerweise aus einem Guss sein, Freude an der Arbeit ausdrücken, und nur darum kommt diese Firma (und einige andere) in jeder Beziehung so zum Tragen. Totale Kommunikation – spezifisch für

die heutige Zeit! Vielleicht heute das Beste vom Besten für die einen und ein Anfang (as the sky is the limit) für die andern ... Die heutigen Möglichkeiten sind enorm. Selbstverständlich braucht es Visionen. Kraft und Durchhaltevermögen, Risikofreude und die Überzeugung, dass man es auch anders machen kann. Es ist ein grosser Unterschied zwischen: nachmachen oder im Trend liegen und neue Lösungen finden, den Zeitgeist spüren, um denselben verbal und optisch umzusetzen; zum Erstaunen und zur Freude des Publikums. Ganz fein im Hintergrund die Menschen spüren, ihren Concern fühlen, das macht das Leben interessant und etwas reicher.

Genau um das geht es in diesem Jahrbuch.

Jetzt habe ich lange genug gesprochen. Blättern Sie bitte um, und freuen Sie sich am Dargebotenen.

FRITZ GOTTSCHALK ist Graphik Designer, Art Director und Berater. Er leitet Gottschalk+Ash Int'l, Design Consultants, in Zürich. Diese Firma hat ausser in Zürich Niederlassungen in Montréal, Toronto und Mailand. Alle Bereiche der Gebrauchsgraphik, einschliesslich Architektur- und Signalisierungsgraphik, die Gestaltung von Jahresberichten, Ausstellungs-Design und Firmenerscheinungsbilder gehören zum Arbeitsbereich von Gottschalk+Ash Int'l.
Fritz Gottschalk, 1937 in Zürich geboren, erhielt seine Ausbildung in Zürich und Basel. 1963 ging er nach Montréal zu Paul Arthur & Associates. Hier war er unter anderem wesentlich an der Vorbereitung der Expo 1967 (in Montréal) beteiligt. 1966 gründete er zusammen mit Stuart Ash die Firma Gottschalk+Ash Int'l in Montréal. 1978 kehrte er in die Schweiz zurück und leitet seitdem die Zürcher Niederlassung, die er mit 5 Mitarbeitern betreut. Fritz Gottschalk ist Bürger der Schweiz und Kanadas.

Qui quoi? Où comment? Combient pourquoi? Meilleur ou moins bon? En progression ou sur le déclin? ----- Toutes ces pensées se sont bousculées dans ma tête lorsque Marty m'a prié d'écrire cette préface.

C'est que ces pensées, et bien d'autres, nous préoccupent jour par jour, avant, pendant, après le travail. C'est bien là le sort du designer: on se sent aussi bien (ou mal) que le dernier travail qu'on a réalisé, la dernière séance à laquelle on a participé. Pourquoi, en somme? Tout simplement parce qu'à chaque nouveau problème, on espère trouver la solution idéale! C'est bien cela, notre tâche: donner une solution optimale au problème et présenter cette solution de manière esthétiquement parfaite! Interviennent des conditions de réalisation, diverses étapes, comme au Tour de France. Le concept, l'idée doivent sonner juste, le verbal doit être spécifique, concis mais léger, au plan visuel tout doit donner l'impression d'être d'un seul jet, nouveau et attrayant, il ne faut pas ménager le poivre et l'origan; ajoutez à cela les désiderata du client qui viennent buter contre les aspirations du designer! C'est qu'il faut aussi essayer de s'entendre! De tirer à la même corde! De temps à autre, on a affaire à un client tenté de prendre un risque personnel et d'essayer quelque chose de radicalement nouveau, mais - son entreprise s'avère tellement conservatrice que la solution retenue serait assurément jugée contre-productive ou douteuse. Que faire? Où est le chemin du juste milieu, cette voie étroite à équidistance de toutes

ces exigences parfaitement raisonnables? Découvrir dans ce fouillis de stipulations la solution optimale, c'est bien le défi que le designer se doit de relever, et c'est aussi - pour paradoxal que cela puisse être - la raison du plaisir que nous procure notre travail. Chercher, expérimenter, peser le pour et le contre, rejeter ce qui ne convient pas, recommencer à zéro si nécessaire, puis, sur le point d'achever le travail, pressentir la réussite parce que tous ces aspects ont été envisagés, considérés, et que la solution en tient compte. Et enfin la finale: le produit achevé! Formidable! Et déjà surgit la pensée: la prochaine fois, il faudra faire mieux. Il aurait fallu voir à temps ces trois petits défauts esthétiques! On est un peu déçu... mais pas vraiment mécontent... et de temps à autre on a même l'impression d'avoir réalisé quelque chose de sensationnel, quelque chose qui va faire tilt!
Et c'est bien de quoi il s'agit dans cet annuel, des succès de l'année 1986!

Comment les a-t-on réalisés? Qui est-ce qui en est responsable, et surtout: qu'y a-t-il de nouveau cette année? C'est bien là le hic. L'art publicitaire a toujours constitué le miroir de l'époque, un instantané de nos attitudes mentales. Ce qui nous amène à un aspect qui n'est guère encourageant: en règle générale, toutes les productions publicitaires se ressemblent, et cela à l'échelle mondiale. La grande masse des travaux de design est carrément mauvaise, et les réalisations hors pair qui nous viennent d'Australie

ressemblent à celles qui proviennent d'Europe, des Etats-Unis ou de Hong Kong. Il est vrai qu'il s'agit de travaux tout à fait exceptionnels, mais est-ce que ça suffit? Une chose est sûre: dans la mesure où ils sont l'aboutissement d'une recherche intègre, ils ne manquent pas d'avoir du caractère, ce qui leur permettra de perdurer par-delà la période d'impact habituelle! Mais si le designer (ce qui est trop souvent le cas, parce que c'est bien plus facile) se laisse piéger par un trend passager, son œuvre ne tardera pas à sombrer dans l'oubli. Permettez-moi une référence personnelle à ce propos: ce qui me plaît tant en Europe après neuf années depuis mon retour, c'est qu'on y attache bien moins d'importance aux trends du moment. Et que ceux-ci exercent bien moins d'influence qu'ailleurs. On ne s'applique pas tant à s'escrimer dans une veine postmoderniste qu'à transposer, à traiter une idée donnée avec la plus grande clarté possible. Pourquoi allons-nous voir des villes moyenâgeuses en Italie? Pourquoi choisissons-nous les vieux maîtres pour modèles, pourquoi nous sentons-nous si petits? Parce que ces gens-là avaient une autre idée de la qualité et bien entendu aussi une autre idée du temps. Tout cela, ça se sent dès qu'on se plonge dans la contemplation d'un tel objet: au fur et à mesure que les détails se révèlent, l'objet gagne en richesse, en vérité, en substance - qu'il s'agisse d'une toile, d'une façade, d'un objet usuel. Retrouver cette qualité, c'est un défi que les designers d'aujourd'hui ont tout intérêt à relever malgré la pression intempestive des

des soucis de délais et d'argent.

C'est de travaux de ce genre qu'il est au fond question dans le présent ouvrage, l'annuel des solutions d'actualité qui ont vu le jour en 1986!

Qu'est-ce qui fait donc qu'une communication visuelle mette en plein dans le mille et aboutisse à des solutions qui lui ouvrent les pages de cet annuel? Il y faut de la part du designer très certainement une bonne dose de talent, avec en plus de l'intelligence et de la tolérance. De la part du client, de la confiance, de l'intelligence, de la tolérance. L'essentiel, pourtant, c'est qu'on ait des atomes crochus, car c'est là que gît la clef du mystère. C'est seulement en se comprenant d'homme à homme qu'on peut collaborer en toute franchise et discuter sans détours des problèmes à résoudre pour aboutir à une réalisation spécifique. C'est là une autre fascination liée à notre domaine d'activité: une fois le travail achevé, on peut encore juger de l'attitude du client au vu du résultat graphique. Prenez l'exemple d'*Esprit*: les produits, l'image publique, les réalisations conceptuelles et les dirigeants de cette entreprise doivent nécessairement être d'un seul tenant, respirer le plaisir du travail bien fait – comment expliquer autrement qu'elle s'impose avec une telle aisance, ce qui vaut aussi pour quelques-unes de ses consoeurs? Un bel exemple de communication totale, une marque spécifique de notre temps! Peut-être aujourd'hui, pour certains, le nec plus ultra, pour d'autres, un début prometteur au sens de la formule anglaise «the sky is the limit»... Les potentialités créatrices sont inouïes de nos jours. Il y faut évidemment une vision. De la force, de la persévérance, le goût du risque et l'intime conviction qu'on peut aussi tenter autre chose. Il y a un abîme entre la simple imitation, la fidélité aux trends passagers, et la mise au point de solutions nouvelles qui s'orientent sur l'esprit du temps, le transposent verbalement et visuellement, pour les délices et le ravissement du public. Affiner sa perception de la motivation intime des êtres humains, de leur sensibilité profonde, voilà ce qui rend la vie intéressante, voilà ce qui l'enrichit quelque peu.

Et c'est bien de quoi il retourne dans cet annuel.

J'ai assez parlé. A vous d'en commencer la lecture. Je vous souhaite beaucoup de plaisir lors de ce parcours inédit!

FRITZ GOTTSCHALK réunit les compétences de designer graphique, de directeur artistique et de conseiller d'entreprises. Il dirige à Zurich la société Gottschalk+Ash Int'l, Design Consultants, qui entretient des succursales à Montréal, Toronto et Milan. Le domaine entier de l'art graphique appliqué, y compris l'architecture et la signalisation, la conception de rapports annuels, le design d'expositions et les images globales de marque, fait partie des activités de Gottschalk+Ash Int'l. Fritz Gottschalk, né à Zurich en 1937, a fait ses écoles à Zurich et à Bâle. En 1963, il rejoint à Montréal l'équipe de Paul Arthur & Associates, où il exerce notamment des responsabilités importantes lors de la préparation de l'Expo 67 à Montréal. En 1966, il fonde avec Stuart Ash la société Gottschalk+Ash Int'l à Montréal. Retourné en Suisse en 1978, il dirige désormais la succursale zurichoise de l'entreprise, aidé de 5 collaborateurs. Fritz Gottschalk a la double citoyenneté de Suisse et du Canada.

BROCHURES

Booklets

Catalogs

Invitations

Announcements

Promotion folders

BROSCHÜREN

Prospekte

Kataloge

Einladungen

Bekanntmachungen

Werbemappen

BROCHURES

Prospectus

Catalogues divers

Invitations

Avis divers

Dossiers publicitaires

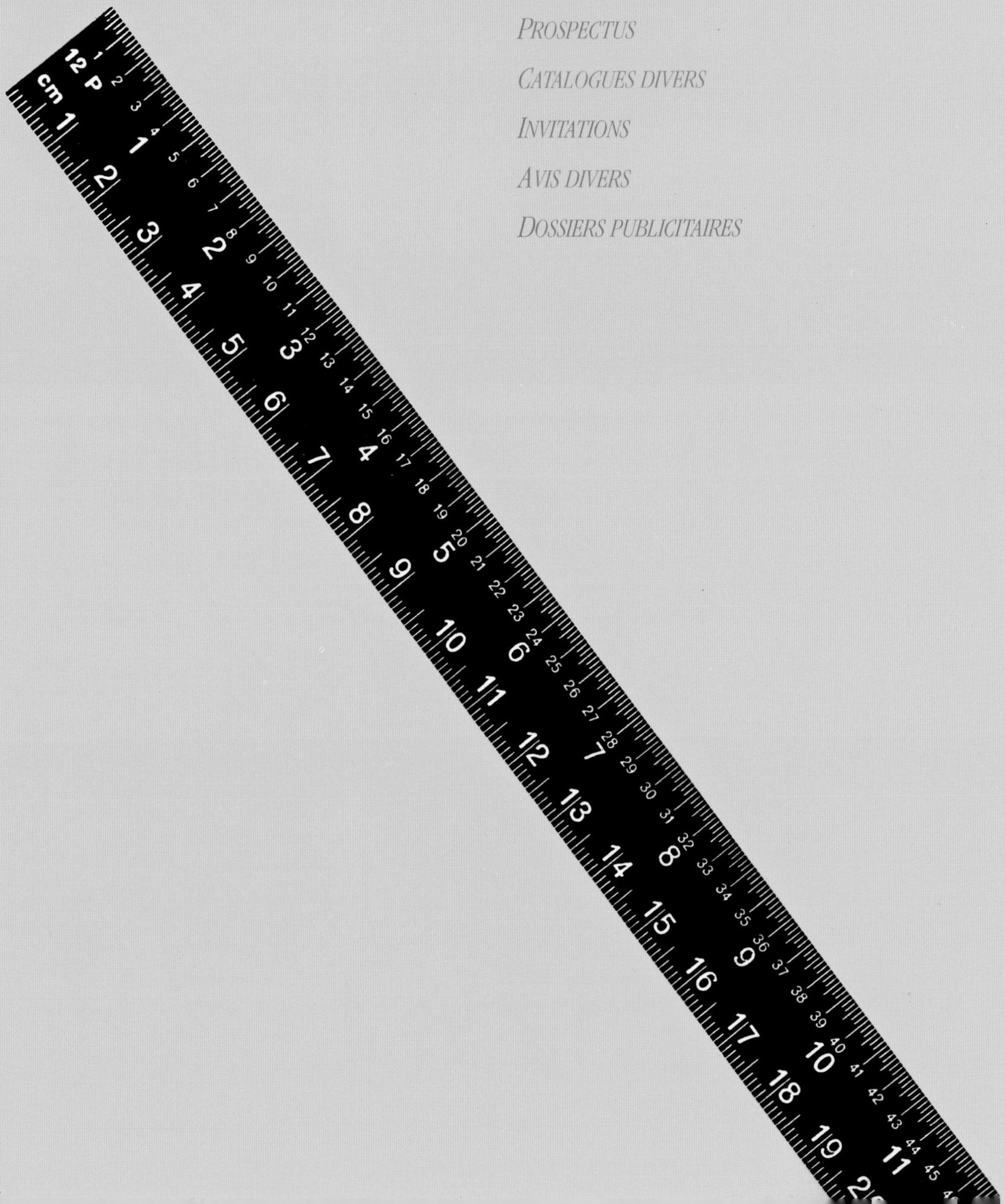

ART DIRECTOR:
James A. Sebastian

DESIGNER:
James Sebastian/Rose Biondi

PHOTOGRAPHER:
Bruce Wolf

AGENCY:
Designframe Inc.

CLIENT:
Martex/West Point Pepperell

■ 1–7

NIGHT CROCODILE · ATELIER MARTEX · PERRY ELLIS

■ **1–7** Front cover and sample spreads showing bed linen (and a list of contents) from the Spring 1987 catalog for *Martex/West Point Pepperell*. (USA)

■ **1–7** Vordere Umschlagseite und Beispiele der Doppelseiten mit Bettwäsche (und dem Inhaltsverzeichnis) aus dem *Martex*-Frühjahrskatalog von *West Point Pepperell*. (USA)

■ **1–7** Ire de couverture et doubles pages types du catalogue de printemps 1987 réalisé pour *Martex/West Point Pepperell*: présentation de linge de maison; sommaire. (USA)

SURFACES

ART DIRECTOR:
Cheryl Heller
DESIGNER:
Cheryl Heller
AGENCY:
HBM/Creamer Design Group
CLIENT:
S.D. Warren Co.
■ 8

ART DIRECTOR:
Michael Vanderbyl
DESIGNER:
Michael Vanderbyl
PHOTOGRAPHER:
Roger Lee
AGENCY:
Vanderbyl Design
CLIENT:
Simpson Paper Company
■ 9–13

■ **8** Cover (with embossed pool balls and die-cut rectangle for the title of "Surfaces") of a promotion brochure for *S.D. Warren* to introduce three paper qualities. (USA)

■ **9–13** Three brochure covers (middle row) and two concertina folders (top belongs to brochure far right and bottom to brochure second from left) for the Simpson Paper Co. The theme throughout is "Quality". (USA)

■ **8** Umschlag (mit geprägten Billardkugeln und ausgeschnittenem Rechteck für den Titel »Oberflächen«) einer Broschüre von *S.D. Warren* für die Einführung von drei Papierqualitäten. (USA)

■ **9–13** Drei Umschläge (rechts, mittlere Reihe) und zwei der darin enthaltenen Leporello-Prospekte für *Simpson*-Papiere. Neben dem gemeinsamen Thema »Qualität« werden Attribute wie Präzision und Vielseitigkeit visualisiert. (USA)

■ **8** Couverture (ornée de boules de billard gaufrées et d'un rectangle en découpe pour le titre »Surfaces«) d'une brochure publicitaire pour trois qualités de papier *S.D. Warren*. (USA)

■ **9–13** Trois couvertures de brochures (au centre) et deux dépliants en accordéon (celui d'en haut fait partie de la brochure tout à droite, celui d'en bas de la 2e depuis la gauche) pour la Simpson Paper Co., sur le thème central de »Qualité«. (USA)

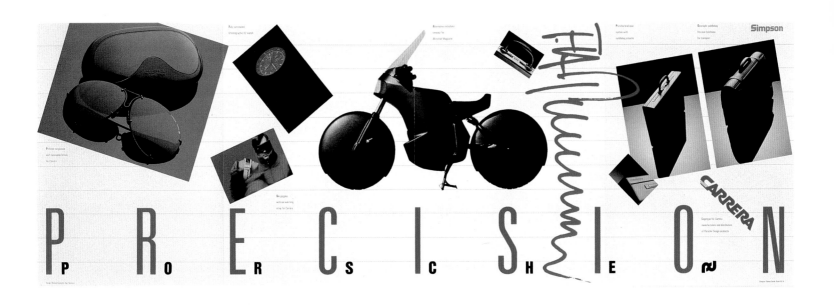

P R E C I S I O N

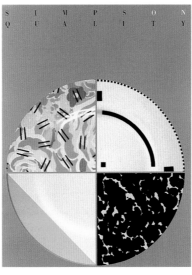

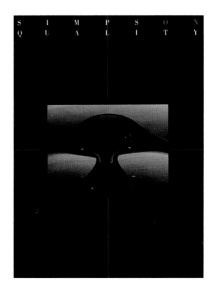

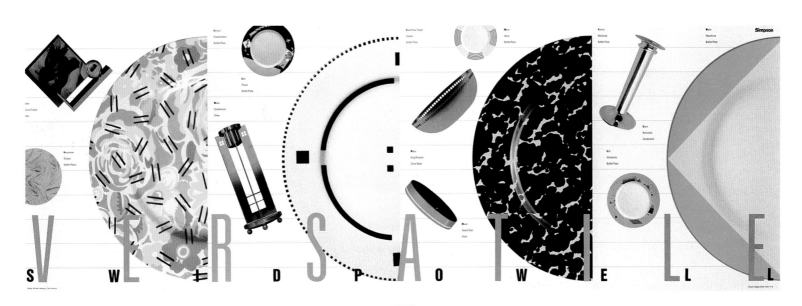

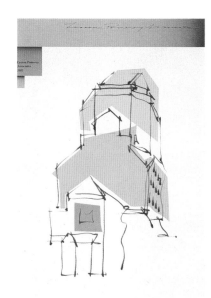

ART DIRECOTOR:
Michael Manwaring
DESIGNER:
Michael Manwaring
AGENCY:
*The Office of
Michael Manwaring*
CLIENT:
Leason Pomeroy Associaties
■ 15-19

S   K   E   T   C   H   E   S

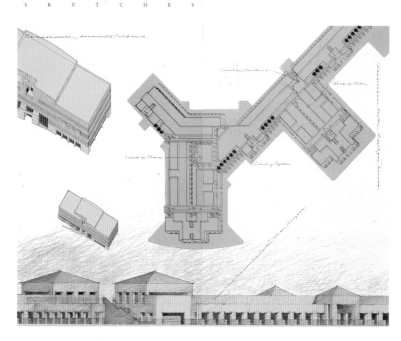

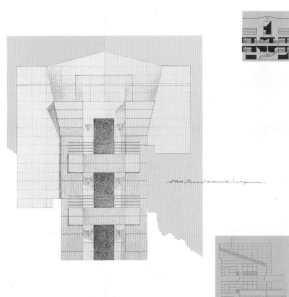

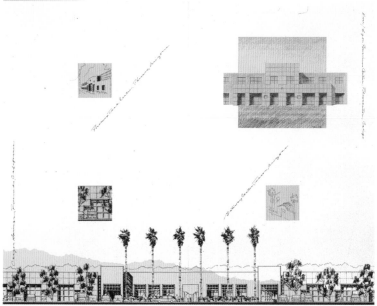

In twenty years, Leason Pomeroy Associates has won over 80 design awards. Not by following architectural fashions or adhering to staid, design formulas. Instead, LPA's awards came through dedication to master plans and building designs that are tailored to individual clients. ● The result of such dedication has been creations that work, inspire and fulfill the needs of each client. In that way, LPA has earned a national reputation for projects and designs that are lasting. ● Founded in 1965 in Orange County, California, LPA now has regional offices in Los Angeles and the San Francisco Bay area. Continually broadening its range of capabilities, planning and interior design specialists now compliment the LPA architectural staff. Twenty-plus years of executing diverse projects have given the firm the experience and insight needed to serve a variety of clients. ● Today, LPA's large and talented staff—assisted by the latest in computer-aided design technology— serves clients ranging from large corporations and development companies to private individuals. Its on-going projects are located throughout the United States—a testament to LPA's ability to perform in a variety of geographic locations. ● To each client, LPA offers a personal and professional design approach. Each project is carried out with strict attention to construction budgets and time schedules. At the same time, LPA maintains the highest standards in solving each architectural challenge. ● Creative architectural solutions are timeless. At Leason Pomeroy Associates, that is one concept that is never out of fashion.

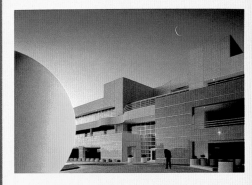

Architecture is the business of designing buildings, open spaces and communities in a way that maximizes their beauty and usefulness. A good architectural business is one that provides personalized service for its individual clients, resulting in projects that last. ● Experienced in the design and management of major commercial projects, municipal offices, data centers, research/manufacturing facilities, residential and specialty retail projects nationwide, LPA provides a full range of architectural services. From early program development to final design documents, including bid processing and site selection, LPA has full-service capabilities. ● The firm's services have been expanded with the addition of the latest in computer-assisted design technology. The Intergraph® Computer-Aided Design & Drafting system (CADD) has increased the quality, precision, and cost-effectiveness of the design process. Utilized as a design tool, the computer facilitates client visualization at an early stage. ● Quality design in combination with personal and professional services are the elements that make architecture long-lasting.

ART DIRECTOR:
Michael Manwaring
DESIGNER:
Michael Manwaring
PHOTOGRAPHER:
Charly Franklin
AGENCY:
The Office of
Michael Manwaring
CLIENT:
Leason Pomeroy Associates
■ **20, 21**

■ **15–19** Cover and sample double spreads from a "Sketch-book" issued by Leason Pomeroy Associates to mark their 20th anniversary in architecture. (USA)

■ **20, 21** Also for the architects Leason Pomeroy Associates, this time a presentation gatefold brochure, shown partially opened and cover only. (USA)

■ **15–19** Umschlag und einige der Doppelseiten aus einem »Skizzen-Buch«, von den Architekten Leason Pomeroy Associates anlässlich ihres 20jährigen Bestehens herausgegeben. (USA)

■ **20, 21** Ein weiteres Werbemittel für die Architekten Leason Pomeroy Associates, hier ein Faltprospekt, halb geöffnet, und dessen Vorderseite. (USA)

■ **15–19** Couverture et doubles pages types d'un »album de croquis« du bureau d'architecture Leason Pomeroy Associates publié pour marquer le 20e anniversaire de l'entreprise. (USA)

■ **20, 21** Un autre moyen publicitaire des architectes Leason Pomeroy Associates: dépliant de présentation montré mi-ouvert; la couverture dudit dépliant. (USA)

22–24 Cover and sample double spreads from a brochure promoting the image of The New Wilshire – a luxurious office building in Los Angeles. (USA)

25–27 Cover and two typical spreads from a leasing brochure for a cathedral-inspired office tower in Montreal "La Maison des Coopérants". (CAN)

22–24 Umschlag und Beispiele der Doppelseiten aus einer Werbebroschüre für The New Wilshire – ein luxuriöses Bürogebäude in Los Angeles. (USA)

25–27 Umschlag und zwei Doppelseiten aus einer Broschüre über einen neuen Büro-Turm in Montréal, dessen Architektur von der benachbarten Kathedrale inspiriert wurde. (CAN)

22–24 Couverture et doubles pages représentatives d'une brochure promotionnelle pour un immeuble de bureaux de grand standing, le New Wilshire à Los Angeles. (USA)

25–27 Couverture et deux doubles pages d'une brochure sur un immeuble-tour de Montréal, à usage de bureaux, qui évoque une cathédrale: «La Maison des Coopérants». (CAN)

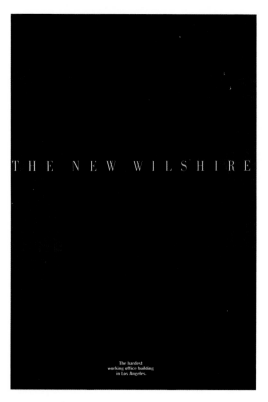

THE NEW WILSHIRE

The hardest
working office building
in Los Angeles.

ART DIRECTOR:
Nicolas Sidjakov/
Jerry Berman
DESIGNER:
Barbara Vick
AGENCY:
Sidjakov Berman & Gomez
CLIENT:
The New Wilshire
■ 22-24

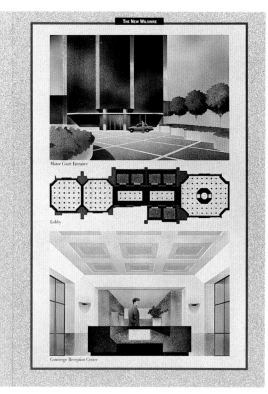

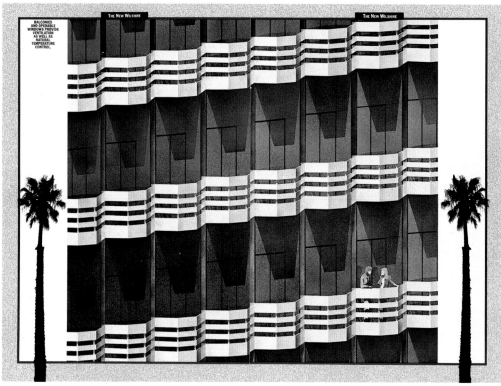

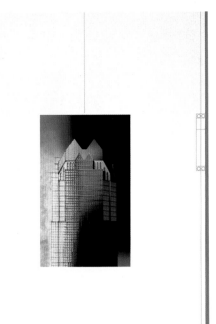

Thirty four storey La Maison des Coopérants, the tallest new building in Montreal, sensitively respects its environment. Pointed arches and porticoes with mullions and columns resting on grey limestone bases relate the tower to the scale and aesthetics of the Cathedral and its Chapter House. Accent mullions, etched in black, subtly define the image of the Cathedral spire.

Responding to the Cathedral, the form of the tower gracefully transforms to smaller floors as it rises, providing three topical floor plates, each with its own characteristics.

The building, clad with a curtain wall of reflective copper glass and aluminum, is a dynamic form against the skyline, ever changing with the interplay of sunlight and cloud on the sculptured tower.

La Maison des Coopérants is surmounted by a distinctive ecclesiastically-inspired twin-peaked roof, assuring its landmark identity from all points of Montreal.

Graceful and uplifting, the dramatic silhouette of the tower is destined to become one of the most photographed images of Montreal's skyline.

ART DIRECTOR:
Paul Browning

DESIGNER:
William Lam

PHOTOGRAPHER:
Peter Christopher/
Paul McCarthy

AGENCY:
Taylor & Browning
Design Associates

CLIENT:
First Quebec Corporation

■ 25–27

La Maison des Coopérants' architects, the Webb Zerafa Menkès Housden Partnership, welcomed the challenge of relating a contemporary design to a nineteenth century church. The result is a brilliant interpretation of the site in both its present and historical context, demonstrating the architects' comprehension and mastery of multi-dimensional urban design issues.

Creating buildings that define their surroundings and capture the imagination has earned international recognition for Webb Zerafa Menkès Housden. The award winning Royal Bank Plaza and the CN Tower in Toronto, the Banque Nationale de Paris in Montreal, and the Edifice Elf Aquitane in Paris are landmarks that have added immensely to the architectural stature of those cities.

Blending contemporary design with historical architectural themes affirms that continuity and change can be equally dynamic forces in a livable city.

Royal Bank Plaza

Edifice Elf Aquitane

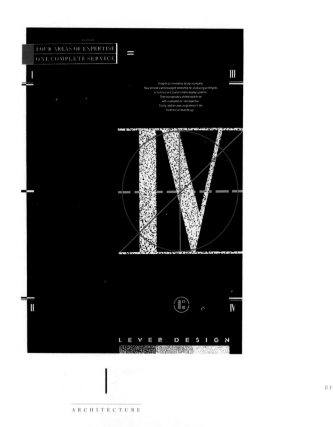

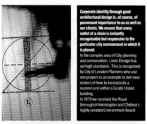

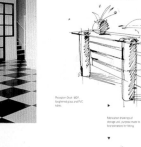

ART DIRECTOR:
Robin Hall

DESIGNER:
Robin Hall

PHOTOGRAPHER:
Julyan Rawlings

AGENCY:
C.Y.B. Design Consultants

CLIENT:
Lever Design

■ **28–30**

■ **28–30** Gatefold brochure as promotion for Lever Design (architects). Shown at top left is the brochure closed; top right with both flaps folded; bottom illustration shows the brochure with back flap opened out. (GBR)

■ **31–34** Cover and spreads from a promotional brochure for the Herring Marathon Group – architects/designers of shopping malls in the sunbelt of the United States. (USA)

■ **28–30** Faltprospekt für die Architekten Lever Design. Hier die Vorderansicht des geschlossenen Prospekts, die beiden nach innen geklappten Ausleger, und die Innenansicht mit einem ausgeklappten Ausleger. (GBR)

■ **31–34** Umschlag und Doppelseiten aus einer Broschüre für die Herring Marathon Group – Architekten/Designer von Einkaufszentren, die mit ihrer Umgebung harmonieren. (USA)

■ **28–30** Dépliant pour le bureau d'architecture Lever Design. En haut: à gauche, recto du prospectus plié; à droite, les deux rabats rabattus; en bas: l'intérieur du dépliant avec le rabat arrière. (GBR)

■ **31–34** Couverture et doubles pages d'une brochure pour le Herring Marathon Group, architectes et designers de centres commerciaux dans le Sud des Etats-Unis. (USA)

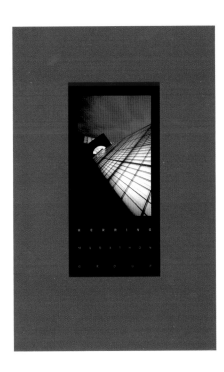

ART DIRECTOR:
Don Sibley

DESIGNER:
Don Sibley

PHOTOGRAPHER:
Steve Brady

AGENCY:
Sibley/Peteet Design.

CLIENT:
*Herring Marathon
Group*

■ 31–34

■ **35–40** Cover and sample spreads from a promotional brochure for the much-honored architectural and graphic design company Media Five Limited of Honolulu. With a typical "Pacific" look, the cover has an applied centerpiece of handmade Japanese papers folded over silken strands. (USA)

■ **41–43** Gloss cover with blind-embossed 11, and spreads from a brochure entitled "Eleven Danes Design" featuring 11 Danish designers and a selection of their work. The pages are all extended tripartite spreads (left side folds out). (DEN)

■ **35–40** Umschlag und Beispiele der Doppelseiten aus einer Broschüre für Media Five Ltd., eine Architektengruppe aus Honolulu, die zahlreiche Auszeichnungen erhalten hat. Typisch für die Pazifik-Länder ist der Umschlag mit einer Applikation aus handgeschöpftem Japanpapier und Seidenbändern. (USA)

■ **41–43** Laminierter Umschlag mit blindgeprägter 11 und Beispiele der jeweils mit einem Ausleger versehenen Innenseiten, aus einer Broschüre, in der elf dänische Designer und ihre Arbeiten vorgestellt werden. (DEN)

■ **35–40** Couverture et doubles pages types d'une brochure pour un groupe d'architectes et de designers réputé, Media Five Ltd. à Honolulu. La couverture caractéristique du look océanien est ornée en son centre de papiers japonais faits main rapportés sur des rubans de soie. (USA)

■ **41–43** Couverture laminée (chiffre 11 gaufré à froid) et doubles pages d'une brochure collective de 11 designers danois, «Eleven Danes Design». Chaque page de gauche se dépliant une fois, toutes les doubles pages sont en fait triples. (DEN)

ART DIRECTOR:
Kunio Hayashi
DESIGNER:
Kunio Hayashi
COVER ARTIST:
The Paper Gallery
ILLUSTRATOR:
Dennis S. Osato/
Donna E. Yuen/ Kunio Hayashi
PHOTOGRAPHER:
Dana Edmunds
AGENCY:
Media Five Ltd.
CLIENT:
Media Five Ltd.
■ **35–40**

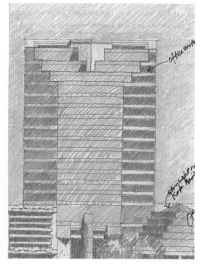

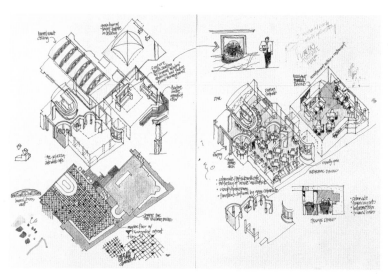

Peter Hiort-Lorenzen, 1943. Industrial Designer (ID)

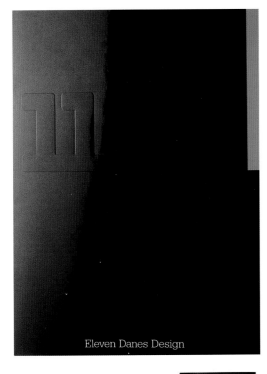

Susse Fischer

Studied history of art as minor subject, University of Copenhagen. 1970. Studied at the Royal Academy of Fine Art, Copenhagen. 1977. Independent design practice. Thon & Fischer. 1983.

Danish Design Council 1978-83

Work for Danish and international companies has included: Exhibitions, shop design, shop display, interior design, fittings, building renovation, and packaging. Clients have included: Danish Design Council, Copenhagen Telephone Co., Fredgaard Radio A/S, Foreign Ministry, Tønsberg Repær A/S, Sony A/S, L'Oreal de Paris, Christianshavns Apotek, Mortensen & Rasmussen Kommunikation, Scandinavian Student Travel Service, Lyngby Storcenter, and Mobilia.

The PRINT Magazine Exhibition Award 1982.

Pipeline Sofa system

Eleven Danes Design

Ole Søndergaard, 1937. Graphic Designer (ID)

Typeface «Pidro»

BRSHNP WGKOXF cyæqngr hdkiobul pxgøzev. mtsfj?!↗ 1652408

Fotex, 1983. Tête-à-tête sofa and chaise-longue. Executed in moulded foam and steel. Manufacturer: Erik Jørgensens Møbelfabrik. Design: Johannes Foersom and Peter Hiort-Lorenzen.

Waiting/Rest furniture, 1984. Part of large furniture series. In beechwood, with painted components and moulded-foam upholstery. Manufacturer: Hong Stolefabrik. Design: Johannes Foersom and Peter Hiort-Lorenzen.

Walking sticks, 1980. For arthritis patients. In laminated beechwood. Manufacturer: Bjørn Nielsen Hospitalsartikler.

Newspaper rack, 1978. In moulded beechwood. Manufacturer: Bjørn Nielsen Hospitalsartikler.

PHOTOGRAPHER:
Louis Schnakenburg/
Per Dreyer

AGENCY:
Eleven Danes Design A/S

CLIENT:
Eleven Danes Design A/S

■ 41–43

ART DIRECTOR:
Don Sibley

DESIGNER:
Don Sibley

ILLUSTRATOR:
Kelly Stribling

PHOTOGRAPHER:
Thom Jackson/John Parrish

AGENCY:
Sibley/Peteet Design, Inc.

CLIENT:
Neiman-Marcus

■ **44–47**

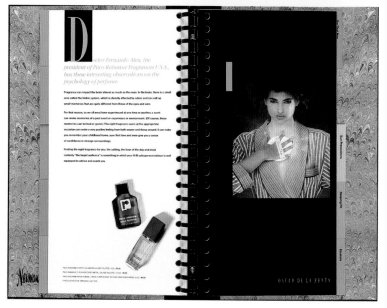

■ **44–47** A hard cloth-bound "Beauty Notebook" to serve as promotion for *Neiman-Marcus*; spiral-binding for clients to add new sheets, the cards offer tips on beauty care and carry ads for cosmetics stocked by this store. (USA)

■ **48, 49** Die-cut and folded portfolio, shown partially opened and fully closed, promoting fashions styled by *Gin Tonic* of Stuttgart. (The folio contains eight separate sheets.) (GER)

■ **44–47** Ringordner mit festem Leineneinband, als »Schön-heits-Notizbuch« von dem Kaufhaus *Neiman-Marcus* an Kunden abgegeben. Die Seiten, deren Anzahl sich beliebig ergänzen lässt, enthalten Schönheitstips und werben für Produkte. (USA)

■ **48, 49** Halb geöffnete und geschlossene Faltmappe, die acht einzelne Blätter enthält, als Werbung für die Kollektion Herbst/Winter 86/87 von *Gin Tonic*. (GER)

■ **44–47** «Agenda de beauté» relié, à feuillets mobiles pour la mise à jour, remis aux clientes des grands magasins *Neiman-Marcus*. Chaque feuillet contient des conseils de beauté et des annonces pour des produits de beauté. (USA)

■ **48, 49** Chemise de dossier, motif en découpe, partiellement ouverte et fermée, pour 8 feuillets de mode de la collection automne/hiver 1986/87 de la marque *Gin Tonic*. (GER)

Stockjacke 2310
Hemd 2267
Hose 2015

Sakko 2000
Pullover 2388
Hemd 2260
Hose 2002

Blouson 2004
Pullover 2315
Hemd 2450
Hose 2003

Lederblouson 2281
Pullover 2060
Hemd 2450
Hose 2006

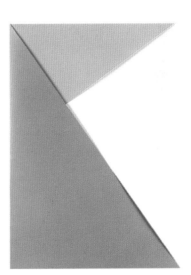

ART DIRECTOR:
Birgit Unterweger

DESIGNER:
Birgit Unterweger

PHOTOGRAPHER:
Conny Winter

AGENCY:
Art Work

CLIENT:
Gin Tonic

■ 48, 49

ART DIRECTOR:
Cheryl Heller

DESIGNER:
Cheryl Heller

PHOTOGRAPHER:
Herb Ritts

AGENCY:
HBM/Creamer Design

CLIENT:
Reebok

■50—52

ART DIRECTOR:
Nando Miglio

PHOTOGRAPHER:
Arthur Elgort

AGENCY:
Nando Miglio S.r.L.

CLIENT:
Genny

■**53, 54**

■**50–52** Double spreads from a large-format brochure to promote active sportswear for men and women by *Reebok* (USA)

■**53, 54** Two covers of large brochures (without text) for fashions by *Genny*: Left, presenting the spring/summer collection; right, the fall/winter collection. (ITA)

■**50–52** Doppelseiten aus einer grossformatigen Broschüre für den Sportbekleidungshersteller *Reebok* (USA)

■**53, 54** Umschläge von zwei grossformatigen Broschüren (ohne Text) für Mode von *Genny*; links für die Frühjahr/Sommer-Kollektion, rechts für die Herbst/Winter-Kollektion. (ITA)

■**50–52** Doubles pages d'une brochure au grand format pour les vêtements de sport hommes et femmes de *Reebok* (USA)

■**53,54** Couverture de deux brochures au grand format sans texte pour les modes *Genny*: à gauche, collection de printemps et d'été; à droite, collection d'automne et d'hiver. (ITA)

ART DIRECTOR:
Kit Hinrichs

DESIGNER:
Kit Hinrichs

PHOTOGRAPHER:
Barry Robinson

AGENCY:
Pentagram Design,

CLIENT:
Pentagram Design

■55–59

PENTAGRAM PAPERS 14

STARS & STRIPES

• Stars & Stripes •

Flags—the ultimate symbol. They instantly identify a nation, rally the troops, personify the spirit of a country. In victory, the emblems are waved triumphantly; in defeat, white flags stripped of any insignia indicate surrender.

Some say that the first flag was implied in the Bible, when God unfurled the multicolored banner of the rainbow after the flood to signal that danger had passed. Certainly, flags have been around since man formed tribal units. Carried into battle and flown on topmasts of ships, they functioned as visual identity to a group. Columbus planted the standard of Spain on American soil in 1492. Neil Armstrong left the Stars and Stripes on the moon in 1969. Flags are clearly the embodiment of a people, a first order of business for any new nation.

Contrary to popular legend, the American flag wasn't the inspired design of a widowed Philadelphia seamstress named Betsy Ross. The official banner of the United States had evolved from the earliest colonial settlement right through the Revolutionary War. These emblems varied in colors, motif, direction of stripes and embroidered slogans. Some pre-Revolutionary liberty flags displayed the New England pine tree, others had a coiled rattlesnake with the warning "Don't tread on me." The Sons of Liberty adopted 13 red and white stripes, representing the colonies.

It wasn't until June 14, 1777, that the Continental Congress "resolved that the Flag of the united states be 13 stripes alternate red and white, that the Union be 13 stars white in a blue field representing a new constellation." The flag was laden with symbolism. Red stood for courage, white for liberty, and blue for loyalty. A star was an ancient Egyptian sign for sovereignty and dominion.

First U.S. flag

• Stars & Stripes •

Congress' design guidelines proved to be so broad, however, that there was liberal interpretation of the stars and stripes, especially in the configuration of stars. Flag artists imaginatively formed star wreaths, arcs, ovals and rows or simply scattered stars across the blue field. Some stars were multi-rayed, others were five-pointed, like the rowel of a knight's spur. The five-pointed star–a pentagram–prevailed.

When Vermont and Kentucky joined the Union in 1795, they demanded representation on the national banner. Despite protests over the "sinful" waste of money, Congress complied, decreeing 15 stars and 15 stripes. After five more states were admitted in 1818, lawmakers decided the design could get out of hand. They voted to return to the 13 original stripes and merely add a star for each state.

During the expansionist period of the 19th century, territories were joining the Union nearly every year. Economy-minded flagmakers often left gaps to "drop in" another star, rather than remake patterns.

Proud of their national banner, Americans freely displayed the Stars and Stripes on all kinds of common objects. The range of expression, which ran from fine art to work of such poor taste that it bordered on desecration, aroused demand for flag codes. In 1912, the first of a series of detailed design standards was approved. In 1934, lawmakers specified official color shades, and in 1942, Congress finally adopted a code of flag etiquette.

More than a century without guidelines, however, allowed for wonderful personal interpretations of the emblem of the United States. The Star-Spangled Banner is an art form in itself and an endearing part of American history.

Current U.S. flag

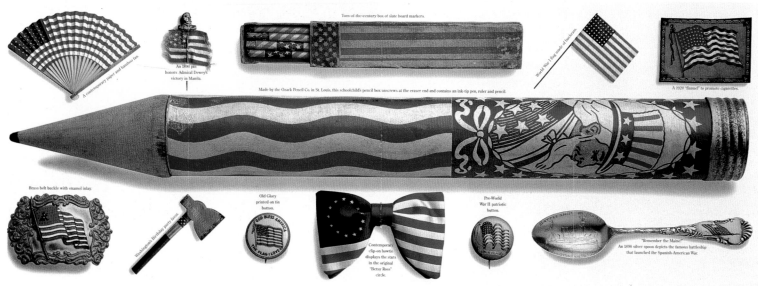

Turn-of-the-century box of slate board markers.

An 1898 pin honors Admiral Dewey's victory in Manila.

Made by the Ozark Pencil Co. in St. Louis, this schoolchild's pencil box unscrews at the eraser end and contains an ink-tip pen, ruler and pencil.

World War I flag made of buckram.

A 1920 "flannel" to promote cigarettes.

Brass belt buckle with enamel inlay.

Washington Birthday party favor.

Old Glory printed on tin button.

GOD BLESS AMERICA THE FLAG I LOVE

Contemporary clip-on bowtie displays the stars in the original "Betsy Ross" circle.

Pre-World War II patriotic button.

"Remember the Maine." An 1898 silver spoon depicts the famous battleship that launched the Spanish-American War.

• Stars & Stripes •

The Stars and Stripes have appeared in every art medium, including decaled on glass against a background of inlaid butterfly wings. Americans used the flag so loosely in commercial advertising that in 1942 Congress passed restrictive flag codes. The Old Glory brand symbol is just one of many uses that became outlawed. The codes forbade displaying the flag for advertising purposes, on cushions and handkerchiefs, or with any writing or design upon it.

OLD GLORY BRAND

Canned asparagus from California, c. 1930.

• Stars & Stripes •

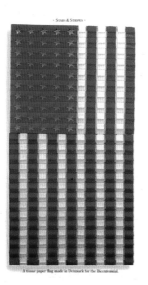

A tissue paper flag made in Denmark for the Bicentennial.

• Stars & Stripes •

Support the war and our store. During World War II, merchants across the United States produced tons of patriotic advertising in support of the war effort.

A Texas construction company distributed a triptych folding fan that covered all the popular themes—a pretty girl in uniform, the familiar red and white stripes, and the Pledge of Allegiance. On the back, it printed its slogan "Put it up to us to put it up for you."

■**55–59** Cover and spreads from *Pentagram* Papers No. 14 "Stars and Stripes"; one of a series. Die-cut cover holds loose flag on pin; center spread (middle illust.) is a gatefold. (USA)

■**60** This concertina folder (with cover) has 20 sides to celebrate the 20th Anniversary of *Rolling Stone* magazine. (USA)

■**61** Mailer for Morrison Productions as promotion for their political television productions. (USA)

■**55–59** Umschlag und Doppelseiten aus der *Pentagram*-Broschüre Nr. 14 über das Sternenbanner. Auf dem Umschlag ist die amerikanische Flagge mit einem Hölzchen eingesteckt. (USA)

■**60** Zwanzigseitiges Leporello mit Umschlag zur Feier des 20jährigen Bestehens der Zeitschrift *Rolling Stone* (USA)

■**61** »Kaum ein Tag vergeht, an dem ich nicht jemanden erschiessen (filmen) möchte.« Für einen TV-Produzenten. (USA)

■**55–59** Couverture et doubles pages du fascicule 14 des *Pentagram* Papers, »Stars and Stripes«. La découpe de la couverture recèle la bannière étoilée fixée à un bâtonnet. (USA)

■**60** Volets d'un dépliant en accordéon (on voit aussi la couverture) pour fêter les 20 ans du magazine *Rolling Stone* (USA)

■**61** Publicité directe pour Morrison Productions et ses émissions TV politiques qui »filment« et »tuent« les gens. (USA)

Hardly a day goes by that I don't want to shoot somebody.

Ken Morrison has an obsession. Take advantage of it. Call Kelly Brown at Morrison Productions. (504) 486-8150.

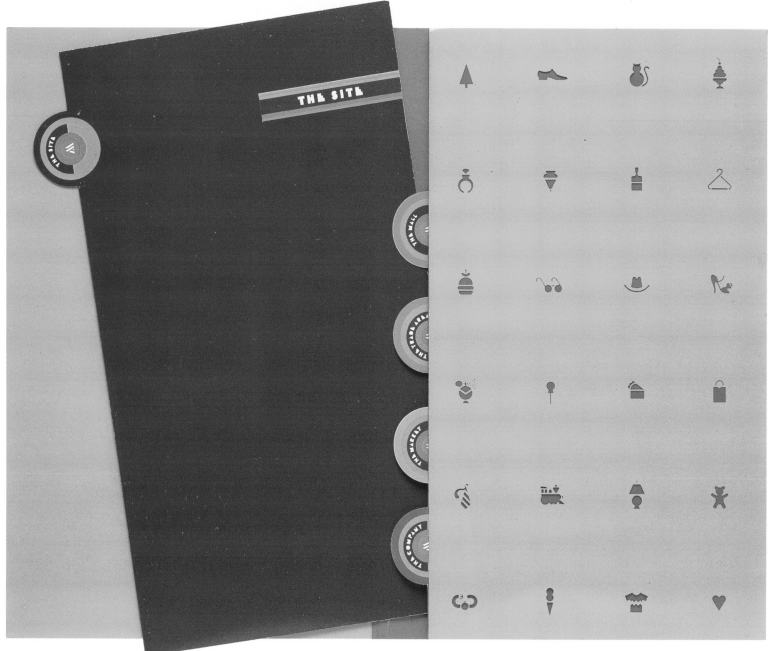

ART DIRECTOR:
Rex Peteet

DESIGNER:
Rex Peteet

AGENCY:
Sibley/Peteet Design, Inc.

CLIENT:
The Herring Group

■**62**

■**62** Herring (architects/builders of shopping malls) issued this glossy envelope (die-cut) containing 5 folders to promote their new expansion to Alexandria Mall, Louisiana. (USA)

■**63–68** Small board book by way of promotion for the *First Bank System* and invitation to a management conference in Minneapolis, under the motto "Partners in Performance". (USA)

■**62** Glanzpapier-Mappe (mit ausgestanzten Gegenständen), die 5 Prospekte enthält, um das neue Projekt der Herring Group – ein Einkaufszentrum in Louisiana - publik zu machen. (USA)

■**63–68** Doppelseiten und Umschlag eines Kartonbüchleins der *First Bank Systems* zum Thema Teamwork, das gleichzeitig als Einladung zu einer Konferenz verwendet wurde. (USA)

■**62** Enveloppe cartonnée laminée et découpée avec 5 dépliants du Herring Group, architectes-réalisateurs de centres commerciaux, pour l'agrandissement d'Alexandria Mall. (USA)

■**63–68** Doubles pages et couverture d'un livret cartonné de *First Bank Systems* invitant à la conférence de gestion bancaire «Associés en réalisations» de Minneapolis. (USA)

THIS BOOK ANNOUNCES
OUR 1987 FIRST BANK
SYSTEM MANAGEMENT
CONFERENCE • THE
WORDS AND IMAGES
YOU FIND HERE REIN-
FORCE THE WORK WE
WILL BEGIN TOGETHER
ON MONDAY MORNING,
FEBRUARY 9TH • WE
INVITE YOU AND YOUR
SPOUSE OR GUEST TO
JOIN US FOR PARTNERS
IN PERFORMANCE AT
MARRIOTT CITY CEN-
TER, MINNEAPOLIS

PARTNERS IN
PERFORMANCE
FIRST BANK
SYSTEM 1987

ART DIRECTOR:
Charles Spencer Anderson
DESIGNER:
Charles Spencer Anderson
ILLUSTRATOR:
Charles Spencer Anderson
AGENCY:
Duffy Design Group
CLIENT:
First Bank Systems
■63–68

PARTNERS PER-
FORM BETTER BY
ACCEPTING, NOT
ERASING, THEIR
DIFFERENCES

I DON'T KNOW
THE KEY TO
SUCCESS, BUT
THE KEY TO
FAILURE IS TRY-
ING TO PLEASE
EVERYONE •
BILL COSBY

GOOD TEAMWORK
CALLS FOR A
VERY SMALL BIT
OF VERY GOOD
LEADERSHIP

THE BEST EX-
ECUTIVE IS
THE ONE WHO
HAS SENSE
ENOUGH TO PICK
GOOD MEN TO
DO WHAT HE
WANTS DONE▸

GOOD TEAMWORK
DOES NOT MEAN
LESS WORK •
JUST MORE PRO-
DUCTIVE WORK

EVEN IF YOU
ARE ON THE
RIGHT TRACK,
YOU WILL GET
RUN OVER
IF YOU JUST
SIT THERE •
WILL ROGERS

AS WE, SIX ADVEN-
TURERS FROM DIFFER-
ENT PARTS OF THE
WORLD, STAND WHERE
THE LINES OF
LONGITUDE OF ALL
COUNTRIES MEET, WE
BELIEVE THIS JOURNEY
STANDS FOR HOPE •
HOPE THAT OTHER
SEEMINGLY IMPOSSIBLE
GOALS CAN BE MET
BY PEOPLE EVERY-
WHERE • THE STEGER
INTERNATIONAL
POLAR EXPEDITION

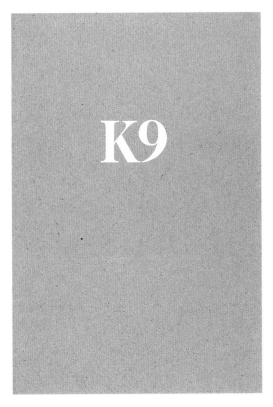

K9

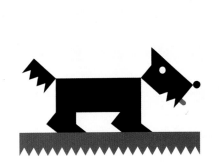

∧ Spike
> Pluto

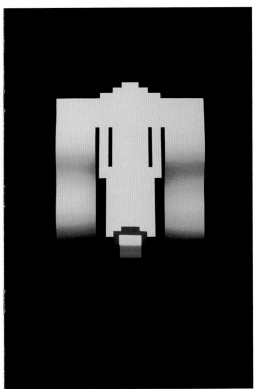

ART DIRECTOR:
Woody Pirtle
DESIGNER:
Woody Pirtle
ILLUSTRATOR:
Woody Pirtle/Gary McCoy
AGENCY:
Pirtle Design
CLIENT:
Pirtle Design
■**70-72**

ART DIRECTOR:
Rex Peteet
DESIGNER:
Rex Peteet/Judy Dolim
AGENCY:
Sibley/Peteet Design, Inc.
CLIENT:
Sibley/Peteet Design, Inc.
◄■**69**

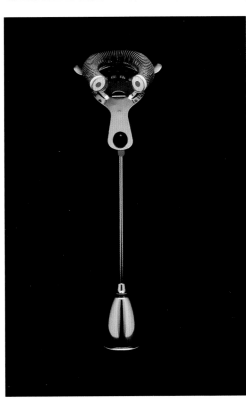

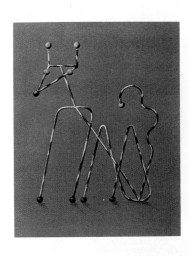

∧ Memphis
< Boozer

■**69** Views of a 3-dimensional case and its contents - a spiral-bound brochure (shown closed and opened) presenting a selection of trademarks designed by Sibley/Peteet Design. (USA)

■**70–72** Cover and spreads from a promotional brochure for Pirtle Design devoted to dogs and presenting 9 artists' impressions of Man's Best Friend. (K9 = Canine.) (USA)

■**69** Ansichten einer Faltschachtel und ihres Inhalts, einer spiralgebundenen Broschüre (hier geschlossen und geöffnet) als Eigenwerbung eines Design-Studios in Dallas. (USA)

■**70–72** Umschlag und Doppelseiten aus einer Werbebroschüre für Pirtle Design. Das Thema ist des Menschen bester Freund, der hier von 9 Künstlern dargestellt ist. (USA)

■**69** Vues d'une boîte pliante et de son contenu – une brochure à reliure spirale (fermée et ouverte) présentant des marques déposées conçues par Sibley/Peteet Design, Dallas. (USA)

■**70–72** Couverture et doubles pages d'une brochure promotionnelle de Pirtle Design, où «K9» se lit «Canine»: 9 artistes y représentent le chien, le meilleur ami de l'homme. (USA)

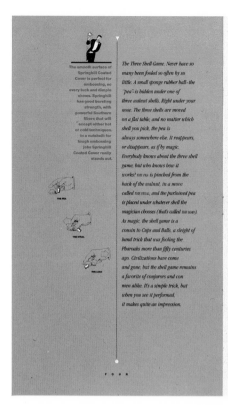

The smooth surface of Springhill Coated Cover is perfect for embossing, so every tuck and dimple shows. Springhill has good bursting strength, with powerful Southern fibers that will accept either hot or cold techniques. In a nutshell: for tough embossing jobs Springhill Coated Cover really stands out.

THE PEA

THE STEAL

THE LOAD

F O U R

The Three Shell Game. Never have so many been fooled so often by so little. A small sponge rubber ball–the "pea"–is hidden under one of three walnut shells. Right under your nose. The three shells are moved on a flat table, and no matter which shell you pick, the pea is always somewhere else. It reappears, or disappears, as if by magic. Everybody knows about the three shell game, but who knows how it works? THE PEA is pinched from the back of the walnut, in a move called THE STEAL; and the purloined pea is placed under whatever shell the magician chooses (that's called THE LOAD). As magic, the shell game is a cousin to Cups and Balls, a sleight of hand trick that was fooling the Pharoahs more than fifty centuries ago. Civilizations have come and gone, but the shell game remains a favorite of conjurors and con men alike. It's a simple trick, but when you see it performed, it makes quite an impression.

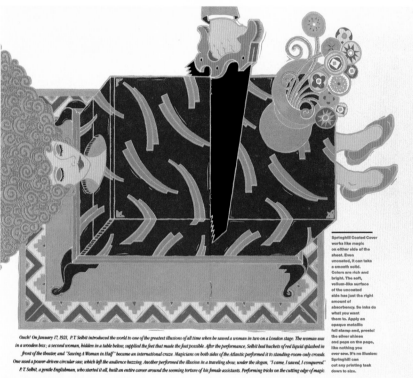

Springhill Coated Cover works like magic on either side of the sheet. Even uncoated, it can take a smooth solid. Colors are rich and bright. The soft, vellum-like surface of the uncoated side has just the right amount of absorbency. So inks do what you want them to. Apply an opaque metallic foil stamp and, presto! the silver shines and pops on the page, like nothing you ever saw. It's no illusion: Springhill can cut any printing task down to size.

Ouch! On January 17, 1921, P.T. Selbit introduced the world to one of the greatest illusions of all time when he sawed a woman in two on a London stage. The woman was in a wooden box; a second woman, hidden in a table below, supplied the feet that made the feat possible. After the performance, Selbit had buckets of red liquid splashed in front of the theater, and "Sawing A Woman in Half" became an international craze. Magicians on both sides of the Atlantic performed it to standing-room-only crowds. One used a power-driven circular saw, which left the audience buzzing. Another performed the illusion in a traveling show, under the slogan, "I came, I sawed, I conquered!" P.T. Selbit, a gentle Englishman, who started it all, built an entire career around the seeming torture of his female assistants. Performing tricks on the cutting edge of magic.

ART DIRECTOR:
Rex Peteet

DESIGNER:
Rex Peteet

ILLUSTRATOR:
Rex Peteet/Michael Schwab

PHOTOGRAPHER:
John Wong

AGENCY:
Sibley/Peteet Design, Inc.

CLIENT:
International Paper Co.

■73, 74

ART DIRECTOR:
Rex Peteet

DESIGNER:
Rex Peteet

ILLUSTRATOR:
Walter Horton

AGENCY:
Sibley/Peteet Design, Inc.

CLIENT:
International paper Co.

■75

■**73–75** "Tricks of the Trade" – cards, tricks and magic form the subject of this advertising material for the International Paper Co. to promote their *Springhill* line. Shown are two double spreads from the brochure itself, and slipcase which contains a giant playing card. (USA)

■**76–79** "Contrast" is the title and shoes are the theme of a promotional brochure for the National Press (printers); one of a series. Shown are the cover and three double spreads. (USA)

■**73–75** Kartentricks und Zauberstücke sind das Thema dieses Werbematerials für die Papierqualität «Springhill» von der International Paper Co. Hier zwei Doppelseiten aus einer Broschüre und ein wie eine Spielkartenschachtel wirkendes Couvert mit einer gigantischen Karte. (USA)

■**76–79** «Kontrast» ist der Titel der Broschüre aus einer Serie für die Druckerei National Press. Das Thema sind Schuhe. Hier der Umschlag und drei Doppelseiten (USA)

■**73–75** «Les trucs du métier», matériel publicitaire à base de cartes et tours magiques pour l'International Paper Co. et sa gamme de papiers *Springhill* Nous montrons ici deux doubles pages de la brochure et emboîtage contenant une carte à jouer géante. (USA)

■**76–79** Brochure sur le sujet de la chaussure intitulée «Contraste» et servant à la publicité de l'imprimerie National Press, ici la couverture, ainsi que trois doubles pages. (USA)

ART DIRECTOR:
Steven Tolleson
DESIGNER:
Steven Tolleson/
Susan Gross
ILLUSTRATOR:
Mark Ulriksen
PHOTOGRAPHER:
Terry Heffernan
COPYWRITER:
Roy Parvin
STUDIO:
Tolleson Design
CLIENT:
National Press
■**76–79**

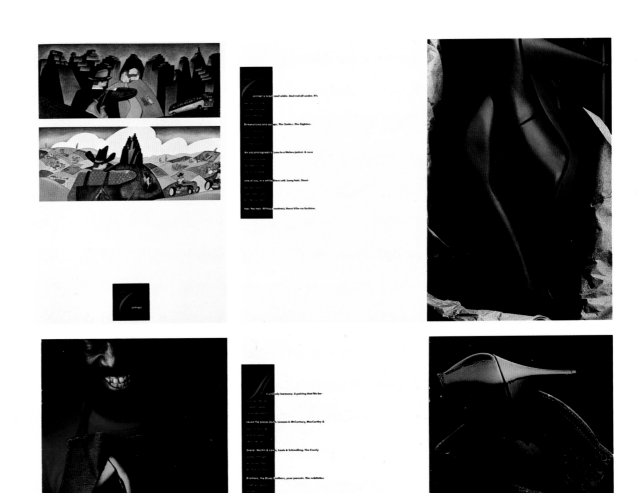

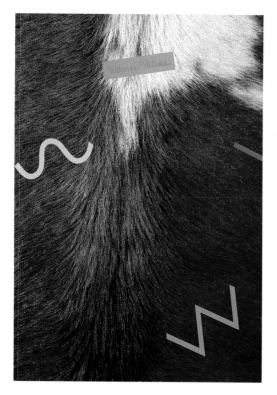

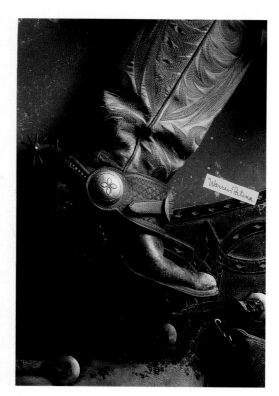

ART DIRECTOR:
Cheryl Heller
DESIGNER:
Cheryl Heller
PHOTOGRAPHER:
Myron/Geoffrey Clifford
Kurt Markus/
William Albert Allard
AGENCY:
HBM/Creamer Design Group
CLIENT:
S.D. Warren
■80-84

Patina is a surface mellowed by age, use, and weather. And in the American Southwest you'll see patina working its most special magic. On work-polished saddles, beaten-up Stetsons, and tarnished spurs... worn Navaho blankets and crumbling adobe... chipped and faded Hopi kachinas and pottery... towering saguaro cacti scarred by birds and bullets. Even the boundless sun-bleached land seems burnished by time. Here is patina without end. And right here, in plain unvarnished 4-color and black-and-white, is Warren Patina, a paper of extraordinary value and runnability ▲▲▲

■**80-84** To promote their *Warren Patina* paper, *S.D. Warren* chose as the subject of their brochure the word it most connotes – surface. This is emphasized with photographs of artifacts from the American Southwest, where surfaces are mellowed by the sun and by long and constant use. (USA)

■**80-84** Als Thema ihrer Werbebroschüre für die Papierqualität *Warren Patina* wählte *S.D. Warren* den Begriff Oberfläche. Die Aufnahmen aus dem Südwesten der USA zeigen Oberflächen, die durch Sonne oder ständigen Gebrauch gezeichnet sind. Der ganze Text ist »handgeschrieben«. (USA)

■**80-84** Pour la promotion de sa qualité de papier *Warren Patina* S.D. Warren a choisi d'interpréter dans cette brochure le sens de »patine = altération de surface avec le temps« au travers de surfaces et d'artefacts du Sud-Ouest des E.-U. polis par l'usage et le soleil. Texte »manuscrit«. (USA)

Patina has always had the reputation of being a workhorse stock, a real performer, economical and not a lick of temperment. A great value for the money, Patina is smooth and gives you an unbroken ink lay across the sheet. You can heavy up on the coverage, without a hint of mottle. And take a good look at the blue/white quality of the unprinted sheet; it will reproduce bright colors, make highlights gleam and details leap out of the shadows. Not at the price of readability either... the non-reflective surface of Patina has a way with words that's gentle on the eye.

Today as in ancient times, corn is the staple of the Southwest. It is food, ornament and sacrament, an integral part of the region's culture and history.

■85 Cover of a brochure to promote *Mead* web printing papers. Bold close-up shots on each page. (USA)

■86–92 Six double spreads and the cover of a spiral-bound brochure for the French Paper Company, printed on and presenting their line of *Speckletone* papers. The illustrations show what is possible with this wood-pulp paper: poster, tickets, guidebooks, bags, containers etc. The text is on narrow interleaves between illustrations. (USA)

■85 Umschlag einer Broschüre für *Mead*-Papier. Ausdrucksstarke Nahaufnahmen unterstützen die Werbeaussage. (USA)

■86–92 Sechs Doppelseiten und Umschlag einer spiralgebundenen Broschüre für einen Papierhersteller. Hier werden eine Papierqualität und ein Design-Studio vorgestellt, das zeigt, wie man das Papier verwenden und als Gestaltungselement einsetzen kann, z.B. für Plakate, Broschüren, Tragtaschen usw. Ein schmales Blatt zwischen den Illustrationen enthält den Text. (USA)

■85 Couverture d'une brochure pour les papiers *Mead* sans fin. Des gros plans expressifs ponctuent chaque page. (USA)

■86–92 Six doubles pages et couverture d'une brochure à reliure spirale pour la French Paper Company, imprimée sur la qualité de papier *Speckletone* mise en vedette. Les illustrations se réfèrent à l'emploi varié de ce papier de pâte: affiches, billets, guides, sacs, conteneurs, etc. Le texte figure sur d'étroits feuillets intercalés entre les illustrations. (USA)

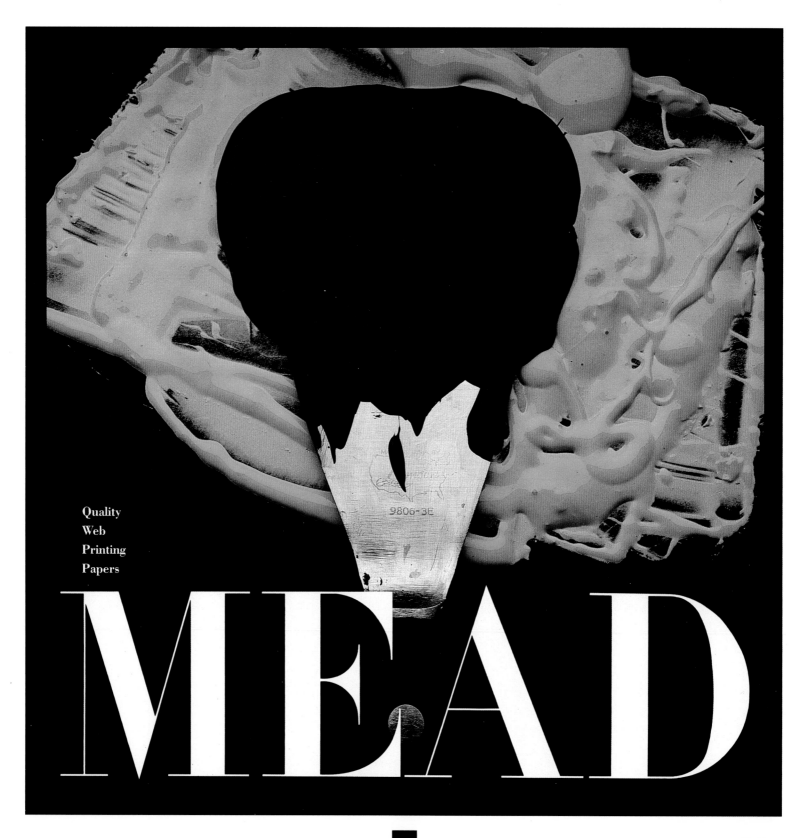

Quality
Web
Printing
Papers

MEAD

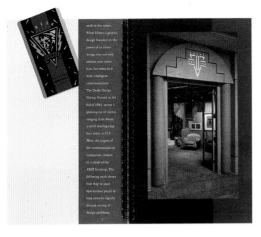 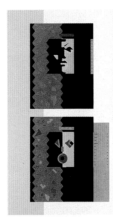  

ART DIRECTOR:
Charles Spencer Anderson

DESIGNER:
Joe Duffy/
Charles Spencer Anderson

ILLUSTRATOR:
Joe Duffy/
Charles Spencer Anderson

AGENCY:
Duffy Design Group

CLIENT:
French Paper Company
■86–92

ART DIRECTOR:
John Van Dyke

DESIGNER:
John Van Dyke

PHOTOGRAPHER:
Terry Heffernan

AGENCY:
Van Dyke Company

CLIENT:
Mead Paper Company
◄■85

ISOMETRIX

Lighting Design

Research + Development

Prototyping

Specialist Manufacture

Luminaire Supply

9 Frederick Mews
Kinnerton Street
London SW1X 8EG
Tel 01 235 5818/9

Lighting Design: a comprehensive design and technical consultancy, encompassing all

aspects of architectural lighting from schemes to fixture design.

—

IT WAS GOOD
& IT GLOWED

—

PLATE VII

Luminaire Supply: competitive suppliers to the trade for all lighting and electrical

equipment.

ART DIRECTOR:
BENITA RAPHAN
DESIGNER:
BENITA RAPHAN
PHOTOGRAPHER:
NICK GEORGHIOU
AGENCY:
GEORGHIOU RAPHAN
CLIENT:
ISOMETRIX LIGHTING +
DESIGN
■93, 94

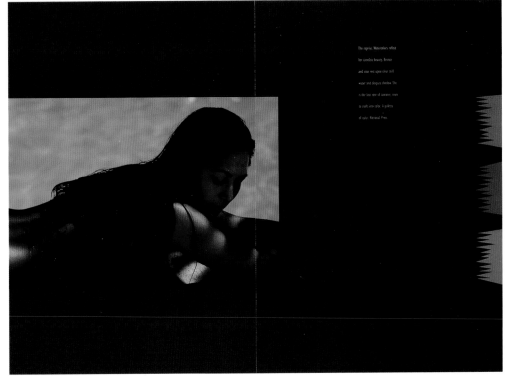

ART DIRECTOR:
Steven Tolleson

DESIGNER:
Steven Tolleson/
Susan Gross

ILLUSTRATOR:
John Hersey

PHOTOGRAPHER:
Steven Unze

COPYWRITER:
Joseph Feldman

STUDIO:
Tolleson Design

CLIENT:
National Press
■95–97

(15) Booklets

■**93, 94** Spreads (and loose sheets with applied photos showing recent projects) from a brochure for Isometrix Lighting Design of London. (GBR)

■**95–97** Cover and spreads from a promotional brochure (series) for the National Press, printers. The subject chosen is the relationship of colors and the emotions they evoke. (USA)

■**93,94** Doppelseiten aus einer Broschüre für das Studio Isometrix und lose Blätter mit Beispielen aus dessen Arbeitsbereich: Technik und Design von Lichtquellen in der Architektur. (GBR)

■**95-97** Umschlag und Doppelseiten aus einer Broschüre (Serie) für eine Druckerei. Das Thema ist die Relation zwischen Farben und Emotionen, die sie hervorrufen. (USA)

■**93, 94** Doubles pages (et feuillets mobiles avec des exemples d'application récents) d'une brochure pour Isometrix Lighting Design (Londres): éclairages d'architecture. (GBR)

■**95–97** Couverture et doubles pages d'une brochure figurant dans une série publicitaire de l'imprimerie National Press: les rapports existant entre la couleur et l'émotion. (USA)

DESIGNER:
Michael Mabry/Peter Soe
ILLUSTRATOR:
Michael Mabry
STUDIO:
Michael Mabry Design
CLIENT:
*AIGA American Institute
of Graphic Arts*
■98

ART DIRECTOR:
Kazumasa Nagai
DESIGNER:
Kazumasa Nagai
AGENCY:
Nippon Design Center
CLIENT:
*The Vatican Exhibition
Executive Committee*
■99

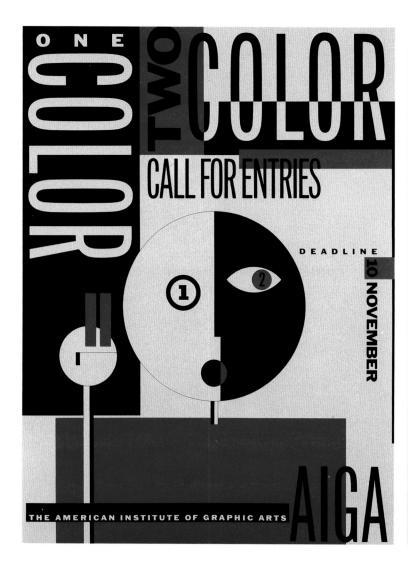

■98 Call for Entries folder to the AIGA One Color/Two Color Show – exhibiting works produced on a limited budget. (USA)

■99 Cover of the catalog for The Vatican Exhibition which took place in Tokyo. (JPN)

■100 Call for Entries to the Art Directors Club 66th Annual Exhibition. (USA)

■101 Folder to promote The American Craft Expo – a juried exposition showing 350 professional designers' handmade crafts – traditional and contemporary. (USA)

■98 Faltprospekt als Einladung der AIGA: Wettbewerb/Ausstellung von ein- und zweifarbigen Design-Lösungen. (USA)

■99 Umschlag des Katalogs für die Vatikan-Ausstellung, die in Tokio stattfand. (JPN)

■100 Einladung zur Teilnahme am jährlichen Wettbewerb bzw. an der 66. Ausstellung des Art Directors Club. (USA)

■101 Faltprospekt für die American Craft Expo – eine jurierte Ausstellung zeitgenössischer und traditioneller Handarbeiten von 350 professionellen amerikanischen Designern. (USA)

■98 Dépliant invitant à participer à la One Color/Two Color Show de l'AIGA = solutions de design à budget réduit. (USA)

■99 Couverture du catalogue de l'Exposition Vaticane organisée à Tokyo. (JPN)

■100 Invitation à participer à la 66e exposition annuelle de l'Art Directors Club. (USA)

■101 Dépliant promotionnel pour l'American Craft Expo – un concours-exposition de travaux artisanaux traditionnels et contemporains réalisés par 350 pros du design américain. (USA)

ART DIRECTOR:
Sheila McCaffery

AGENCY:
McCaffery & Partner

CLIENT:
*The Art Directors Club,
New York*

■100

ART DIRECTOR:
Julie Koch-Beinke

DESIGNER:
Julie Koch-Beinke

AGENCY:
Alternatives

CLIENT:
American Craft Enterprises

■101

The Art Directors Club 66th Annual Exhibition

■**102** Folder/poster to publicize a show on special effects issued by the Communicating Arts Group of Arizona (CAGA). (USA)

■**103, 104** "It's a Girl." Concertina folder (opened and cover) with cigars all round for the new (female) addition to an all-male design staff of a studio. (USA)

■**105–107** Cover, partially-opened and fully-opened views of a prospectus for Morison Asset Management offering flexible portfolios for large private and corporate investors. (USA)

■**102** Faltprospekt/Plakat für die Ankündigung einer Präsentation von Spezialeffekten in der visuellen Kommunikation. (USA)

■**103, 104** «Es ist ein Mädchen.» Leporello-Prospekt (geöffnet und Vorderseite) einer Werbeagentur, deren männliche Belegschaft durch eine weibliche Mitarbeiterin ergänzt wurde. (USA)

■**105–107** Umschlag und Ansichten des halb und ganz geöffneten Prospekts für einen Anlageberater, der ein flexibles Angebot für grosse Privat- und Firmenanleger verspricht. (USA)

■**102** Dépliant-affiche du Communicating Arts Group d'Arizona annonçant une démonstration d'effets visuels spéciaux. (USA)

■**103, 104** «C'est une fille» – nouvelle venue dans un studio de design exclusivement masculin et cigarophile. Dépliant en accordéon et sa couverture. (USA)

■**105–107** Couverture d'un prospectus montré mi-ouvert et complètement ouvert. Morison Asset Management y offre un portefeuille de placements flexible pour gros clients. (USA)

ART DIRECTOR:
Dennis Merritt

DESIGNER:
Dennis Merritt

PHOTOGRAPHER:
Rick Gayle

AGENCY:
Dennis Merrit Group

CLIENT:
*Communicating Arts Group
of Arizona*

◄ ■102

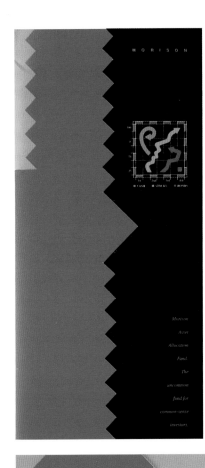

ART DIRECTOR:
Angela Dunkle

AGENCY:
Fallon McElligott

CLIENT:
Fallon McElligott

◄ ■103, 104

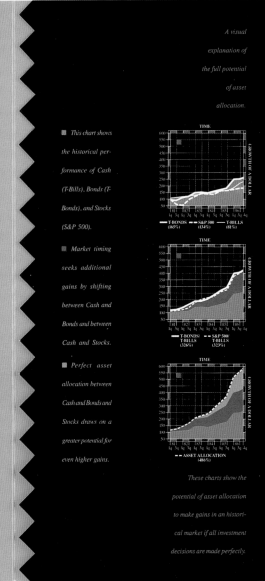

ART DIRECTOR:
Charles Spencer Anderson

DESIGNER:
Sharon Werner

ILLUSTRATOR:
Charles Spencer Anderson

AGENCY:
Duffy Design Group

CLIENT:
*Morison Asset
Allocation Fund*

■105–107

Holiday Memories

Samata Associates

Christmas comes with a basketful
of memories. Some of them are tattered
with time, some are still fresh
with the sweetness of yesterday.
No matter how far we have moved away
from our Christmas roots,
the holiday season beckons us
to relive our childhood traditions.
As this time of year, the smells, sounds,
images and emotions of holidays past
rush to confront our present.
The fragrance of baking cookies,
the sight of a familiar ornament,
the chord of a carol, or
the voice of an old friend
return us to our roots.
Samata Associates is a creative and
professional family bound together
by a commitment to design excellence.
Each of us has learned the meaning
of Christmas in a special way.
This year, we're sending our
warmest holiday wishes and
our favorite Christmas memories
to you.

Ann Tsoo

"The night the tree is decorated
has always been special to me.
Each year we would make a party of it
and the whole family joined in.
We put our favorite ornaments in
'strategic' places so they were easily seen
and the tinsel would go on
one strand at a time
(unless Dad was looking the other way).
This is one of my happiest memories
from when I was little. And
our home was, and still is,
the best decorated house
on the block."

K. C. Yoon

"Under the mistletoe.
A special moment that
brings new meaning to a friendship.
And that friendship is a gift
from God to cherish and love.
I will secretly hang my mistletoe
in hope that I will find
that special someone blowing a kiss
my way."

Cooper

"As the design dog, I've trained
my staff to be responsive to
my canine needs at Christmas.
During the holiday season
mail arrives in cardboard tubes
that Connie gives me to chew apart.
Cookies, nuts and apples appear
in abundance and Norm shares them
with me when no one is watching.
Last year Jim left a huge rawhide bone
for me under the tree.
Even Jennifer, who sneezes whenever
I come near, gives me a pat on the head,
adding to the general love and affection
I receive from Ann, Susan and Jeanne.
My New Year's resolution is to work
on K.C. in 1987. He still resists
my sad brown eyes when I beg for food,
but he'll come around.
It's not easy running a design business
and keeping these people in line
during the holidays, but
it's my favorite time of year!"

ART DIRECTOR:
Pat & Greg Samata

DESIGNER:
Pat & Greg Samata

PHOTOGRAPHER:
Jean Moss

AGENCY:
Samata Associates

CLIENT:
Samata Associates

■108—112

■**108–112** Cover and spreads from a tall seasonal brochure given to clients of Samata Associates, designers; photos of staff members plus their thoughts on Christmas. (USA)

■**113** Die-cut invitation to the UCLA Graduate School of Architecture and Urban Planning's annual dinner. (USA)

■**108–112** Umschlag und Doppelseiten aus einer Weihnachts-broschüre für Kunden des Design-Studios Samata Associates, mit Bildern der Mitglieder und deren Gedanken zu diesem Fest. (USA)

■**113** Dreidimensionale, mit Ausstanzungen versehene Einladung der Fakultät für Architektur, University of California. (USA)

■**108–112** Couverture et doubles pages d'une brochure de fin d'année au grand format destinée aux clients des designers Samata Associates: vœux de Noël de l'équipe. (USA)

■**113** Invitation tridimensionnelle au dîner annuel de la Graduate School d'architecture et d'urbanisme de Los Angeles. (USA)

ART DIRECTOR:
John Coy
DESIGNER:
John Coy
AGENCY:
Coy
CLIENT:
University of California
■**113**

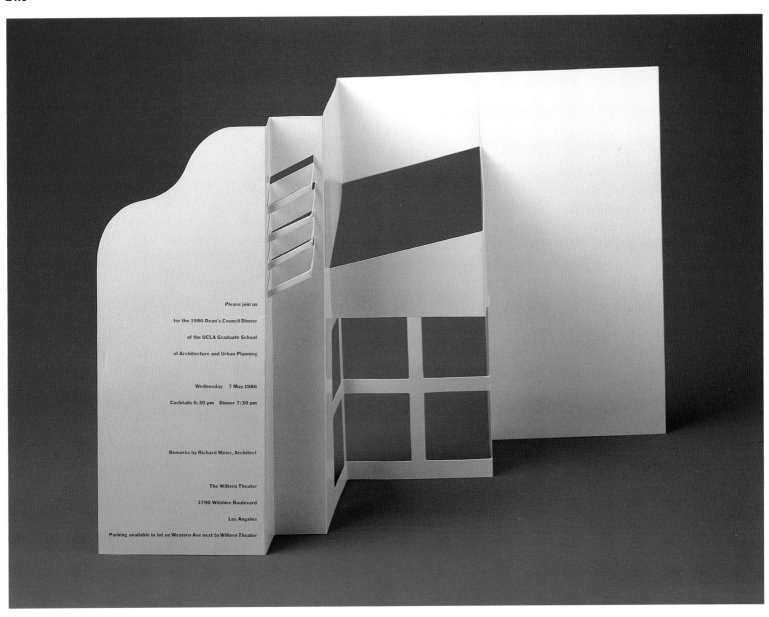

ART DIRECTOR:
Massimo Vignelli
DESIGNER:
Michael Bierut
CLIENT:
*The International Design
Center, New York*
■ 114, 115

SEE HOW EVERY PICTURE TELLS A STORY.

4 DAYS. 55 SHOWROOMS. 73 CHARTER TENANTS. 228 JOURNALISTS. 8,000 LUNCHES. 8,000+ GOERS. 4,000 DC RS. 850 DES HEAR MARIO BOTTA SPEAK. 7,600+ REGISTERED. 1,000,000 SQUARE FEET. 2 BUILDINGS. 1 IDCNY.

ART DIRECTOR:
Jean McCartney
PHOTOGRAPHER:
Bruce Wolf
CLIENT:
WestPoint Pepperell
■ 116, 117

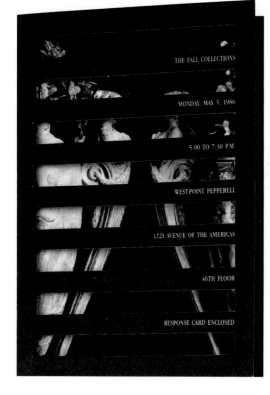

THE FALL COLLECTIONS

MONDAY, MAY 5, 1986

5:00 TO 7:30 P.M.

WESTPOINT PEPPERELL

1221 AVENUE OF THE AMERICAS

46TH FLOOR

RESPONSE CARD ENCLOSED

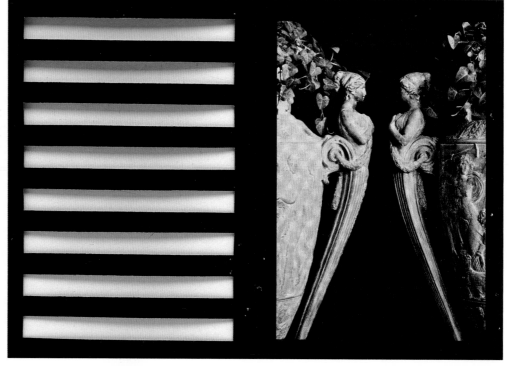

Change
of a
dress.

71 Park Place
New Canaan
Connecticut
06840

Gina Federico
graphic designer
203.966.7603

DESIGNER:
Gina Federico
AGENCY:
Gina Federico Graphic Design
CLIENT:
Gina Federico Graphic Design
■ 118

■ **114, 115** Square sheets which, when opened out, reveal loose cards with photos and facts of the Grand Opening of the IDCNY (International Design Center New York) as promotion for the leasing and services this organization offers. (USA)

■ **116, 117** Die-cut folder enclosing response card as invitation to clients to the fall collections by *Westpoint Pepperell.* (USA)

■ **118** "Change of a Dress" – pun on a change-of-address card for a graphic designer. (USA)

■ **114,115** Quadratische Blätter, hier geöffnet, die lose Karten mit Photos und Informationen enthalten. Es geht um die Eröffnung des Internationalen Design Center in New York, die Ausstellungsmöglichkeiten und Dienstleistungen. (USA)

■ **116, 117** Doppelkarte mit Ausstanzungen und einer losen Antwortkarte für *Westpoint Pepperell.* (USA)

■ **118** Bekanntgabe der Adressänderung einer Graphik-Designerin. Wortspiel: A dress (Kleid) = Address. (USA)

■ **114,115** Feuilles carrées dépliées, contenant en vrac des fiches illustrées décrivant l'inauguration solennelle de l'International Design Center New York. Matériel promotionnel pour les expositions et services offerts par le centre. (USA)

■ **116, 117** Dépliant découpé, avec carte-réponse, pour les créations de mode *Westpoint Pepperell* pour l'automne. (USA)

■ **118** «Changement d'adresse/de dress (vêtement)» – jeu de mots sur la carte d'une artiste graphique. (USA)

ART DIRECTOR:
Felipe Taborda/
Marciso Carvalho

DESIGNER:
Felipe Taborda/
Marciso Carvalho

CLIENT:
Showbras

■ 119

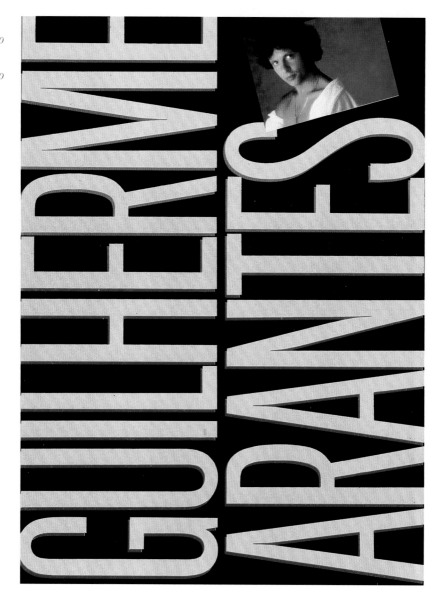

ART DIRECTOR:
Keizo Matsui

DESIGNER:
Keizo Matsui/Eiji Shimizu

AGENCY:
Keizo Matsui & Associates

CLIENT:
Hiroko Koshino
International Corp.

■ 120,121

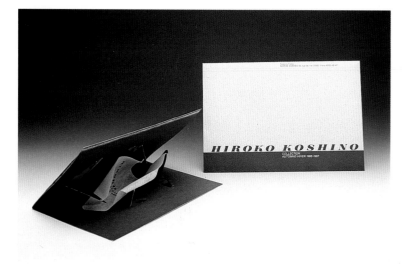

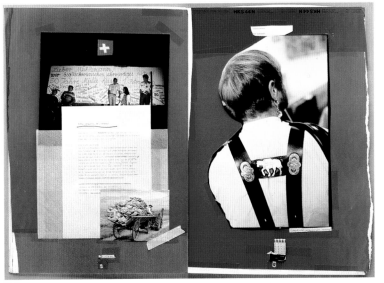

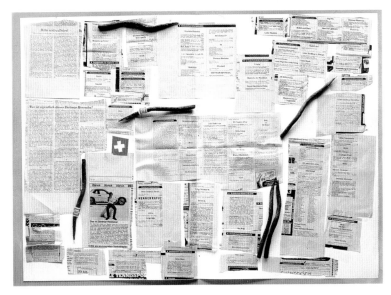
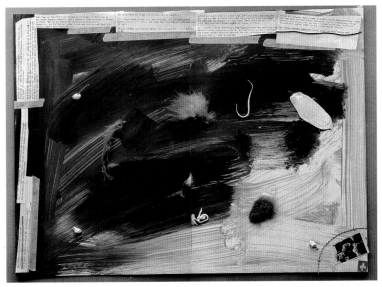

ART DIRECTOR:
Urs Schwerzmann/
Hanspeter Kamm

DESIGNER:
Ute Vogt-Vollenweider

PHOTOGRAPHER:
Dietmar Henneka

COPYWRITER:
Claudia Jaekel/Sithara Atasoy

AGENCY:
Büro Schwerzmann

CLIENT:
Dietmar Henneka/
PSL Hamburg

■**122–125**

■**119** Cover of a program for a pop concert featuring Guilherme Arantes in Rio de Janeiro. (BRA)

■**120, 121** Views of a card with 3-dimensional soft-tissue inset as an invitation to the fall/winter Paris collection of Japanese (lady) fashion designer Hiroko Koshino. (JPN)

■**122–125** Spreads and, bottom right, complete cover of a large promotional "magazine" issued by a German photographer. Called "Switzerland", it comprises collages of labels, letters, cards and artifacts from the photographer's collection. (GER)

■**119** Umschlag eines Programms für ein Pop-Konzert mit Guilherme Arantes in Rio de Janeiro. (BRA)

■**120, 121** Ansichten einer dreidimensionalen Karte mit Seiden-Papier, als Einladung zu einer Präsentation der Herbst-/Winter-Kollektion des Modeschöpfers Hiroko Koshino. (JPN)

■**122–125** Doppelseiten und (unten rechts) der komplette Umschlag der Ausgabe »Schweiz« von *Auss/Puff*, dem grossformatigen Kundenmagazin des Photographen Dietmar Henneka, der hier anschaulich aus seinem Berufsalltag berichtet. (GER)

■**119** Couverture de programme pour un concert pop de Guilherme Arantes à Rio de Janeiro. (BRA)

■**120,121** Vues d'une carte incrustée de papier mousseline tri-dimensionnel, invitant à un défilé de mode du couturier japonais Hiroko Koshino à Paris (collection automne/hiver). (JPN) ·

■**122–125** Doubles pages et (en bas, à droite) couverture d'un »magazine« promotionnel au grand format réalisé par un photographe allemand sous le titre de »Suisse«. Il se compose de collages d'étiquettes, de lettres, de cartes et d'artefacts.' (GER)

ART DIRECTOR:
John Coy

DESIGNER:
John Coy

PHOTOGRAPHER:
Steven A. Gunther/
Craig Schmitt

AGENCY:
COY

CLIENT:
California Institute
of the Arts

■**126, 127**

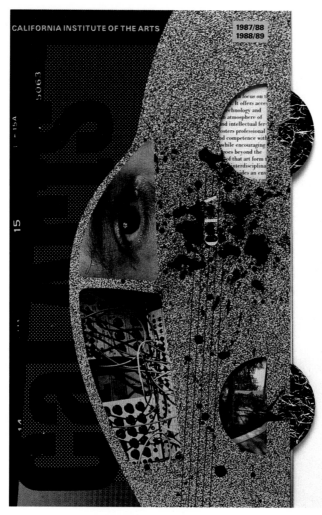

■**126,127** Die-cut cover and spread from the "Viewbook" – an information brochure issued by the California Institute of the Arts, giving details of the various course programs. (USA)

■**128,129** Cover and spread from a catalog for the Washington College (one of the ten oldest colleges in the USA) dedicated to the study of the liberal arts and sciences. (USA)

■**126, 127** Umschlag mit ausgestanzten Halbkreisen und Doppelseite aus einer Informationsbroschüre mit Einzelheiten über das Lehrprogramm des California Institute of the Arts. (USA)

■**128, 129** Umschlag und Doppelseite aus einem Katalog für das Washington College, das seinen Namen und eine Unterstützung von George Washington erhielt. (USA)

■**126, 127** Couverture aux motifs en découpe et double page de «Viewbook», brochure informative publiée par le California Institute of the Arts avec le programme des cours. (USA)

■**128, 129** Couverture et double page d'un catalogue du Washington College (l'un des dix plus anciens aux E.-U.) spécialisé dans les beaux-arts et les sciences. (USA)

ART DIRECTOR:
Anthony Rutka
DESIGNER:
Kate Berquist
ILLUSTRATOR:
Kim Parr
PHOTOGRAPHER:
Bill Denison
AGENCY:
Rutka Weadock Design
CLIENT:
Washington College
■**128, 129**

Washington

Washington College

Founded in 1782 by the Reverend William Smith, Washington College is one of the ten oldest colleges in the country. General George Washington gave the College his name, 50 guineas, and six years of service on the Board of Visitors and Governors.

Today, in an eighteenth-century setting, Washington College educates young men and women for life in the twenty-first century.

Chestertown, Maryland

The Clifton B. Miller Library, the academic heart of the campus, contains more than 168,000 volumes, 700 periodicals, and an extensive microform collection. An efficient interlibrary loan system, open stacks, abundant study carrels, a rare book collection, and the helpful services of the staff are other important features of the library. The library also offers an on-line text/bibliographic/general information data base search service (DIALOG) and public access to six Macintosh microcomputers.

Living accommodations at Washington College are diverse. Students may choose to live in coed residences, residences organized by academic interest, and dorms organized around fraternity and sorority chapters. Housing includes modern apartment suites and charming old dorms — twelve residence halls in all — with 30 to 143 students in each house.

Athletic facilities include the Cain Athletic Center's two gymnasiums which accommodate basketball, tennis, volleyball, badminton, weight lifting, aerobic exercise, and dance; tennis and platform tennis courts; a quarter-mile track, playing fields for soccer, field hockey, baseball, softball, and lacrosse. In 1984 the College opened the Eugene B. Casey Swim Center, which features a 42 by 75-foot pool with six lanes and both one-meter and three-meter diving boards.

Another facility, the Truslow Boathouse on the Chester River, has become part of the Washington College Boating Park. The Park provides a center for both men's and women's crews, the sailing club, and other waterfront activities, and is the site of the Lelia Hynson Boat Pavilion, which serves as a special gathering place for student and faculty social activities.

"Living in Chestertown gave me a perspective on life that I never would have had if I attended school in a large city. Washington College was a most positive experience at a very important stage of my life."

Peter J. Rosen '68
Physician, Anesthesiologist

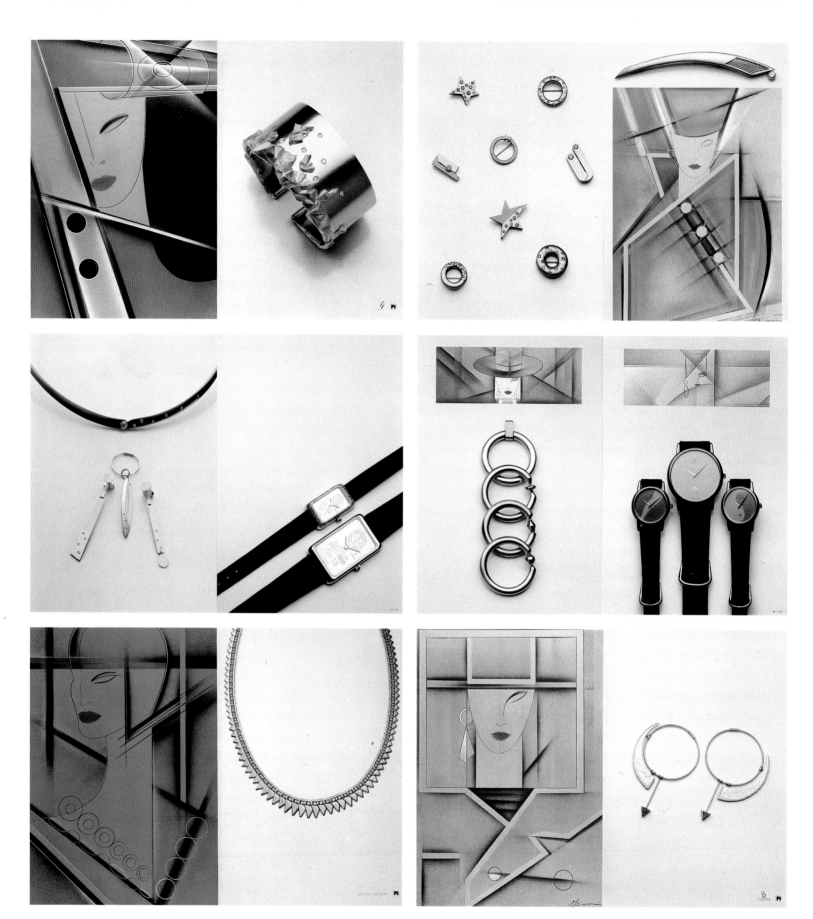

ART DIRECTOR:
Moni Lutz

ILLUSTRATOR:
Jane Kleinman

PHOTOGRAPHER:
Mane Weigand

AGENCY:
J. Walter Thompson

■ **130-135**

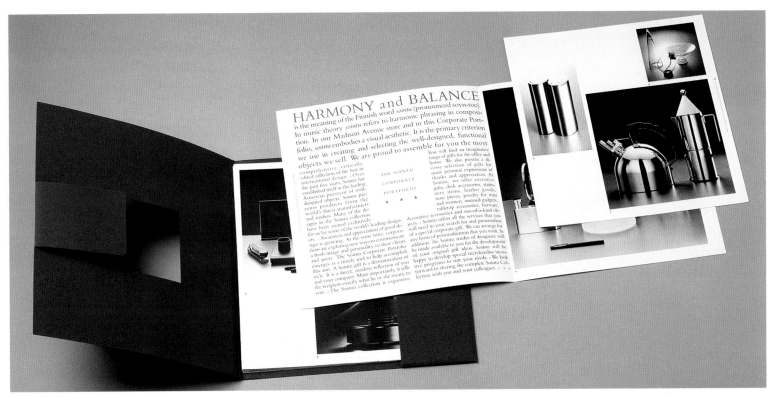

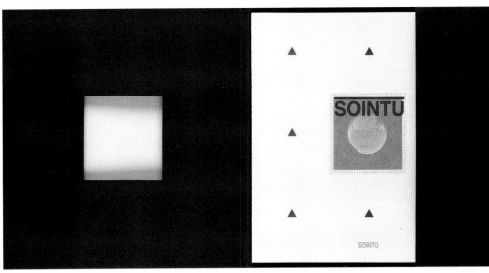

ART DIRECTOR:
STEPHEN DOYLE
DESIGNER:
STEPHEN DOYLE
AGENCY:
DRENTTEL DOYLE PARTNERS
CLIENT:
SOINTU
■**136–138**

■**130–135** Sample double spreads from a jewellery catalog (No. 9) issued by the Platinum Guild of Germany presenting their latest creations. (GER)

■**136–138** Views of the *Sointu* corporate portfolio – a die-cut folder containing loose spreads showing international designer wares from the collection on sale at this Madison Avenue store. The Finnish word "sointu" means harmony and balance. (USA)

■**130–135** Beispiele der Doppelseiten aus »Platin Edition No. 9«, einem Katalog der Platin Gilde International, Deutschland, mit den neuesten Schmuckkreationen. (GER)

■**136–138** Mappe, die aus losen Blättern für die in diesem Laden erhältlichen Designer-Artikel und einem Umschlag mit ausgestanztem Viereck und einer Lasche besteht. Das finnische Wort »sointu« bedeutet Harmonie und Ausgewogenheit. (USA)

■**130–135** Doubles pages spécimens du catalogue de joaillerie no 9 de la section allemande de la Guilde internationale du platine, avec les dernières créations en platine. (GER)

■**136–138** Album *Sointu.* Ce classeur aux motifs en découpe renferme des feuillets mobiles où sont illustrées les créations de design mises en vente dans ce magasin de Madison Avenue. En finnois, «sointu» signifie équilibre, harmonie. (USA)

■**139, 140** Cover and double spread from a tall catalog presenting the range of pens made by *Parker.* (USA)

■**141–144** Cover and spreads from the *Apple* collection catalog, showing some of the in-house "famous name" merchandise bearing the *Apple* logo. (USA)

■**139, 140** Umschlag und Doppelseite aus einem schmalen Katalog mit einer Auswahl von *Parker*-Schreibgeräten. (USA)

■**141–144** Umschlag und Doppelseiten aus einem Katalog für die *Apple*-Kollektion, Markenprodukte, die von *Apple*-Computers mit dem *Apple*-Logo vertrieben werden. (USA)

■**139, 140** Couverture et double page d'un catalogue au grand format des stylos et matériels d'écriture *Parker.* (USA)

■**141–144** Couverture et doubles pages du catalogue de la collection *Apple*, où figurent quelques-uns des articles commercialisés sous la célèbre marque d'ordinateurs. (USA)

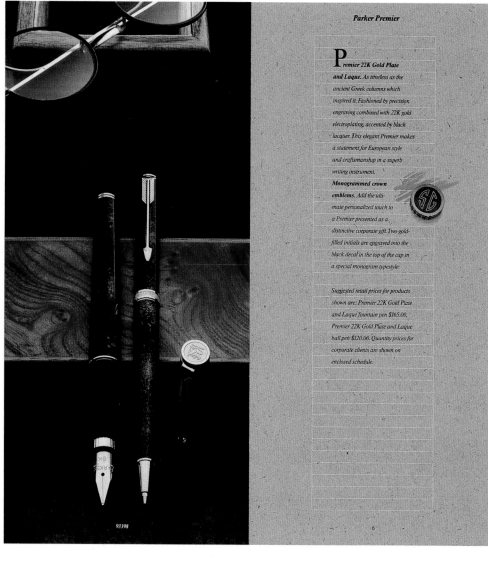

ART DIRECTOR:
Pat & Greg Samata
PHOTOGRAPHER:
Terry Heffernan/
Denis Dooley
AGENCY:
Samata Associates
CLIENT:
Parker Pen Company
■**139,140**

THE APPLE COLLE CTION

ART DIRECTOR:
Clement Mok

DESIGNER:
Jill Savini

PHOTOGRAPHER:
Paul Matsuda

AGENCY:
*Apple Computer/
Creative Services*

CLIENT:
Apple Computer

■141–144

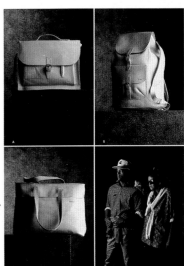

A. You know how they used to make things in the olden days? Well, in Germany a company named Bree still does. Our Bree brief is hand-crafted from the sturdiest natural leather that darkens with age. It has two outer pockets, brass fittings, a handle, and a shoulder strap. **Leather Brief #9525, $125.**

B. Another small masterwork from the hands of the German craftsmen at Bree—the Leather daypack. All natural vegetable-tanned leather with brass fittings make this a personal treasure you're likely to have for the rest of your life. **Leather Daypack #9526, $154.**

C. The Bree all-leather satchel is exactly what you need for a hard day's shopping. Its main pocket has brass zipper closure to hold almost everything; a side pocket holds the rest. Shoulder straps are stitched and brass-riveted for extra strength. **Leather Satchel #9527, $149.**

The Segrets Collection. All natural fibers and hand silk-screening are trademarks of these unique designs. Each piece in the collection features painstaking attention to fine detail. Segrets sweatshirts and flannel shirts all work together as perfect color coordinates.

D. The softest 100% cotton flannel you ever felt, and they perfectly match our Segrets sweatshirts. They're cut a little big and feel sooo good. Each is silk-screened by hand, so each is unique. Special unisex sizes (S/M, M/L, L/XL) in teal print or purple print. Please specify size and color. **Segrets Flannel Shirt #710, $42.**

11

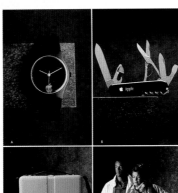

A. Take a dive. The Apple watch is water-resistant to 100 feet. Comes with quartz movement and a 90-day warranty. **Apple Watch #0287, $35.**

B. Amazing how often you'll use the 12 features of this Victorinox knife. Open wine. Pull splinters. Turn screws. Open cans. Strip wires. Pick teeth. Even use it as a knife. **Swiss Army Knife #0288, $34.**

C. Very hot lunch. High-tech lunch box of high-impact—virtually indestructible—plastic. Yellow with black shoulder strap. **Lunch Box #0185, $9.50.**

D. Sink your hands into the double-entry pockets of this oversized, fashionable yet-functional jacket. Hot stuff for women or men, from Mistral. 100% cotton unisex sizes (S–XL) in white or yellow. **Mistral Jacket #0920, $78.**

E. Clean design distinguishes the Braun wall clock. Made in Germany, the black clock boasts a quartz movement. **Braun Wall Clock #0430, $42.**

F. This compact kit can turn your airline seat or hotel room into an office. It contains a scaled-down stapler, scissors, tape dispenser, tape measure, razor cutter, ruler, glue stick, and holder for paper clips and rubber bands. **Travel Kit #0175, $12.**

G. This daypack is made by Caribou from tough 420-denier nylon packcloth. It measures 15" x 8" x 5" and has two front zipper pockets and adjustable shoulder straps. Choose plum, teal, or royal blue. **Nylon Daypack #0400, $36.**

H. This plastic Loose-leaf notebook by Cadic has a locking compartment inside the front cover to hold notes, letters, and all the things you want to have handy. With pencil compartment, four divider tabs, and 30 sheets of letter-quality writing paper. **Loose-leaf Notebook #0505, $12.50. 70-page Loose-leaf Notebook Refills #0506, $2.95.**

H. This may be the world's best-designed notebook. The cover serves two purposes: an envelope in back stores things like floppy disks, and a wraparound flap completely seals in the notebook. In three sizes, by Cadic. Please specify size. 8½" x 11" **Writing Folder #0507, $10.** 7" x 10" **Writing Folder #0508, $7.50.** 3½" x 6" **Writing Folder #0509, $3.50.**

I. This bag is also great for carrying your sweats to the gym as it is for holding them in an overhead compartment on a flight to Aspen—or Cancun. In black, navy, or teal, with padded shoulder strap. **Nylon Duffle #9430, $32.**

J. Nylon sport wallet with Velcro closure is available in black, red, or teal. **Sport Wallet #0295, $9.50.**

12   13

A. The sleek Rona briefcase will help you be as organized as it makes you look. Its patented design features a lambskin exterior, sheepskin lining, hidden combination locks, secret compartment, and a debossed Apple logo. Hand made in Spain. **Rona Briefcase #0223, $449.**

B. How much work do you take home with you? It really doesn't matter, because this Stuart Kern briefcase's gusseted pockets allow it to expand to hold as much as you can carry. Black calfskin with retractable handles and removable shoulder strap. **Leather Expandable Briefcase #0657, $290.**

C. Three-piece set includes an upright holder with nickel-plated steel scissors and a magnifying glass/letter opener of pressed zinc. **Standing Desk Set #0346, $32.**

23

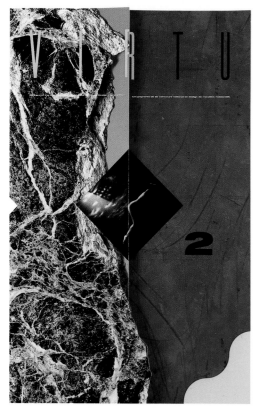

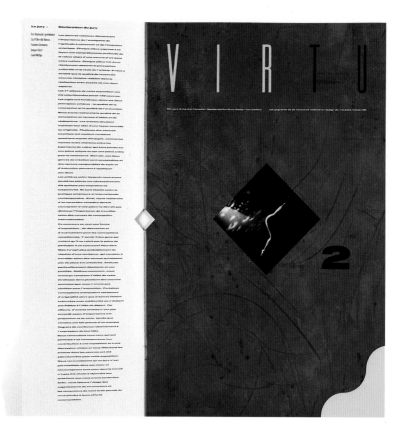

ART DIRECTOR:
Del Terrelonge
DESIGNER:
Del Terrelonge
PHOTOGRAPHER:
Ron Baxter Smith
AGENCY:
Terrelonge Design
CLIENT:
Virtu Forum & Function
■ **145–148**

■**145–148** Die-cut catalog of winners in an annual designer's exhibition *Virtu* organized by Forum and Function Directions in Canadian Design. Shown is the half-width outer cover, the outer cover opened, and two spreads. (CAN)

■**149–151** Front and two views of a catalog presenting architect/designer items in the *Swid Powell* collection. (USA)

■**145–148** Katalog mit Ausstanzungen für die Präsentation von Gewinnern eines Produkt-Design-Wettbewerbs. Gezeigt ist die über die halbe Breite reichende Vorderseite, geschlossen und geöffnet, und zwei Doppelseiten. (CAN)

■**149–151** Vorderseite und zwei Ansichten eines Leporellos mit Gegenständen aus der *Swid-Powell*-Kollektion. (USA)

■**145–148** Catalogue (motifs en découpe) des lauréats de l'exposition annuelle de design *Virtu* de Forum and Function Directions in Canadian Design: demi-couverture extérieure fermée et ouverte; deux doubles pages. (CAN)

■**149–151** Recto et deux vues d'un catalogue d'articles d'architecture et de design, collection *Swid Powell*. (USA)

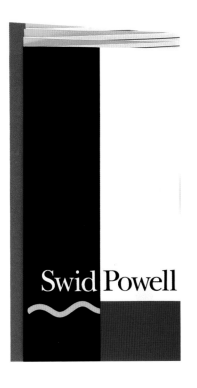

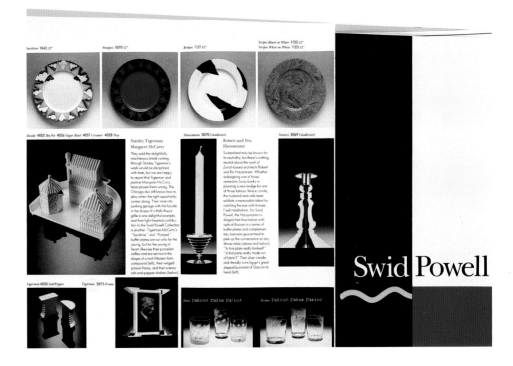

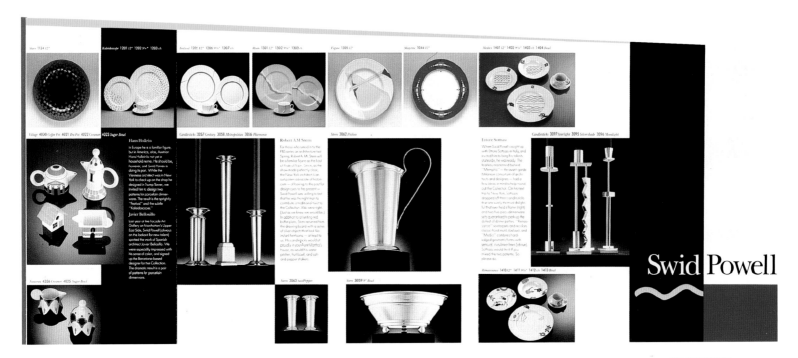

ART DIRECTOR:
NANCY SKOLOS

DESIGNER:
NANCY SKOLOS/CHERYL SHEA/
LAURA SILVERMAN

PHOTOGRAPHER:
TOM WEDELL/KEN RAYNOR

AGENCY:
SKOLOS, WEDELL + RAYNOR

CLIENT:
SWID POWELL

■149–151

Die ästhetische Wirkung von Linea beruht auf einem formalen Dreiklang: Podest, Korpus, Türen. Aus wenigen Gestaltungselementen ergeben sich Möbel von seltener Ausgewogenheit und Schönheit. Ein Sideboard 245 cm x 78 cm, schwarz-Hochglanzlack mit Türen aus exclusivem Myrtenwurzel-Maserfurnier.

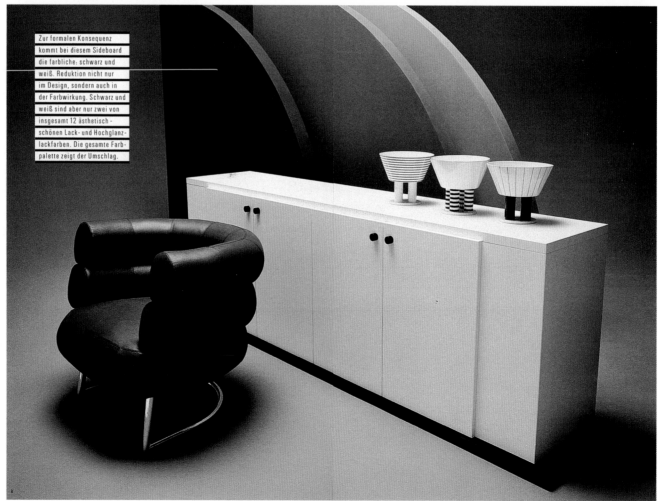

Zur formalen Konsequenz kommt bei diesem Sideboard die farbliche: schwarz und weiß. Reduktion nicht nur im Design, sondern auch in der Farbwirkung. Schwarz und weiß sind aber nur zwei von insgesamt 12 ästhetisch-schönen Lack- und Hochglanzlackfarben. Die gesamte Farbpalette zeigt der Umschlag.

■152,153 Two spreads from a catalog presenting *Linea* furniture made by *Stüker*. Top: a sideboard in black high-gloss lacquer with doors of exclusive gnarled myrtlewood veneer; bottom: black and white high-gloss lacquered sideboard. (GER)

■154–156 Cover and double spreads from a catalog for *Erco* Lighting. Spreads show *Eclipse* halogen spotlights. (GER)

■152,153 Doppelseiten aus einem Katalog für das *Linea*-Möbelprogramm von *Stüker*. Die ästhetische Wirkung wird als formaler Dreiklang aus Podest, Korpus und Türen umschrieben. Das Thema: «Alles wirklich Schöne ist einfach.» (Sokrates). (GER)

■154–156 Umschlag und Doppelseiten mit *Eclipse*-Strahlern für Halogenlampen, aus einem Katalog für *Erco*-Leuchten. (GER)

■152,153 Deux doubles pages d'un catalogue d'ameublements *Linea* de *Stüker* (Allemagne). En haut: buffet verni noir extrabrillant, portes plaquées de hêtre australien noueux; en bas: buffet verni noir et blanc extra-brillant. (GER)

■154–156 Couverture et doubles pages d'un catalogue d'éclairages *Erco*. Doubles pages: spots *Eclipse* à halogène. (GER)

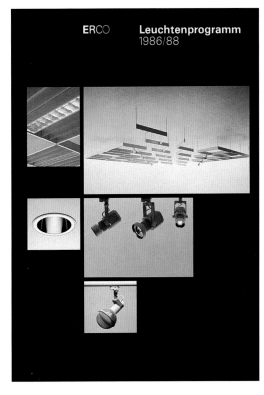

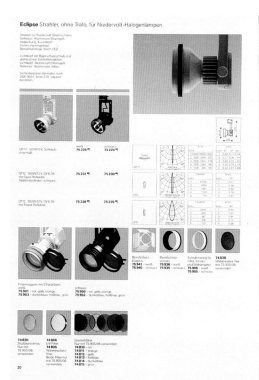

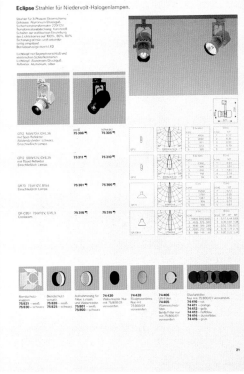

ART DIRECTOR:
HEINZ-H. ZÖLLER
DESIGNER:
HEINZ-H. ZÖLLER
PHOTOGRAPHER:
FOTOGRAFEN-TEAM
AGENCY:
ERCO/MARKTVORBEREITUNG
CLIENT:
ERCO LEUCHTEN GMBH
■154–156

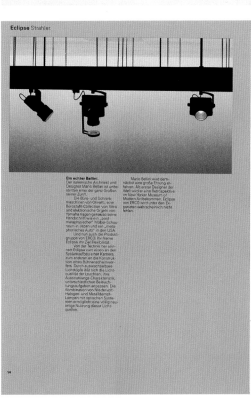

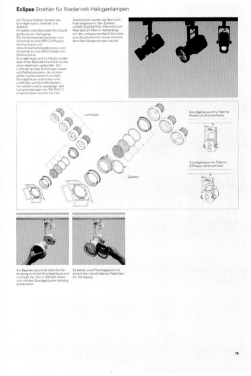

ART DIRECTOR:
WERNER WÜRDINGER
DESIGNER:
WERNER WÜRDINGER
PHOTOGRAPHER:
RUDI SCHMUTZ
AGENCY:
GOTTSCHLING & WÜRDINGER
CLIENT:
STÜKER GMBH
◄■152,153

ART DIRECTOR:
Randolph Nolte

DESIGNER:
Randolph Nolte

PHOTOGRAPHER:
Hans Hansen

AGENCY:
Randolph Nolte
Creative Consultants

CLIENT:
B.T. Dibbern

■**157–160**

ART DIRECTOR:
Michael Vanderbyl

DESIGNER:
Michael Vanderbyl

AGENCY:
Vanderbyl Design

CLIENT:
Bernhardt Furniture Co.

■**161** ▶

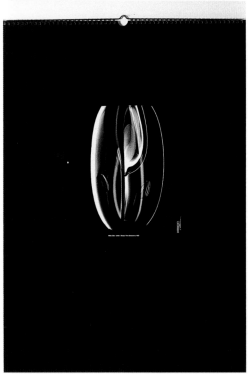

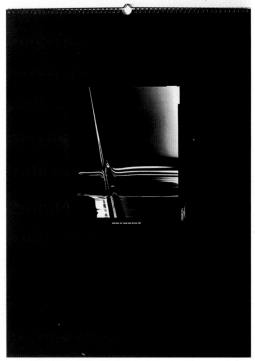

■**157–160** Cover sheets, introductory sheet and two sample sheets from a catalog in the form of a calendar for *Dibbern* presenting a collection of rare *Iittala* glassware photographed in an unconventional manner. (GER)

■**161** Sample covers and spreads from a series (16) of product brochures for exclusive furniture made by the Bernhardt Furniture Co. The *Bernhardt* conference table (Anigre series) is portrayed at bottom left of illustration. (USA)

■**157–160** Deckblatt, einleitende Seite und Beispiele der Inhaltsseiten aus einem Katalog in Kalenderform. Die unkonventionelle Verarbeitung der *Iittala*-Glaskollektion von *Dibbern* (Hamburg) wird durch die Photographie unterstützt. (GER)

■**161** Beispiele von Umschlägen und Doppelseiten aus einer Serie von Broschüren für exklusive Möbel der Bernhardt Furniture Co. Wie die Umschlagaufnahmen deutlich machen, ist jede Broschüre einem bestimmten Programm gewidmet. (USA)

■**157–160** Feuillet de couverture, feuillet initial et deux feuillets types d'un catalogue *Dibbern* sous forme de calendrier, avec une collection rare de verrerie *Iittala* photographiée de manière peu conventionnelle. (GER)

■**161** Exemples des couvertures et doubles pages réalisées pour une série de 16 brochures en faveur des ameublements exclusifs de la Bernhardt Furniture Co. La table de conférence *Bernhardt* (série Anigre) est visible en bas, à gauche. (USA)

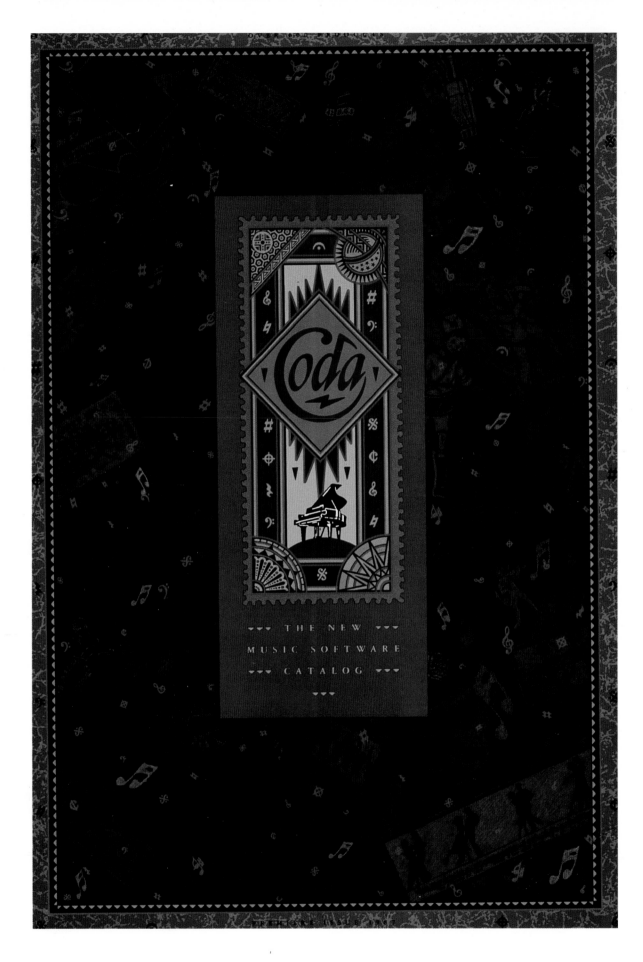

ART DIRECTOR:
Charles Spencer Anderson

AGENCY:
Duffy Design Group

CLIENT:
Wenger Corporation

■162–168

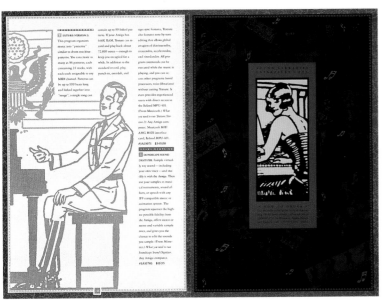

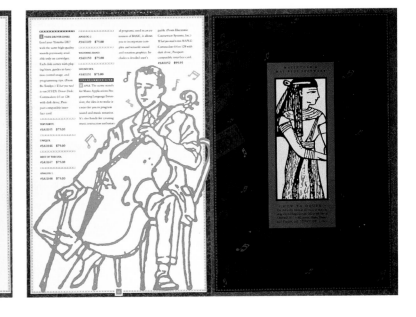

■ **162–168** Cover and double spreads from *Coda* - catalog of music software stocked by the Wenger Corp. New-fashioned technology is presented with old-fashioned pictures. (USA)

■ **162–168** Umschlag und typische Doppelseiten aus *Coda*, einem Katalog für Musik-Software der Wenger-Corporation. Nostalgische Bilder, eingesetzt für neue Technologie. (USA)

■ **162–168** Couverture et doubles pages caractéristiques du catalogue *Coda* de logiciels musicaux de la Wenger Corporation: une technologie de pointe illustrée d'images rétro. (USA)

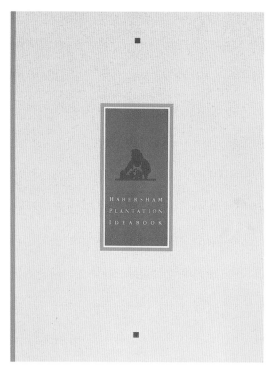

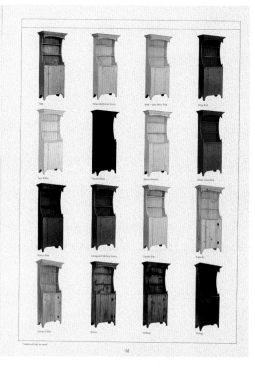

ART DIRECTOR:
Brad Copeland/
Kathi Roberts

DESIGNER:
Brad Copeland/
Kathi Roberts

PHOTOGRAPHER:
Mike Granberry

AGENCY:
Cooper Copeland Inc.

CLIENT:
Habersham Plantation Corp.

■**169–171**

■**169–171** Cover and double spreads from a catalog for Habersham Plantation Corporation showing their various pieces of traditionally-flavoured colonial-style furniture. (USA)

■**169–171** Umschlag und Doppelseiten aus einem Katalog für Habersham Plantation Corporation, Hersteller von traditionellen Möbeln im Kolonialstil. (USA)

■**169–171** Couverture et doubles pages d'un catalogue de la Habersham Plantation Corporation, qui fabrique des meubles de style colonial à la manière du temps jadis. (USA)

ADVERTISING

Magazine Advertisements

Newspaper Advertisements

WERBUNG

Zeitschrifteninserate

Zeitungsinserate

PUBLICITÉ

Annonces de magazines

Annonces de journaux

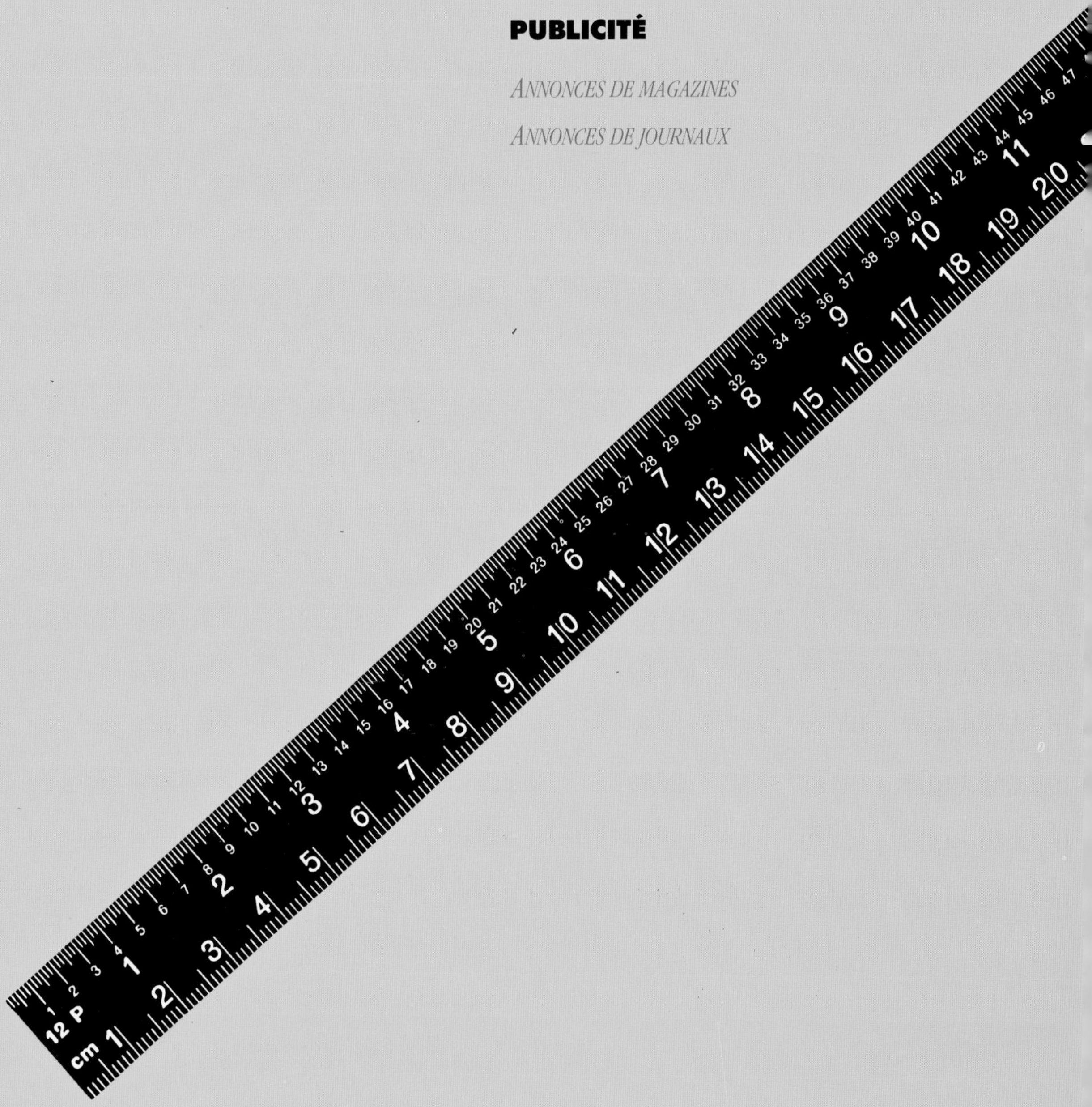

ART DIRECTOR:
Robert Probst

DESIGNER:
Robert Probst/Joel Conison

PHOTOGRAPHER:
Joel Conison

AGENCY:
Schenker Probst Barensfeld

CLIENT:
Market at Garfield Place Restaurant

■ 172–175

ART DIRECTOR:
Steve Jaeger

DESIGNER:
Steve Jaeger

PHOTOGRAPHER:
Martin Mistretta

AGENCY:
DDB Needham Worldwide

CLIENT:
*National Federation of
Coffee Growers of Columbia*

■**176**

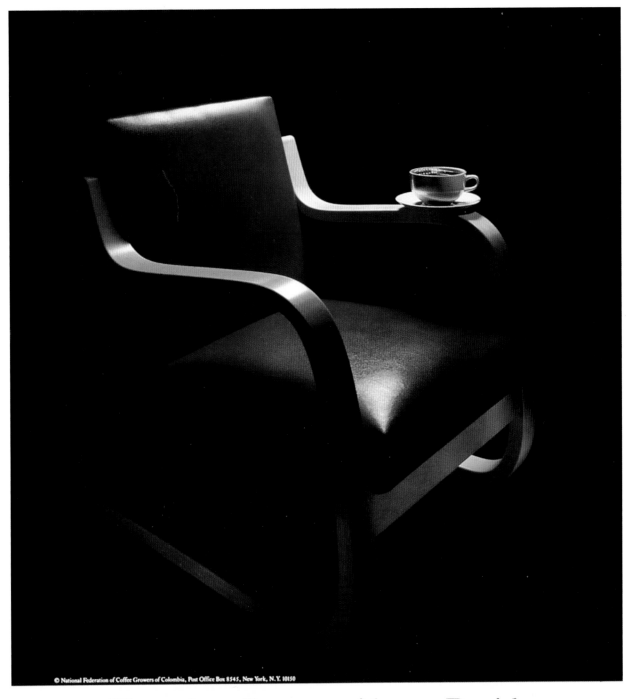

© National Federation of Coffee Growers of Colombia, Post Office Box 8545, New York, N.Y. 10150

The only coffee to go with your Danish.

100% Colombian Coffee

The richest coffee in the world.™

■**172–175** Series of advertisements to publicize a market at Garfield Place Restaurant (Cincinnati). (USA)

■**176** Magazine ad issued by the National Federation of Coffee Growers of Colombia to promote Colombian coffee; a graphic solution, intensive lighting and sophistication to complement the copy. (USA)

■**172–175** Beispiele aus einer Anzeigenkampagne für das Garfield Place Restaurant in Cincinnati. (USA)

■**176** Magazinanzeige für kolumbianischen Kaffee: «Der einzige Kaffee, der zu Ihrem dänischen (Gebäck und Design) passt.» Die graphische Lösung, Licht und Text unterstreichen den Stil des Inserats. (USA)

■**172–175** Série d'annonces pour l'ouverture d'un marché au Garfield Place Restaurant de Cincinnati. (USA)

■**176** Annonce de magazine de la Fédération nationale des planteurs de café de Colombie, pour la promotion du café colombien: une solution graphique, un éclairage intense, un doigt de sophistication pour arrondir le texte. (USA)

ART DIRECTOR:
Gary Goldsmith

DESIGNER:
Gary Goldsmith

ILLUSTRATOR:
Gary Goldsmith

AGENCY:
Geers Gross

CLIENT:
Lender's Bagels

■ **177**

Two ideas that changed America.

Lender's
We brought America the bagel.

■ **177** Full-page advertisement to promote bagels (a very popular type of pastry eaten in the USA) made by *Lender's*. (USA)

■ **178–180** Full-page advertisements from a series for *Hero* conserves. Headers: "Instant Pasta"; "It simply belongs to pasta. Basta"; and "No Banquet without Pearls". (SWI)

■ **177** «Zwei Ideen, die Amerika verändert haben.» Ganzseitiges Inserat für ein in den USA populäres Gebäck. (USA)

■ **178–180** Beispiele aus einer Reihe von ganzseitigen Inseraten für *Hero*-Konserven, hier für italienische Teigwaren, eine Sauce nach italienischem Rezept und für «erlesene» Erbsen. (SWI)

■ **177** Annonce pleine page pour la promotion d'un type de biscuit *Lender's*: «Deux idées qui ont changé l'Amérique.» (USA)

■ **178–180** Pour une série des Conserves *Hero*: pâtes minute; une sauce qui ne se discute pas pour accompagner les pâtes; pas de banquet sans les «perles» des petits pois fins. (SWI)

Pasta subito.

Die gehört einfach zu Pasta. Basta.

Dass unsere Teigwaren wie Pasta schmecken, dass sie molto delicato munden, darauf legen wir grossen Wert. Deshalb bereiten wir sie nur mit ausgesuchten Rohstoffen, nur mit erlesenen Beilagen zu. Die Subitoparaten, die Ravioli, die Triangoli, Tortellini und Cannelloni.

Hero
Freude am Essen
1886–1986

Für eine gute italienische Sauce braucht es ein gutes italienisches Rezept. Haben wir! Man darf nur auserlesene Zutaten verwenden. Machen wir! Dann muss sie lange, sehr lange köcheln. Tut sie bei uns! Nun kann man sie servieren. Können Sie, buon appetito!

Hero
Freude am Essen
1886–1986

Kein Festessen ohne Perlen.

Zart muss Gemüse sein, zart aber ja nicht ohne Biss. Und nach Gemüse muss Gemüse schmecken. Bohnen nach Bohnen, Erbsen nach Erbsen. Und vollwertig muss es sein, voll von Nährwerten und Mineralstoffen. Sonst hat es keine Chance zum Gourmets-Gemüse zu werden. Da sind wir stur!

Hero
Freude am Essen
1886–1986

ART DIRECTOR:
M. Weber
DESIGNER:
T. Bolliger
PHOTOGRAPHER:
Patrick Rohner
AGENCY:
Adolf Wirz AG
CLIENT:
Hero Conserven
■**178–180**

ART DIRECTOR:
Graham Watson
DESIGNER:
James Marsh
ILLUSTRATOR:
James Marsh
COPYWRITER:
Mike Cuzens
AGENCY:
Bartle Bogle & Hegarty
CLIENT:
Courvoisier
■ **181, 182**

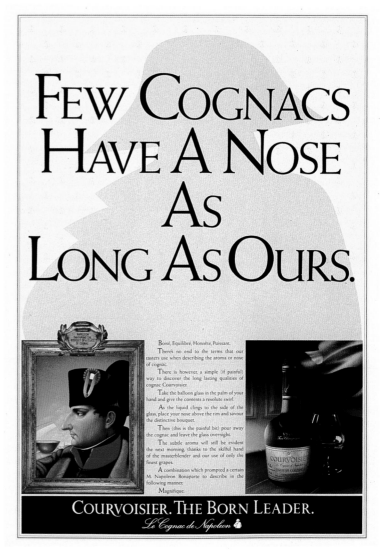

DESIGNER:
Kaspar Hiltbrand

PHOTOGRAPHER:
Christoph Markwalder

AGENCY:
Urs Tschan AG

CLIENT:
Haecky Import AG

■183

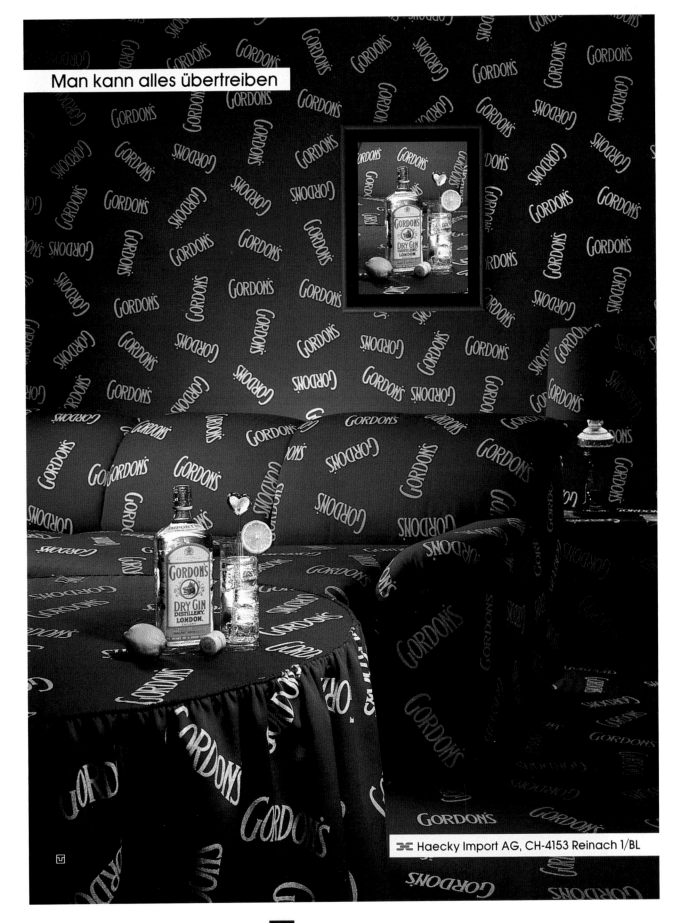

Man kann alles übertreiben

Haecky Import AG, CH-4153 Reinach 1/BL

Dessert your diet.

Try Blue Bell®Light.
It has the same great homemade taste you'd expect
from the Little Creamery.
The big difference is Blue Bell Light is 97% fat free.
So now you can diet and get your just deserts.

We eat all we can.
We sell the rest.

Blue Bell'Ice Cream
From the Little Creamery in Brenham.

ART DIRECTOR:
Lyle Metzdorf
DESIGNER:
Lyle Metzdorf
PHOTOGRAPHER:
Barry Seidman
AGENCY:
*Jonson Pirtle Pedersen
Alcorn Metzdorf & Hess*
CLIENT:
Blue Bell Creameries, Inc.
■**184, 185**

ART DIRECTOR:
Michael McLaughlin
DESIGNER:
Michael McLaughlin
ILLUSTRATOR:
John Martin
COPYWRTITER:
Stephen Creet
AGENCY:
Carder Gray Advertising Inc.
CLIENT:
H.J. Heinz
■**186**

■**184, 185** Advertisements for Blue Bell Creameries, Inc. to promote their *Blue Bell* brand ice cream. Left, a 97% fat-free ice cream which can be eaten while on a diet. (USA)

■**186** Single page advertisement for *Heinz Ketchup*, sponsors of music awards in Canada. (CAN)

■**184, 185** Anzeigen für Speiseeis. Der Slogan für die kalorien-arme Sorte (links) basiert auf einem Wortspiel. Rechts: «Wir essen soviel wir können. Den Rest verkaufen wir.» (USA)

■**186** «Glückwünsche an alle, die sich einen Namen gemacht haben. Wir wissen, was Sie durchgemacht haben.» (USA)

■**184, 185** Annonces pour les glaces *Blue Bell* de Blue Bell Creameries, Inc. A gauche, une glace à teneur en graisse réduite de 97%, idéale pour un régime alimentaire. (USA)

■**186** Annonce sur page simple pour *Heinz Ketchup*, qui parraine des concours de musique au Canada. (CAN)

To all of you who have succeeded in becoming a famous name, congratulations.

We know what you went through.

Heinz Ketchup, sponsor of the 1986 Casby Music Awards.

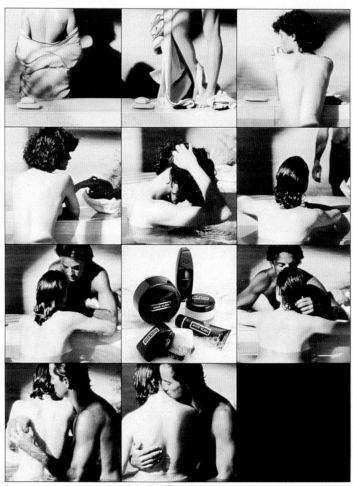

ANNE KLEIN
for body and bath.

ANNE KLEIN
PARFUM

ART DIRECTOR:
Sheila McCaffery
DESIGNER:
Sheila McCaffery
PHOTOGRAPHER:
Neil Barr
AGENCY:
McCaffery & Ratner
CLIENT:
Anne Klein
■**187, 188**

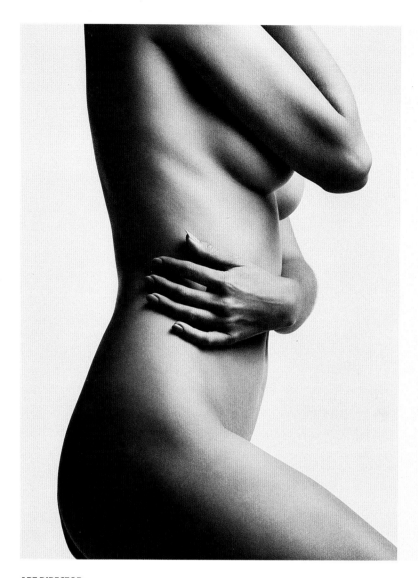

FEW PEOPLE KNOW WHAT THE BODY'S LARGEST ORGAN IS. FEWER STILL KNOW HOW TO TAKE CARE OF IT.

The largest organ of the body is skin and if your skin is dry, it should have the best care possible. Keri Hand and Body Lotion is a therapeutic lotion made with beneficial ingredients. Its concentrated formula penetrates skin and quickly provides relief. Keri soothes, softens and moisturizes; your skin will feel good all day. Countless women use Keri, many of them on a dermatologist's recommendation. Keri: the best way to care for a vital part of your body.

KERI HAND AND BODY LOTION.
Keri for your dry skin.

ART DIRECTOR:
Michael McLaughlin

PHOTOGRAPHER:
John Mastromonaco

COPYWRITER:
Stephen Creet

AGENCY:
Carder Gray Advertising Inc.

CLIENT:
Keri Lotion

■ **189**

■**187, 188** Two magazine advertisements for *Anne Klein* - bath and skin products and perfume. (USA)

■**189** Double-spread magazine advertisement in black and white for *Keri* lotion, a hand and body therapeutic lotion to soothe, soften and moisturize the skin. (USA)

■**187, 188** Magazinanzeigen für Bade- und Körperlotionen sowie für Parfum der Marke *Anne Klein.* (USA)

■**189** Zeitschrifteninserat für *Keri*-Körperlotion. «Nur wenige wissen, welches das grösste Organ des Körpers ist. Noch weniger Leute wissen etwas über die notwendige Pflege.» (USA)

■**187, 188** Deux annonces de magazines pour les produits de bain et de beauté et les parfums *Anne Klein.* (USA)

■**189** Annonce de magazine, noir et blanc, pour la lotion *Keri* qui soigne, adoucit et humidifie la peau: «peu de gens savent quel est le plus grand organe, et comment le soigner.» (USA)

82

Mailand Welch Glanz

bei dieser Exibition:

Rockin' Doreen in der

Ehrenloge des Clubs.

REGINA/
INNSBRUCK
HÖFINGER/
KITZBÜHEL
RIEDHERR/
SALZBURG
CIRRA/GRAZ
LAMEE/WELS

Unüblich dieser Perla mare.

ART DIRECTOR:
Sigi Mayer
DESIGNER:
Sigi Mayer
PHOTOGRAPHER:
Horst Stasny
AGENCY:
Die Agentur
CLIENT:
Modern Times
Markus Mahringer
■190–193

■**190–193** Four spreads advertising *Perla Mare* swimwear, from a ten-page running advertisement in the Austrian quarterly *Modern Times*, a sports and fashion magazine. (AUT)

■**190–193** Vier doppelseitige Anzeigen für *Perla-Mare*-Bademode, aus einer zehnseitigen Anzeigenreihe in *Modern Times*, einem sogenannten »Zeitgeist«-Magazin. (AUT)

■**190–193** Doubles pages publicitaires pour les costumes de bain *Perla Mare* dans une section promotionnelle de 10 pp. Magazine trimestriel des sports et de la mode *Modern Times*. (AUT)

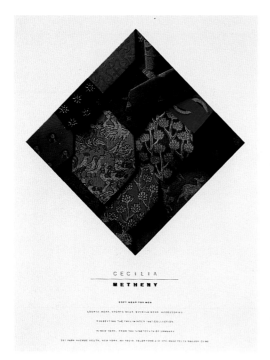

ART DIRECTOR:
Tyler Smith
DESIGNER:
Tyler Smith
PHOTOGRAPHER:
Myron
AGENCY:
Tyler Smith
CLIENT:
Cecilia Metheny
■**194–196**

ART DIRECTOR:
Petra Prem
DESIGNER:
RG Wiesmeier GmbH
PHOTOGRAPHER:
Jost Wildbolz
COPYWRITER:
Carlos Obers
AGENCY:
RG Wiesmeier GmbH
CLIENT:
Bi Strumpffabrik GmbH
■**197,198** ▶

■**194–196** Series of advertisements with the fashion trade as target to promote the Fall/Winter Collection of *Cecilia Metheny's* "Soft Wear for Men". (USA)

■**197, 198** Two double-spread advertisements from the German *Vogue* to promote *Bi* ladies' stockings and tights, with a list in each case of the German stockists. (GER)

■**194–196** Beispiele aus einer an den Textilhandel gerichteten Anzeigenkampagne für die Herbst/Winter-Kollektion von *Cecilia Metheny*: «Soft Wear für Männer». (USA)

■**197, 198** Zwei in der deutschen Vogue veröffentlichte, doppelseitige Anzeigen für *Bi*-Strümpfe und Strumpfhosen, mit einer Liste der Geschäfte, die diese Marke führen. (GER)

■**194–196** Série d'annonces destinées à l'industrie de la mode, pour la promotion de la collection d'automne et d'hiver de *Cecilia Metheny*, «Soft Wear for Men». (USA)

■**197, 198** Deux annonces double page dans l'édition allemande de *Vogue*, pour les bas et collants *Bi*. Les listes renferment les noms et adresses des dépositaires allemands. (GER)

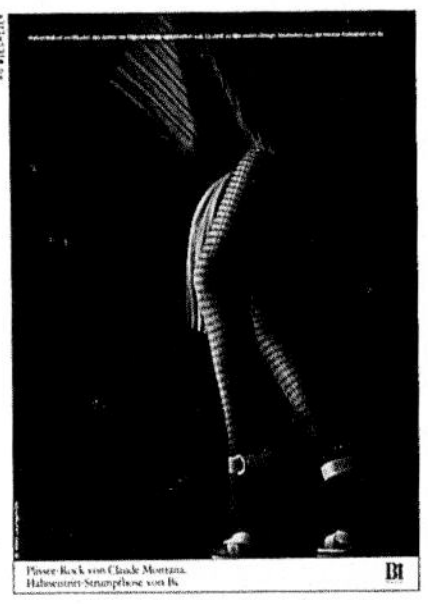

Plissee Rock von Claude Montana.
Hahnentritt-Strumpfhose von Bi.

Beine, die mit der neuen Herbst-Mode gehen, gehen in eines dieser Geschäfte:

1000 Berlin 30 Strumpfladen Europacenter, KaDeWe
2000 Hamburg 1 Hans Buck
2000 Hamburg 13 Der Wollkorb
2000 Hamburg 36 Alsterhaus, Strumpf & Mode Havermann, Ferdinand Schaffner
2000 Hamburg 54 Hoyer-Moden
2000 Hamburg 55 Harald Adolff
2000 Hamburg 56 Isa Weyrich
2000 Hamburg 67 Sanitätshaus Thiede
2000 Hamburg 73 Schuhhaus Hittcher
2000 Hamburg 76 Paulette-Damenwäsche
2000 Norderstedt Parfümerie Exclusive
2054 Geesthacht H. F. Franck
2057 Reinbek Ina-Moden
2084 Rellingen Feminin
2085 Quickborn Schuhhaus Sahling
2100 Hamburg 90 Der Strumpf Thomas Dallmann, Arnold Dierbach
2110 Buchholz Nina F.
2120 Lüneburg Boutique Angelique
2150 Buxtehude Ernst Stackmann
2160 Stade Hans Henrizi
2190 Cuxhaven Modehaus Jelden
2202 Barmstedt Barmstedter Modestübchen Bruhn
2240 Heide Mode-Meißner
2252 St. Peter-Ording Kosmetik Sassen
2280 Westerland Ma Petite
2300 Kiel Ferdinand Meislahn
2720 Rotenburg Sonja Frings
2730 Zeven Franck
2740 Bremervörde Modehaus Burfeind
2800 Bremen 1 Haita, Corset-Friedel, Modehaus F. H. Harms, Schuhhaus Lattemann
2800 Bremen 44 Colby
2808 Syke Schuhhaus Eickhoff
2810 Verden Wäsche-Wenzel
2830 Bassum Christa Mindermann
2842 Lohne Haider-Moden
2848 Vechta Schuhhaus Eickhoff
2850 Bremerhaven Strumpfecke Habuch, Otto May
2870 Delmenhorst J. H. Hohenböken
2902 Rastede Haus der Mode Tams
2903 Bad Zwischenahn Lieselotte Hillje
2930 Varel Spezialhaus Harfst, G. Schlicht
2970 Emden Modehaus De Wall & Co.
2972 Borkum C. H. Meyer
2982 Norderney Haus der Mode Tams, Ingeborg Medebach
3000 Hannover 1 Haita, Karstadt, I. G. von der Linde, Magis, Nora, Helene Warzecha, Bally-Deutschland
3000 Hannover 71 Gerti Stolzenbach
3006 Burgwedel Moden-Werner
3040 Soltau Chez Cathrine
3042 Munster Lady M
3052 Bad Nenndorf Miedermoden Schaar
3057 Neustadt Helga Felsch
3070 Nienburg Rosemarie Brahmstädt
3100 Celle Im Spiegel
3167 Burgdorf Mode-Tenne
3180 Wolfsburg August Haerder & Co.
3200 Hildesheim Textilhaus Kressmann, Miederhaus Sleek
3250 Hameln Hermann Lohmann, Sanitätshaus Meyer
3260 Rinteln Schuhhaus Neumann, Modehaus Sasse
3280 Bad Pyrmont Ellen Uhlmann
3300 Braunschweig Exclusive Damenmode Lothar
3380 Goslar Clare Kuhl, bei Stephanie
3388 Bad Harzburg Farber-Dessous, Haus der Dame
3410 Northeim J. u. S. Kulenkampff
3440 Eschwege Strumpf-Salon Knauf
3500 Kassel Miederstube Dieter Heinze, Heinsius & Sander
3508 Melsungen Schuhschachtel Mand
3550 Marburg City-Schuh, Richard Kaphingst, Schuhhaus Kranz, Helene Rhiel
3575 Kirchhain Hess & Hoffmann
4000 Düsseldorf 1 Haita Königsallee, Modehaus Heinemann, Hörhager-Laimböck, Strumpfmoden Mohnfeld, Schuhhaus Prange, Ela Be
4000 Düsseldorf 31 Damenmoden Stork
4005 Meerbusch Up to Date
4006 Erkrath Dress-Shop
4010 Hilden Modeladchen
4030 Ratingen Schuhhaus Juppen
4040 Neuss Heinemann & Co.
4050 Mönchengladbach 1 Schuhhaus Siemes
4050 Mönchengladbach 2 Rheydter Strumpfmoden
4100 Duisburg 1 Femina-Moden, Haita, Strumpf-Voigt
4100 Duisburg 14 Pelz- und Ledermoden
4100 Duisburg 28 Fußbehandlungen Dekkers
4130 Moers Schuhgalerie Pelzl
4150 Krefeld Burian-Moden, Strumpfhaus Stelkes
4152 Kempen Mode & Antik Lu
4180 Goch Damenmoden Lueb
4190 Kleve Dessous-Kommode
4200 Oberhausen Bischof-Moden
4280 Borken Pelz-Vierhaus
4300 Essen Margit Pollerberg
4400 Münster Wäschehaus Reichel, Schuhhaus Zumnorde, Mieder-Rödiger, Thomas Koberg
4410 Warendorf Mode-Ebbers
4500 Osnabrück Christian Otto Kurtz, Schuhhaus Zumnorde
4600 Dortmund Haita Westenhellweg, Schuhhaus Vogelsang
4650 Gelsenkirchen 1 Gebr. Sinn
4690 Herne 2 Sanitätshaus Hohlfeld
4722 Ennigerloh Textilhaus Beumker
4770 Soest August Pier
4780 Lippstadt Fellmer
4790 Paderborn Efi-Moden
4800 Bielefeld Schuhhaus Degen, Zumnorde-Studio
4837 Verl Modehaus Ebbinghaus
4930 Detmold Strumpfkästchen Lippok
4950 Minden Corset-Moden Hassenmeier
4970 Bad Oeynhausen Miederwaren Guder, Mieder-Wäsche Sandmann
4990 Lübbecke Modehaus von Stiften
5000 Köln 1 Bartels & Rieger, Mode-Halbreiter, Franz Sauer, Strumpfgeschäft Schneider, Stegmann-Wittig, Philo's Moden
5000 Köln 41 Miederhaus Stephan
5000 Köln 80 Sabina-Moden
5000 Köln 90 Griesberg
5030 Hürth Sanitätshaus Heinzen
5060 Bergisch Gladbach 1 Exquisite Schuhmoden Pickert
5060 Bergisch Gladbach 2 Schirm-Beitus
5100 Aachen Strumpf-Magazin Göpfert, Pour elle, Bally Deutschland, Strumpfpalette Buffleben
5208 Eitorf Elisabeth Husges
5216 Niederkassel Modehaus Tober
5300 Bonn 1 Schuhhaus Bally, B. H. Blömer, Haita
5300 Bonn 2 Hans Schmitz, Modehaus Voggenreiter
5420 Lahnstein Textil und Mode Kramer
5450 Neuwied Mieder-Wäsche Kruft
5600 Wuppertal 1 Schuhhaus Voss GmbH
5600 Wuppertal 11 Marion Müller
5630 Remscheid Goll & Schracke
5650 Solingen Klasing & Baumann
5788 Winterberg Mode im Fachwerkhaus
5790 Brilon Modenhaus Frink
5882 Meinerzhagen Rili-Moden
5900 Siegen Mode-Arkade Golbach
5952 Attendorn Mode und Heim Kohl
5960 Olpe MR-Moden
6000 Frankfurt 1 Haita Kaiserstraße, Lingerie Lemler, Alfons Michels, Mi Schulte, Valentina, Madame, Hertie Zeil, Modetruhe Neumann, Schuhhaus Prange
6000 Frankfurt 50 Erni Losert
6000 Frankfurt 60 Valentina
6000 Frankfurt 71 Modetruhe Hauck
6050 Offenbach Conny, Simone, Georg Wuschanski, Katha Kurt
6056 Heusenstamm Modesalon Desideria
6070 Langen Wäsche-Mieder-Bademoden Jacobs
6072 Dreieich Barbara van den Boom, Edith Theis
6082 Mörfelden-Walldorf Waltraud Schuler
6085 Nauheim Ruth Vogt
6100 Darmstadt Strumpfhaus Geppert, Henschel + Ropertz
6140 Bensheim Schuhhaus Rohr
6200 Wiesbaden Strumpfladen Fuchs, La Mano, Modehaus Poulet, Theodor Werner
6230 Frankfurt 80 Mode-Pavillon Weiss
6233 Kelkheim Modehaus Horn
6238 Hofheim City-Moden
6240 Königstein Yasmin
6242 Kronberg Gertrude Karls & Co
6290 Weilburg Modehaus Stroh
6308 Butzbach Modehaus Schäfer
6330 Wetzlar Miederhaus Albold
6340 Dillenburg Curt Brauns
6348 Herborn Curt Brauns
6350 Bad Nauheim Das Strumpfkästchen
6374 Steinbach Modetruhe Barth
6380 Bad Homburg Mabe
6382 Friedrichsdorf Modehaus Hornig
6400 Fulda Institut Fendel
6450 Hanau Waldschmidt
6460 Gelnhausen Kaufhaus Joh
6482 Bad Orb Stick- u. Strumpfladchen Baumgarten
6500 Mainz Marz-Moden
6550 Bad Kreuznach Strumpf-Vitrine Coldewey, Mode-Centrum Heimrich
6600 Saarbrücken Gebr. Sinn, Wäschehaus Weinhold
6620 Völklingen Boutique Pour Elle
6630 Saarlouis Ludwig Pieper
6650 Homburg Modesalon Morsch & Martin
6660 Zweibrücken Minna Ambos
6710 Frankenthal Schuh-Schachtel
6720 Speyer Ladychic
6730 Neustadt Strumpfland
6733 Haßloch Boutique Christine
6750 Kaiserslautern Strumpfvitrine Gramer
6780 Pirmasens Textilhaus Forster
6800 Mannheim Handschuh-Eckert, Engelhorn & Sturm, Gaby-Moden, Haita
6900 Heidelberg Gätschenberger, Textilhaus Kraus
6909 Walldorf Textilhaus Veronelli
6920 Sinsheim Tricot
6950 Mosbach Exquisit Junge Mode Palm
6972 Tauberbischofsheim Lucky Lady
6980 Wertheim Textilhaus Witt
7000 Stuttgart 1 Handschuh-Luickert, G. Maute-Benger, Modehaus Spiecker, Marett Schule
7000 Stuttgart 50 Miederwaren Zerrweck
7014 Kornwestheim Franz Ott
7070 Schwäbisch Gmünd Die Commode
7090 Ellwangen Textilhaus Bruder
7100 Heilbronn Eugen Palm
7110 Öhringen Schuhhaus Kleinhans
7118 Künzelsau Medico-Vitrine
7140 Ludwigsburg Mieder- und Wäschesalon Madame
7290 Freudenstadt Strumpfvitrine Piehl
7300 Esslingen Miederhaus Schmid
7312 Kirchheim Strumpfmoden Klotz
7440 Albstadt 1 Rosa Haug
7500 Karlsruhe Damenboutique Domino, Wäschehaus Schmitt, Strumpfmoden Harich
7506 Bad Herrenalb Die Dame, Modepavillon Thoma
7530 Pforzheim Strumpfhaus Hirzel, Gisela Staib, Modehaus Stober
7555 Bietigheim Bietigheimer Boutique
7560 Gaggenau Strumpfmoden Marion
7570 Baden-Baden Strumpfsalon Bresagk, Damenwäsche Caroline
7600 Offenburg Modehaus Keilbach
7630 Lahr Max Caroli
7730 Villingen-Schwenningen Strumpfhaus Abigt
7750 Konstanz Wäschetruhe Artmann
7770 Überlingen Emmy Bischoff
7798 Pfullendorf Moden-Langer
7800 Freiburg Viktoria Hustedt, Jacqueline van der Vliet, Modehaus Carl Fabel
7889 Grenzach-Wyhlen Modehaus Rubin & Co.
7900 Ulm Modehaus Rank, Woll-Wanner
7920 Heidenheim Paul Frey, Paul Hausser, Modewaren Reiber
7950 Biberach Ruth Leu
7967 Bad Waldsee Damenmoden Hofmann
7980 Ravensburg Modehaus Sommer
8000 München 2 Bally-Deutschland, Mieder-Wäsche Erlanger, Hertie Bahnhofsplatz, Beck am Rathauseck, Karstadt-Oberpollinger, J. M. Edel, City 22, Loden-Frey, F. Ludwig Kubler, Strumpfsalon Kudelka, Grete Ziernfuß
8000 München 40 Strumpfboutique Schwabing
8000 München 71 Schuhpavillon Charlott
8000 München 80 Barbara Ondrusch
8032 Gräfelfing Textil-Schmidt
8035 Gauting Wäschetruhe Hähr & Nefzger
8100 Garmisch-Partenkirchen Textilhaus Hartenstein, Damenmoden Paul
8183 Rottach-Egern Gretel Schultes
8220 Traunstein Therese Geiger
8230 Bad Reichenhall Strumpfhaus Kindersberger, Strumpf-Walter
8300 Landshut Mieder-Evi
8397 Bad Füssing Gisela-Moden
8400 Regensburg Regensburger Gewürzstube, Modehaus Schottl
8500 Nürnberg 1 Korsett-Denis
8500 Nürnberg 60 Kosmetikboutique Cerny
8502 Zirndorf Regina
8510 Fürth Modehaus Fiedler
8520 Erlangen Modehaus Storr
8532 Bad Windsheim Helga Opolka
8540 Schwabach Boutique Elle
8580 Bayreuth Strumpf-Scholl
8600 Bamberg Strumpf-Queen
8620 Lichtenfels Barth & Schüller
8630 Coburg Strumpfecke Töpfer
8650 Kulmbach Mode-Rudel
8672 Selb Resi Feig
8700 Würzburg Modehaus Seisser, Carl Schlier
8720 Schweinfurt Inge Then
8750 Aschaffenburg Wäsche-Mäder, Modeboutique Schenk
8760 Miltenberg Modehaus Brand
8803 Rothenburg Anny Müller
8900 Augsburg Modehaus Caro, Kröll & Nill, Zentral-Kaufhaus
8939 Bad Wörishofen Pia Neudel
8940 Memmingen Hauser-Moden
8950 Kaufbeuren Strumpf-Maschke
8960 Kempten Mode-Steinhart
8980 Oberstdorf Strumpfecke Cenia Haag

Bi Strümpfe und Strumpfhosen erhalten Sie auch in Benelux, Italien, Österreich, Schweiz und Skandinavien.

Hahnentritt ist ein Muster, das bisher der Männer-Mode vorbehalten war. Es zählt zu den vielen Design-Neuheiten aus der Herbst-Kollektion von Bi.
Bi, 8882 Lauingen/Do.

Plissee-Rock von Claude Montana.
Hahnentritt-Strumpfhose von Bi.

Das ist die kommende Mode: Print-Strumpfhosen, mehrfarbig bedruckt. Im Bild: die neue Bi „Print Manhattan", die Sie wahlweise in schwarz-rot-grau, schwarz-blau-grau und schwarz-grün-grau kaufen können (22 dtex/20 den, mit unverstärkter Spitze und Ferse). Das augenfällige Fenstermuster läßt Ihre Beine lang und schlank wie Manhattan-Wolkenkratzer wirken. Nur eben schöner.

Beine, die mit der neuesten Mode gehen, gehen in eines dieser Geschäfte:

1 1000 Berlin 12, Karstadt, Schuh-Tick. 1000 Berlin 15, Schuhhaus Bally, Knopf + Schnalle, Schaum der Tage, Strumpfladen. 1000 Berlin 30, KaDeWe, Schuhhaus Bally, Strumpfladen. 1000 Berlin 41, Warenhaus Wertheim. 1000 Berlin 65, Karstadt, Wäsche und Mieder Ständer. 2 2000 Hamburg 1, Elsner-Schuhe, Jäger & Mirow, Karstadt, Peek & Cloppenburg, Penndorf Das Hamburger Modehaus. 2000 Hamburg 36, Alsterhaus, Strumpf und Mode Havermann, Jäger & Mirow, Schuhhaus Wilhelm Prange, Ferdinand Schaffner. 2000 Hamburg 54, Hoyer-Moden. 2000 Hamburg 65, Jäger & Mirow. 2000 Hamburg 70, Karstadt. 2000 Hamburg 73, Schuhhaus Hittcher. 2000 Hamburg 76, Karstadt. 2070 Ahrensburg, Kaufhaus Nessler, Mompti. 2085 Quickborn, Schuhhaus Sahling. 2100 Hamburg 90, Jäger & Mirow, Karstadt, Der Strumpff Thomas Dallmann. 2110 Buchholz, Nina F. 2120 Lüneburg, Mode und Textil Hedemann. 2160 Stade, Hans Henrizi. 2190 Cuxhaven, Cosmetic & Dessous Marlene. 2448 Burg, Bei Marte. 2800 Bremen, Avanti, Horten. 2850 Bremerhaven, Strumpfecke Habuch. 2930 Varel, G. Schlicht. 2990 Papenburg, Modehaus Averdung. 3 3000 Hannover 1, Schuhhaus Bally, Boutique Charade, Meister Eilert, Karstadt, I. G. von der Linde. Magis. 3006 Burgwedel, Noblesse Sigrid Strauch, Moden-Werner. 3915 Wennigsen, Christina's Mode und Kosmetik. 3040 Soltau, Chez Cathrine. 3052 Bad Nenndorf, Miedermoden Schaar. 3057 Neustadt, Helga Felsch. 3060 Stadthagen, Modenhaus Schilling. 3070 Nienburg, Rosemarie Brahmstädt. 3100 Celle, Strumpfhaus Arndt. 3200 Hildesheim, Textilhaus Kressmann. 3260 Rinteln, Schuhhaus Neumann. 3300 Braunschweig, Carl Langerfeldt, Lothar. 3352 Einbeck, J. u. S. Kulenkampff. 3380 Goslar, Bei Stephanie. 3400 Göttingen, Schuhhaus Nahme. 3410 Northeim, J. u. S. Kulenkampff. 3500 Kassel, Heinsius & Sander. 4 4000 Düsseldorf, Böhmer-Schuhe, Filou, Fiori-Bender, Hörhager-Laimböck, Schuhhaus Juppen, Schuhhaus Paul Prange. 4005 Meerbusch, Up to Date. 4030 Ratingen, Schuhhaus Juppen. 4040 Neuss, Donna. 4050 Mönchengladbach, Mönchengladbacher Strumpfhaus. 4100 Duisburg, Strumpf-Voigt. 4150 Krefeld, La Difference. 4300 Essen, Schuhhaus Grüterich, Horten. 4330 Mülheim, Jeanette. 4400 Münster, Doris Falk, Heinrich Petzhold. 4410 Warendorf, Mode-Ebbers. 4450 Lingen, Mode-Löning. 4500 Osnabrück, Christian Otto Kurtz, Lengermann & Trieschmann. 4590 Cloppenburg, C. A. Thole. 4630 Bochum, Textilhaus Baltz, Anna Maria Kracht, Die Wäschekiste. 4690 Herne 2, Hohlfeld. 4770 Soest, August Pier. 4790 Paderborn, Efi-Moden, F. Klingenthal. 4800 Bielefeld 11, Helmold-Moden. 4830 Gütersloh, Modehaus Tholen. 4900 Herford, Franz Klingenthal. 4930 Detmold, Strumpf-Kästchen Lippok. 4970 Bad Oeynhausen, Mieder-Wäsche Sandmann. 4990 Lübbecke, Modehaus von Stiften. 5 5000 Köln 1, Hertie, Schuhhaus Kämpgen, Philo's Moden, Strumpfhaus Schneider. 5000 Köln 80, Sabina-Moden. 5000 Köln 90, Griesberg. 5030 Hürth, Heinzen. 5040 Brühl, Strumpf-Schatulle Hübner. 5090 Leverkusen 3, Bio's Schuhgarten. 5100 Aachen, Schuhhaus Bally, Strumpf-Barth, Strumpf-Palette Buffleben, Strumpf-Magazin Göpfert, Pour elle, Gebr. Sinn. 5138 Heinsberg, Strumpf-Vitrine Nötlichs. 5160 Düren, Fantasy. 5270 Gummersbach, Modekaufhaus Engelbertz. 5300 Bonn 2, Strumpfmoden Paus. 5400 Koblenz, Fiori-Bender. 5450 Neuwied, Modehaus Leininger. 5470 Andernach, Modehaus Schäfer. 5600 Wuppertal 1, Strumpf-Palette Dostalek, Schuhhaus Voss. 5600 Wuppertal 11, Strumpfhaus Marion Müller. 5630 Remscheid, Goll & Schracke. 5650 Solingen, Klasing & Baumann. 5657 Haan, Cleo. 5790 Brilon, Damenmodenhaus Frink. 5800 Hagen, Gebr. Sinn. 5810 Witten, Gebr. Hömberg. 5820 Gevelsberg, Textilhaus Kemmler. 5900 Siegen, Mode-Arkade Golbach. 6 6000 Frankfurt 1, Boutique Chez Hella, Haita Kaiserstraße, Hako-Schuh, Madame, Alfons Michels, Mi Schulte, Valentina Jenny Schäfer. 6000 Frankfurt 50, Erni Losert. 6000 Frankfurt 60, Valentina Jenny Schäfer. 6000 Frankfurt 90, Maria Beller. 6050 Offenbach, Modehaus C. Hassert, Mode und Textil Zwicklbauer. 6056 Heusenstamm, Modesalon Desideria. 6070 Langen, Wäsche-Mieder-Bademoden Jacobs. 6078 Neu-Isenburg, Wilhelm Bohl, Sisi-Wäschemoden. 6082 Mörfelden-Walldorf, Waltraud Schuler. 6100 Darmstadt, Strumpfhaus Geppert, Henschel & Ropertz. 6140 Bensheim, Schuhhaus Rohr. 6200 Wiesbaden, Strumpfladen Fuchs, Karstadt, Modehaus Poulet. 6238 Hofheim, City-Moden Haun. 6240 Königstein, Yasmin Gertrud Schwager. 6300 Gießen, Nr. 2 Sibylle Ludwig. 6330 Wetzlar, Miederhaus Fritz Albold. 6340 Dillenburg, Curt Brauns. 6350 Bad Nauheim, Das Strumpfkästchen. 6368 Bad Vilbel, G. u. M. Müller. 6380 Bad Homburg, Mabe Mathilde Bender. 6450 Hanau, Waldschmidt. 6500 Mainz, C. O. Reuter. 6550 Bad Kreuznach, Bi-Boutique Doll. 6600 Saarbrücken, Gebr. Sinn. 6630 Saarlouis, Ludwig Pieper. 6640 Merzig, Salon Rita. 6670 St. Ingbert, Gebr. Sinn. 6680 Neunkirchen, Gebr. Sinn. 6700 Ludwigshafen, Hanny's Moden. 6720 Speyer, Ladychic. 6733 Haßloch, Boutique Christine, Mode-Shop. 6800 Mannheim, Handschuh-Eckert, Tausendfüssler. 6900 Heidelberg, Gätschenberger, Textilhaus Kraus. 6950 Mosbach, Exquisit Junge Mode. 7 7000 Stuttgart 1, Bally-Capitol, C. F. Braun, Handschuh-Luickert, Marett. 7000 Stuttgart 50, Textilhaus Baitinger, Miederwaren Zerrweck. 7000 Stuttgart 80, Schuh-Wolf. 7014 Kornwestheim, Franz Ott. 7022 Leinfelden-Echterdingen, Eberhard Boden. 7030 Böblingen, Hermann Knoll. 7100 Heilbronn, Eugen Palm. 7110 Öhringen, Schuhhaus Kleinhans. 7118 Künzelsau, Medico-Vitrine. 7140 Ludwigsburg, Modehaus Kodweiss, Mieder- u. Wäschesalon Madame. 7150 Backnang, Schuhhaus Boss. 7180 Crailsheim, TC-Buckenmaier, Bekleidungshaus Burkardt, Geschenklädle Carmen Veit. 7230 Schramberg, Bekleidungshaus Vogelmann. 7290 Freudenstadt, Strumpfvitrine Fred Piehl. 7300 Esslingen, Miederhaus Schmid. 7312 Kirchheim, Strumpfmoden Klotz. 7450 Hechingen, Strumpf-Boutique Winkler. 7460 Balingen, Mode-Treff Behne. 7500 Karlsruhe, Schuhhaus Bally, Strumpfmoden. 7530 Pforzheim, Stumpfhaus Hirzel, Gisela Staib. 7547 Wildbad, Mieder-Fleig. 7560 Gaggenau, Strumpfmoden Marion. 7570 Baden-Baden, Strumpfsalon Bresagk, Caroline. 7594 Kappelrodeck, Schuh-Galerie Lorenz. 7750 Konstanz, Wäschetruhe Artmann. 7760 Radolfzell, Strumpfparadies Häusler. 7770 Überlingen, Emmy Bischoff. 7798 Pfullendorf, Moden-Langer. 7800 Freiburg, Modehaus Carl Fabel, Viktoria Hustedt, Boutique Sitterle, Strumpf-Kommode, Jacqueline van der Vliet. 7809 Denzlingen, Damenmoden Diegel-Deisler. 7812 Bad Krozingen, Hans Hoch. 7830 Emmendingen, Modehaus Blum & Jundt. 7850 Lörrach, Elise Unverzagt. 7890 Waldshut-Tiengen, Modehaus Stulz. 7920 Heidenheim, Strumpfmoden Paul Hausser. 7950 Biberach, Strumpfbouitque Hauser. 7954 Bad Wurzach, M. Hauber. 7980 Ravensburg, Bekleidungshaus Bredl, Strumpf-Bühler, Modehaus Sommer. 8 8000 München 2, Ludwig Beck, City 22, Fiori-Bender, Hertie, Karstadt. 8000 München 40, Lebas, L'etoile Brigitte Weyrauch. 8000 München 80, Brigitte Ondrusch. 8000 München 81, Mode fürs Bein. 8012 Ottobrunn, Strumpfparadies Frank Moore. 8035 Gauting, Wäschetruhe Hähr & Nefzger. 8183 Rottach-Egern, Gretel Schultes. 8400 Regensburg, Bleyle-Elbeo Wäsche-Strumpf-Studio, Regensburger Gewürzstube Weigert. 8450 Amberg, M. & M. Mode-Accessoires. 8500 Nürnberg, Karstadt. 8600 Bamberg, Strumpf-Queen. 8630 Coburg, Strumpfecke Töpfer. 8672 Selb, Strumpfvitrine Feig. 8720 Schweinfurt, Inge Then. 8750 Aschaffenburg, Cinderella, Emma's feiner Laden, Wäsche-Mäder. 8900 Augsburg, Kröll & Nill. 8950 Kaufbeuren, Strumpf-Maschke. Bi Strümpfe und Strumpfhosen erhalten Sie auch in Benelux, Italien, Österreich, Schweiz und Skandinavien.

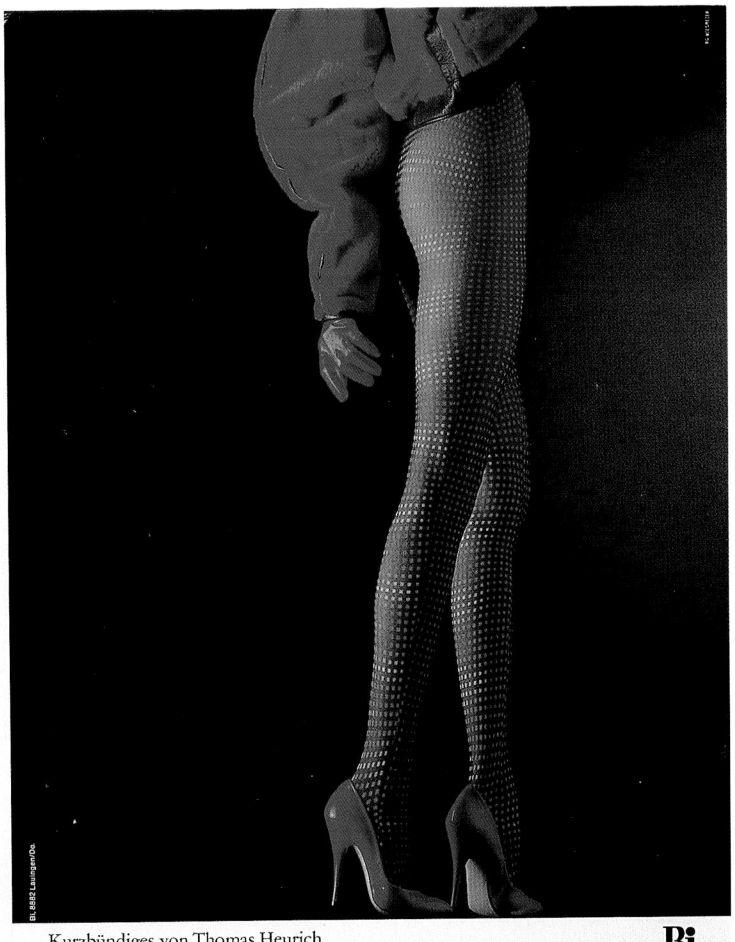

Bi, 8882 Lauingen/Do.

Kurzbündiges von Thomas Heurich.
Langbeiniges von Bi.

ART DIRECTOR:
DIETRICH EBERT

DESIGNER:
DIETRICH EBERT

PHOTOGRAPHER:
DIETMAR HENNEKA

COPYWRITER:
RUDOLF REICHARD

AGENCY:
ALAIN FION

CLIENT:
YELLO SPORT GMBH
■199

Wie der Fuß.

Tennis wird mit dem Arm
gespielt, aber auf den Füßen
ausgetragen. Und dabei muß
der Tennisschuh dem Fuß auf
die Sprünge helfen. Er muß

also Rennschuh, Bremsschuh,
Stoppschuh, Sprungschuh,
Stützschuh, Sicherheitsschuh,
Kontaktschuh und Klima-
schuh in einem sein. Und

dabei noch so wohlgeformt,
ausdauernd und feinfühlig
wie der Fuß selbst. Oder
wie der Lacoste unter den
Tennisschuhen. **LACOSTE**

ART DIRECTOR:
DIETRICH EBERT

DESIGNER:
DIETRICH EBERT

ILLUSTRATOR:
DIETRICH EBERT

COPYWRITER:
RUDOLF REICHARD

AGENCY:
ALAIN FION

CLIENT:
YELLO SPORT GMBH
■200

Das Krokodil zeigt Urlaubsflagge
zu Lande und zu *Wasser.

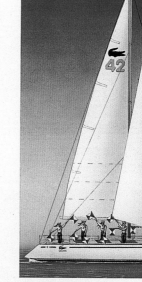

„L"
wie Lachen, Lagune, Liebe,
Lust, Langusten, Luft, Lieder,
Lido, Lagerfeuer, Liegestuhl,
Lebensgeister, Luftverände-
rung, La dolce vita ....

„O"
wie Oase, Ozean, Ouzo,
Ostfriesland, Osso buco,
Oleander, O sole mio,
Olivenhain, Orientexpress,
Oberdeck, Orvieto, Oahu ...

„E"
wie Erholung, Expedition,
Echo, Escudo, Elefanten,
Eisberge, Eigernordwand,
Engelsburg, Enzian ....
Darüber hinaus wünscht das
Krokodil allzeit eine Hand-
breit Wasser unter dem Kiel.
✱ Die Hochseeyacht
„Lacoste 42" – eine 42-Fuß-
Segelyacht vom amerikani-
schen Bootsbauer-Team
Sparkman & Stephens im
Auftrag von Lacoste
gezeichnet und in französi-
schen Werften gebaut – gibt
es übrigens auch als Poster.
Im Format 60 x 84 cm in
Ihrem Lacoste-Geschäft,
oder – wenn nicht vorrätig –
gegen DM 5,– in Brief-
marken unter dem Stich-
wort „Lacoste 42" direkt von
YELLO SPORT
GmbH, Post-
fach 30 14 40,
5000 Köln 30. **LACOSTE**

„A"
wie Abenteuer, Aussicht,
Ausspannen, Ausziehen,
Anziehen, Ausgehen,
Akropolis, Alpenglühen,
Austern schlürfen, Arri-
verderci, Abendspaziergang,
Antipasti, Andenken, Alm-
rausch, Acapulco ....

„S"
wie Sand, Surfen, Schatz-
insel, Schlemmen, Segeln,
Sonne, Strand, Sombrero,
Schwarzwaldklinik, Safari,
Souvenir, Sonnenuntergang,
Südsee, Steuerbord, Spaß,
Spiel, Swimmingpool ....

„C"
wie Café crème, Camping,
Capuccino, Casanova,
Chancen, Charme, Chalet,
Champagner, Calamares,
Caprifischer, C'est la vie,
Candlelight-Dinner, Chablis,
Champs-Elysées ....

„T"
wie Tanzen, Traumschiff,
Tarzan, Tête-à-tête, Taran-
tella, Theater, Tirolerhut,
Tauchen, Tapas, Titicacasee,
Tausendundeine Nacht,
Tanga, Tahiti, Tadsch Mahal,
Ticket, Transfer, Trekking ...

■**199–202** Spreads which appeared in the German magazine
Der Spiegel for *Lacoste* sportswear. Slogans read, this page - "As
the foot itself" and "The crocodile flies holiday flags on land and
water." Opposite – "The crocodile, a winter fairytale." and "Evergreen at golf." (GER)

■**199–202** Doppelseitige Anzeigen für *Lacoste*-Sportartikel
aus einer Kampagne im *Spiegel*. Auf dieser Seite: Der *Lacoste*-
Tennisschuh ist wie der Fuss. Die Hochseeyacht *Lacoste 42* wird
in französischen Werften gebaut. Rechte Seite: Die Erfolgs-Story
als Märchen verpackt und die Golftradition. (GER)

■**199–202** Doubles pages du magazine allemand *Der Spiegel*
pour les vêtements de sport *Lacoste*. Les slogans: «comme le
pied»; «le crocodile bat pavillon à terre comme sur l'eau.» Ci-
contre: «le crocodile, un conte d'hiver» et «la tradition en matière
de golf.» (GER)

ART DIRECTOR:
Dietrich Ebert

DESIGNER:
Dietrich Ebert

ILLUSTRATOR:
Dietrich Ebert

COPYWRITER:
Rudolf Reichard

AGENCY:
Alain Fion

CLIENT:
Yello Sport GmbH

■ 201

Das Krokodil, ein Wintermärchen.

Es war einmal ein schönes, grünes Krokodil. Das lebte im Lande Ägypten, tummelte sich in den Wassern des Nils und ruhte im heißen Sand seiner Ufer. Oft schaute es dabei den Schiffen nach, die auf dem Flusse dahinfuhren. An einem Abend erblickte es ein Schiff, das vor lauter Lichtern nur so funkelte. Das Schönste aber war das Lied, das herübertönte und von der Winterszeit, von Schneeflocken und weißer Weihnacht erzählte. Da wurde dem Krokodil ganz sonderbar ums Herz und sehnsüchtig sah es zu den Pyramiden hinüber und träumte davon, was es wohl hinter den hohen gelben Sandbergen geben mochte. Eines Tages traf es einen großen Zauberer, dem es über die Maßen gefiel. Er lud es ein, mit ihm zu kommen und die ganze Welt zu sehen. Das Krokodil sah seine Stunde gekommen, sagte ja, und der Zauberer versetzte es flugs auf prachtvolle Hemden und andere schöne Kleidungsstücke. Die bot er in vielen Ländern feil, so daß das Krokodil weit herumkam und so zu einem berühmten Zeichen wurde. Nie vergaß es aber, was es damals am Nil vom Winter, vom Schnee und von Weihnachten gehört hatte. Als sich wieder einmal der Sommer neigte, erzählte es dem Zauberer davon und bat ihn, es sich wie immer in den Winterschlaf zu legen, sondern ihm Kleider zu machen, auf denen es auch im Schnee mit den Menschen sein könnte. Der Zauberer freute sich sehr über diesen Vorschlag, rief alle seine Helfer zusammen und wies sie an, das Nötige zu tun.

Da ging ein Arbeiten los, daß es nur so eine Art hatte.

Die Schneider erdachten vornehme Schnitte und Formen. Die Maler schufen prächtige Farben und Muster. Die Stricker strickten wunderbare Pullover und Jacken. Die Näher mühten elegante Blousons und Hosen. Und die Wirker gaben dem berühmten Hemd des großen Zauberers lange Ärmel, damit man es auch im Winter tragen konnte. Alle waren sie glücklich und freuten sich, daß die Leute rechten Gefallen an ihrer Arbeit fanden. Am glücklichsten aber war das Krokodil. Und wenn es vergnügt auf einem schönen, warmen Pullover saß und die weißen Berge und verschneiten Wälder ringsumher betrachtete, und der Schnee glitzerte und die Wintersonne vom blauen Himmel lachte, dann dachte es an seine Heimat… **LACOSTE**

ART DIRECTOR:
Dietrich Ebert

DESIGNER:
Dietrich Ebert

ILLUSTRATOR:
Dietrich Ebert

COPYWRITER:
Rudolf Reichard

AGENCY:
Alain Fion

CLIENT:
Yello Sport GmbH

■ 202

Evergreen beim Golf.

Daß Lacoste seit über 5 Jahrzehnten zum Tennis gehört wie das Krokodil aufs Lacoste-Hemd, zählt schon zur Allgemeinbildung. Daß Lacoste auch eine fast ebenso lange und erfolgreiche Golftradition hat, ist eher ein Geheimtip. Denn Madame René Lacoste war eine der weltbesten Golferinnen ihrer Zeit, vielfache Meisterin und die erste Nichtengländerin, die das British Ladies Open gewann. Tochter Catherine Lacoste, „das kleine Krokodil" genannt, wurde eine ebenbürtige Nachfolgerin und sorgte für eine Sensation, als sie 1967, mit 22 Jahren, bei den U.S. Women's Open siegte und sich 1969 die internationalen Amateur-Meisterschaften der USA, Großbritanniens und Frankreichs holte.

Ein Grund zur Freude, doch kein Grund zur Schaffung einer uniformen „Golf-Mode". Das gibt es von Lacoste bis heute nicht. Dafür golfgerechte Funktionalität, sporterfahrene Qualität und stilsicheres Erscheinungsbild durch die gesamte Kollektion. Denn jeder Aktive weiß: Den guten Golfer erkennt man selten an der modischen Kleidung.

Wenn Ihnen unser Bild hier gefällt – Sie bekommen es als Poster im Format 60 x 84 cm. Gegen 5 Mark in bar in dem Geschäft, wo Sie auch sonst Lacoste kaufen oder gegen 5 Mark in Briefmarken direkt von: Yello Sport GmbH, Postfach 30 14 40, 5000 Köln 30. Bitte Stichwort „Evergreen beim Golf" angeben. **LACOSTE**

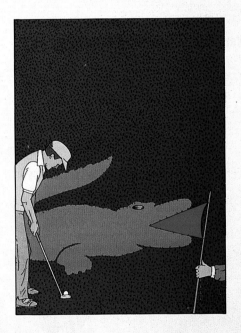

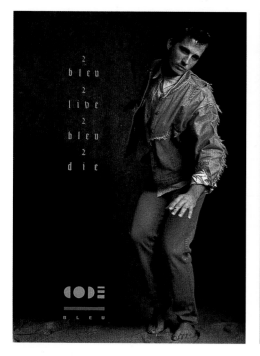 

ART DIRECTOR:
David & Nancy Edelstein
Lanny French

DESIGNER:
David & Nancy Edelstein
Lanny French
Carol Davidson

PHOTOGRAPHER:
Ben Kerns

COPYWRITER:
David Edelstein/
Lanny French

AGENCY:
Edelstein Associates
Advertising Inc.

CLIENT:
Code Bleu Sportswear

■ **203, 204**

■ **203, 204** Page and double spread from a magazine advertising campaign for *Code Bleu* sportswear, Seattle. (USA)

■ **205, 206** Magazine ads for *h.i.s.* jeans. Slogans: "Immortals wear *h.i.s.* jeans, they are forever," and "For this reason, whoever ties the knot forever, should prove whether the *h.i.s.* jeans match." (Latter is a play on a Schiller epigram.) (GER)

■ **203, 204** Seite und Doppelseite aus einer Werbekampagne in Zeitschriften für *Code-Bleu*-Sportkleidung. (USA)

■ **205, 206** Doppelseitige Zeitschriftenanzeigen aus einer Werbekampagne für *h.i.s.*-Jeans. Hier machte man sich die aktuelle Popularität Mozarts und ein häufig gebrauchtes Schiller-Zitat für den Slogan zunutze. Die Motive sind als Plakate erhältlich. (GER)

■ **203, 204** Page et double page dans une campagne de magazine en faveur des vêtements de sport *Code Bleu*. (USA)

■ **205, 206** Annonces double page pour les jeans *h.i.s.*: «les immortels portent des jeans *h.i.s.*, qui durent éternellement»; «un oui pour toujours – mais vos jeans *h.i.s.* vont-ils ensemble?» (allusion à une épigramme du poète Schiller). (GER)

ART DIRECTOR:
Feico Derschow

PHOTOGRAPHER:
Rainer Bald

AGENCY:
RG Wiesmeier

CLIENT:
H.I.S. Sportswear GmbH

■ 205

ART DIRECTOR:
Feico Derschow

PHOTOGRAPHER:
Rainer Bald

AGENCY:
RG Wiesmeier

CLIENT:
H.I.S. Sportswear GmbH

■ 206

ART DIRECTOR:
Mary Rose

DESIGNER:
Michael Mabry Design

PHOTOGRAPHER:
Michael Utterbach/
Brad Mollath

AGENCY:
Santa Cruz/In House

CLIENT:
Santa Cruz

■ 207–209

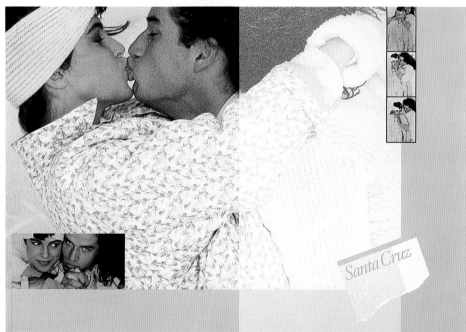

■ **207–209** Double-spread magazine ads for *Santa Cruz*, manufacturer of junior women's sportswear. (USA)

■ **210** *Payer* presents the world's first electric shaver made from the precious metal titan in this magazine ad. (GER)

■ **207–209** Doppelseitige Anzeigen für *Santa Cruz*, Hersteller sportlicher, jugendlicher Mode. (USA)

■ **210** In dieser Zeitschriftenanzeige stellt *Payer* den ersten Elektro-Rasierer aus Titan vor. (GER)

■ **207–209** Annonces double page pour *Santa Cruz*, qui fabrique des vêtements sport pour les jeunes femmes. (USA)

■ **210** Cette annonce de magazine sert à présenter le premier rasoir électrique du monde réalisé en titane pour *Payer*. (USA)

ART DIRECTOR:
GüNTHER TIBI
DESIGNER:
GüNTHER TIBI
PHOTOGRAPHER:
AXEL WALDECKER
AGENCY:
WENSAUER & PARTNER
CLIENT:
PAYER
■ **210**

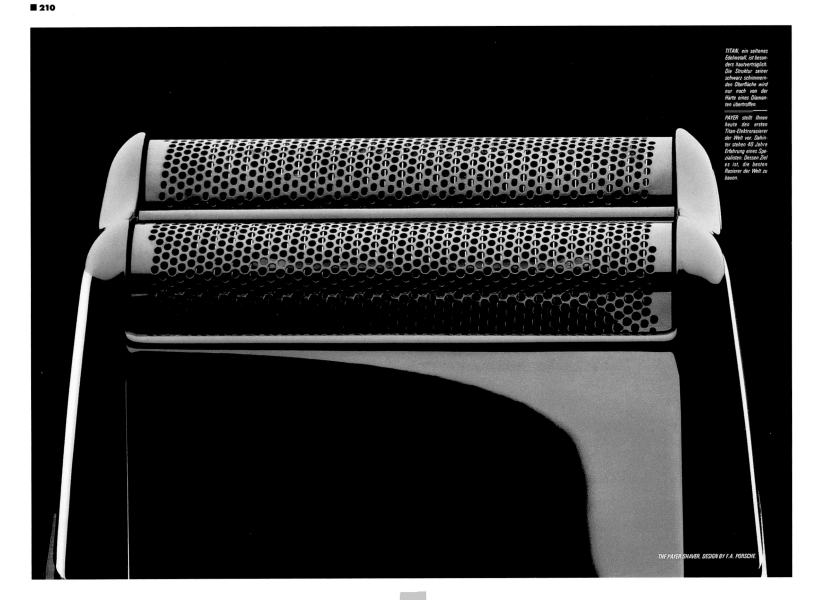

TITAN, ein seltenes Edelmetall, ist besonders hautverträglich. Die Struktur seiner schwarz schimmernden Oberfläche wird nur noch von der Härte eines Diamanten übertroffen.

PAYER stellt Ihnen heute den ersten Titan-Elektrorasierer der Welt vor. Dahinter stehen 40 Jahre Erfahrung eines Spezialisten. Dessen Ziel es ist, die besten Rasierer der Welt zu bauen.

THE PAYER SHAVER. DESIGN BY F.A. PORSCHE.

VOM PORSCHEFAHREN

»Es war schon immer etwas
beruhigender, jederzeit über ausreichende
Sicherheitsreserven zu verfügen.«

Daß Porschefahren einiges mit besonderer Fahrfreude zu tun haben muß,
erkennt man auch daran, daß viele Porsche-Fahrer auf hohe km-Leistungen
im Jahr kommen. Um bei den hohen Belastungen im Alltag die Begeisterung
nicht zu trüben, verfügt ein Porsche über besondere Reserven. Dabei kann sich
der Fahrer auf ein ausgewogenes Verhältnis von aktiver und passiver Sicherheit verlassen, die der Leistungsfähigkeit des Fahrzeugs immer voll entsprechen.

FAHREN IN SEINER SCHÖNSTEN FORM

VOM PORSCHEFAHREN
»Wenn Kundenwünsche ernst genommen
werden, kann dabei ein so interessantes Fahrzeug
wie der Porsche 944 Turbo entstehen.«

Immer mehr Autofahrer möchten ihr automobiles Verständnis weniger
durch einen spektakulären Auftritt, sondern mehr durch die Summe technischer Feinheiten ausdrücken. Es war Porsche ein Vergnügen, ein Fahrzeug
zu entwickeln, das dieses zeitgemäße Understatement sportlicher Fahrweise
perfekt verkörpert. Und allen eine Alternative bietet, die das sportliche Fahren
komfortabel oder das komfortable Fahren sportlich erleben möchten.

PORSCHE
FAHREN IN SEINER SCHÖNSTEN FORM

VOM PORSCHEFAHREN
»Früher oder später kommt man
dahinter, daß Leben auch
etwas mit Erlebnis zu tun hat.«

Porschefahren bedeutet für den einen Freiheit, für andere wiederum Freude an
einem faszinierenden Fahrgefühl. Oder ganz einfach Erfüllung eines Wunschtraums.
Dieses Erlebnis zu erhalten, ist eines der Ziele von Porsche. Selbst, wenn es sich
im Alltag oft nur um eine Form von »Kurzurlaub« zwischen zwei Geschäftsterminen
handelt, ist es für so manchen immerhin die Anschaffung eines Porsche wert.

PORSCHE
FAHREN IN SEINER SCHÖNSTEN FORM

ART DIRECTOR:
Günther Tibi
DESIGNER:
Günther Tibi
PHOTOGRAPHER:
Dietmar Henneka
COPYWRITER:
Jürgen Schippers
AGENCY:
Wensauer & Partner
CLIENT:
Porsche AG
■211–216

»Zur Abwechslung einmal ein wenig
vergleichende Werbung.«

Aus wettbewerbsrechtlichen Gründen ist es uns nicht gestattet, die neue limitierte
Baureihe 959 mit anderen Fahrzeugen zu vergleichen. Daher erlauben Sie uns den
Vergleich mit einer Legende – dem PORSCHE 356. Auch er war seiner Zeit voraus. Auch
sind beide nach dem gleichen Prinzip konstruiert, jedoch auf verschiedene Art
faszinierend. Der Unterschied: Während der 356 bereits Geschichte schrieb, zeigt der
PORSCHE 959, was heute und morgen im Automobilbau technisch möglich ist.

PORSCHE
FAHREN IN SEINER SCHÖNSTEN FORM

*Porsche zeigt mit dem 924 S, wie
man Bewährtes nicht nur verändert,
sondern verbessert.*

Der Porsche 924 gilt als Sportfahrzeug, mit dem man sich unter der Woche
im Geschäft, samstags an der Oper und sonntags auch an der Rennstrecke
zeigen kann. Weil man bei Porsche Bewährtes nicht verändert, sondern
verbessert, wird er jetzt zum Porsche 924 S. Der zusätzliche Buchstabe steht für
einen neuen, leistungsstarken 2,5-Liter-Motor, ein optimiertes, nach sichereres
Fahrwerk und viele verbesserte Details.

PORSCHE
FAHREN IN SEINER SCHÖNSTEN FORM

*Porschefahren hat nicht nur etwas mit
der Form des Fahrens zu tun, sondern auch
mit dem Format des Fahrers.*

Die ständige Weiterentwicklung fortschrittlicher Automobil-Technik bei Porsche bewirkt
unter anderem, daß fahrerische Leistung weniger aktiven Fahreinsatz bedeutet. Allein
das Wissen um außergewöhnliche Reserven führt zu einer neuen Form der Gelassenheit.
Der PORSCHE 944 Turbo erfüllt dabei sowohl höchste Ansprüche an zukunftsweisende
Technik als auch an zukunftsorientierte Fahrweise.

PORSCHE
FAHREN IN SEINER SCHÖNSTEN FORM

■**211–216** Examples from a campaign for *Porsche*. The slogan
throughout is: "Porsche – driving in its most beautiful form."
Presented in the campaign are various models including the *944
Turbo*, the *959*, the legendary *356* and the *924S*. (GER)

■**211–216** Beispiele aus einer Magazin-Werbekampagne für
Porsche unter dem Slogan *»Porsche – Fahren in seiner schönsten
Form«*. Es werden verschiedene Modelle vorgestellt, darunter der
944 Turbo, der *959*, der legendäre *356* und der *924S*. (GER)

■**211–216** Annonces dans une campagne de magazines pour
Porsche avec ce slogan unique « *Porsche* – la conduite sous sa
forme la plus achevée » et divers modèles dont la *944 Turbo* la
959 la légendaire *356* et la *924S* (GER)

ART DIRECTOR:
Morton Kirschner

PHOTOGRAPHER:
Ronald van Teunebroek

COPYWRITER:
Henk Roozendaal

AGENCY:
GGK Amsterdam

CLIENT:
IBM

■217

Het ene goede idee leidt tot het andere.

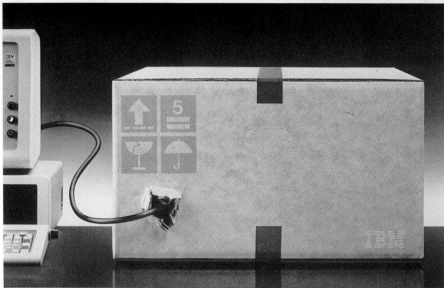

Hoe haalt u het maximum uit uw IBM Personal Computer?

Door er gewoon een of meer IBM PC Printers aan te koppelen.

Want die zijn bedacht, ontwikkeld en gemaakt door de bedenkers en makers van de IBM PC.

Zodat u er zeker van kunt zijn dat er geen onverwachte kink in de kabel komt.

Extra voordelig.

Optimale afstemming en betrouwbaarheid zijn echter bij lange na niet de enige voordelen.

IBM PC Printers zijn berekend op hoge afdruksnelheden, nu tegen een extra lage kostprijs.

Welke printer voor u het best is, hangt overigens absoluut niet van uw portemonnee af.

Elke IBM PC Printer heeft namelijk zijn eigen specialiteiten. Laten we even het rijtje afgaan.

De snelste en veelzijdigste is de IBM Proprinter. Tevens de goedkoopste. Zowel geschikt voor tekst als grafische voorstellingen.

Afdruksnelheid instelbaar van 200 tekens per seconde voor een ruwe uitdraai, tot 40 tekens per seconde voor een mooie kwaliteit.

De Proprinter verwerkt probleemloos losse vellen, meervoudige formulieren, kettingpapier, enveloppen, etiketten, enz.

Heeft u correspondentiekwaliteit nodig? Dan is de IBM Wheelprinter (25 tekens per seconde) een goed idee.

De Wheelprinter wordt standaard geleverd met twee voorzieningen: voor invoer van kettingformulieren én losse vellen.

Is rust een vereiste, dan komt u automatisch terecht bij de stille IBM Quietwriter.

De revolutionaire afdruktechniek van de Quietwriter levert zelfs bij een snelheid van 60 tekens per seconde een superieur schrift op.

Bovendien kunt u letters 2 x zo groot afdrukken. Mooi voor bladtitels en tussenkopjes.

Wat doet u ten slotte met tekst en grafische voorstellingen in kleur?

Die kunt u op z'n voordeligst afdrukken met de zeer bijzondere IBM Kleuren Ink-Jet Printer.

Vier spuitkoppen, gestuurd door een 8-bits microprocessor, zorgen voor haarscherpe details en mooie, strakke kleurvlakken.

Ook mengkleuren behoren tot de mogelijkheden.

De sneldrogende inkt wordt probleemloos en vlekkeloos aangebracht op papier aan de rol, maar ook op losse vellen of doorslagformulieren. Ja, zelfs op overhead transparanten.

U ziet, achter elke IBM PC Printer zit een ander idee. Maar wat u er ook mee gaat afdrukken, IBM heeft in ieder geval de prijs gedrukt.

Wilt u een IBM PC Printer aan het werk zien?

Ga dan eens kijken bij een geautoriseerde IBM Personal Computer Dealer. Bel 020-565 3300 voor een complete dealerlijst. **IBM**

■**217** Newspaper ad in black and white for IBM. The slogan reads: "One good idea leads to another." (NLD)

■**218-220** Three spreads in a magazine ad campaign for *Sony* Slogans from top to bottom: "What a businessman needs when he is travelling"; " *Sony UX-Pro*squeezes out what other tapes leave behind"; " *Sony*introduces *Micro Black Trinitron*; "Where does that leave the competition." (NLD)

■**217** Zeitungsanzeige in Schwarzweiss für IBM. Der Slogan: «Eine gute Idee führt zu einer anderen.» (NLD)

■**218–220** Doppelseitige Anzeigen aus einer Magazinkampagne für *Sony* Slogans von oben nach unten: «Was ein Geschäftsmann braucht, wenn er reist.» «Was andere Tonbänder zurücklassen, bringt *Sony UX-Pro*noch heraus.» « *Sony*stellt *Micro Black Trinitron*vor. Wo bleibt da die Konkurrenz.» (NLD)

■**217** Annonce de journal, noir et blanc, pour IBM: «une bonne idée en entraîne une autre.» (NLD)

■**218–220** Trois doubles pages dans une campagne d'annonces de magazines pour *Sony* De haut en bas: «ce qu'il faut à un homme d'affaires qui voyage»; «l' *UX-Pro de Sony*exprime les résidus des autres bandes»; « *Sony*présente le *Micro Black Trinitron* La concurrence en est où?» (NLD)

SONY UX-PRO PERST ERUIT WAT ANDERE TAPES LATEN ZITTEN

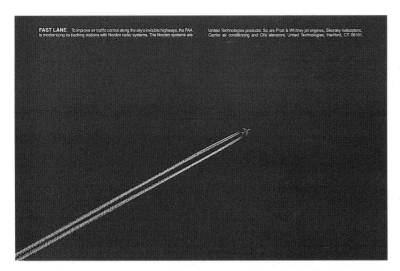

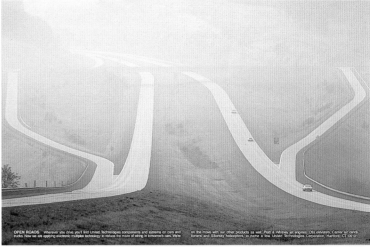

ART DIRECTOR:
Gordon Bowman

PHOTOGRAPHER:
Jay Maisel

CLIENT:
United Technologies Corp.

■**221–224**

■**221–224** Double-spread photographs promote diverse business units belonging to United Technologies Corp.: *Norden* radar systems, electronic components for cars, *Pratt & Whitney* jet engines and *Carrier Transicold* refrigeration systems. (USA)

■**225** "13 years of development for 30 milliseconds." Daimler-Benz AG presents its "airbag" safety system located in the steering column. By frontal collision an electronic sensor releases a gas generator and within 30 thousandth of a second the airbag fills with gas to protect the driver. (GER)

■**221–224** Anzeigen für verschiedene Erzeugnisse der United Technologies Corporation: Norden-Radar-Systeme, elektronische Teile für Autos, *Pratt-&-Whitney*-Düsenmotoren und *Carrier-Transicold*-Kühlsysteme und -Klimaanlagen. (USA)

■**225** Doppelseitige Zeitschriftenanzeige für *Daimler-Benz*. Vorgestellt wird das neuentwickelte Luftsack-Sicherheitssystem. Beim Frontalaufprall löst ein elektronischer Sensor einen Gasgenerator aus, der den Luftsack innerhalb von nur 30 Millisekunden mit ungefährlichem Gas füllt. (GER)

■**221–224** Annonces pour divers produits de la United Technologies Corp.: les systèmes radar *Norden*, les composants électroniques pour l'automobile, les turboréacteurs *Pratt & Whitney*, les systèmes de réfrigération *Carrier Transicold* (USA)

■**225** «13 années de R & D pour 30 millisecondes.» La Daimler-Benz AG présente son système de sécurité dit «airbag» logé dans la colonne de direction. En cas de collision frontale, un palpeur électronique déclenche un générateur de gaz qui remplit en l'espace de 30 ms le sac d'air censé protéger le conducteur. (GER)

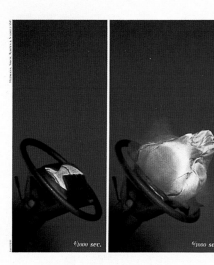

13 Jahre Entwicklung für 30 Millisekunden.

Sicherheit im Automobil ist ein Thema von ganz besonderer Bedeutung. Zumindest für uns.

Das zeigen nicht nur unsere vielen Entwicklungen von Sicherheitselementen aus der Vergangenheit, die nicht selten für den Automobilbau wegweisend waren: wie gestaltfester Fahrgastraum, Knautschzone, Sicherheitslenkung oder Antiblockier-System.

Das zeigt vor allem auch die Entwicklung des Airbag, eines Luftsack-Sicherheits-Systems zur Ergänzung des Sicherheitsgurts, die uns 13 Jahre beschäftigt hat und seit 1980 von uns angeboten wird.

Warum diese Entwicklung so schwierig war, versteht man erst, wenn man weiß, wie sie funktioniert.

Der Luftsack befindet sich im Lenkrad. Bei einem Frontalaufprall löst ein elektronischer Sensor einen Gasgenerator aus, der den Luftsack innerhalb von nur 30 Millisekunden mit ungefährlichem Gas füllt.

Gerade rechtzeitig genug, um Brust-korb und Kopf des Fahrers sicher aufzufangen und das Verletzungsrisiko noch weiter zu verringern. 150 Millisekunden nach dem Aufprall ist der Luftsack schon wieder leer. Das geht also alles in einer so kurzen Zeit vor sich, daß man kaum merkt, was passiert ist.

Eine der Aufgaben, die wir bei der Entwicklung lösen mußten, war, daß dieses hochsensible System nicht schon bei kleineren Karambolagen losgeht. Zum Beispiel auf Parkplätzen. Daß es aber dann, wenn es eines Tages wirklich gebraucht wird, auch in Millisekunden funktioniert. Selbst nach Jahren.

Zusammen mit dem Sicherheitsgurt und dem elektronisch gesteuerten Gurtstraffer, der serienmäßig in allen Mercedes-Benz Personenwagen eingebaut wird, ist der Airbag das heute denkbar beste Sicherheitssystem für den Fahrer eines Automobils.

Eine Sicherheit, der wir schon immer besondere Beachtung geschenkt haben. Und daran wird sich auch in Zukunft mit Sicherheit nichts ändern.

DAIMLER-BENZ AG

ART DIRECTOR:
Rainer Held
PHOTOGRAPHER:
Bernhardt Brill
COPYWRITER:
Gerd Simon
AGENCY:
Hildmann, Simon, Rempen & Schmitz/SMS
CLIENT:
Daimler-Benz AG
■225

DONGHIA

The Luna Arm Chair.
Like a rising moon, now resting gracefully
on conical legs. Illusionary, especially in PAWTUXET
rib weave, the newest addition to Donghia's
domestic wool collection.

Circle 65

DONGHIA FURNITURE AND TEXTILES: 485 Broadway, New York 10013 212.925.2777
Atlanta, Boston, Chicago, Cleveland, Dallas, Denver, Houston, Los Angeles, Miami, New York,
Philadelphia, San Francisco, Seattle, Washington, DC

■**226–229** Full-page and spreads from the magazine advertising for *Donghia* furniture and textiles. Shown: the Luna armchair; the Madison swivel chair; fabrics from the Nuovo collection and the Urbane chair. (USA)

■**226–229** Anzeigen aus einer Zeitschriftenkampagne für *Donghia*-Möbel und -Textilien. Abgebildet sind der «Luna»-Sessel, der «Madison»-Drehstuhl, Stoffe der «Nuovo Collection» und der «Urbane Chair», ein vielseitiger Stuhl aus Birkenholz. (USA)

■**226–229** Annonces de magazines pleine et double page pour les ameublements et textiles *Donghia* Sont représentés: le fauteuil «Luna», le siège pivotant «Madison», des tissus de la collection «Nuovo», la chaise «Urbain». (USA)

ART DIRECTOR:
Susan Slover

DESIGNER:
Susan Slover

PHOTOGRAPHER:
Raenne Giovanni

AGENCY:
Susan Slover Design

CLIENT:
Donghia

■226–229

The
average high
induced
by cocaine
lasts
thirty
minutes.

The
average death
induced
by cocaine
lasts
slightly
longer.

Citizens Against Cocaine Abuse

ART DIRECTOR:
GARY GOLDSMITH
DESIGNER:
GARY GOLDSMITH
COPYWRITER:
NEAL GOMBERG
AGENCY:
GOLDSMITH/JEFFREY
CLIENT:
CITIZENS AGAINST
COCAINE ABUSE
■230

ART DIRECTOR:
DEAN HANSON
PHOTOGRAPHER:
RICK DUBLIN
COPYWRITER:
TOM MCELLIGOTT
AGENCY:
FALLON MCELLIGOTT
CLIENT:
THE EPISCOPAL CHURCH
■232–234

■230 Black-and-white double spread from a campaign on behalf of the *Citizens Against Cocaine Abuse* organization. (USA)

■231 Portrait of Stevie Wonder and a quotation to bring home the message about the dangers of driving after drinking, for the *Reader's Digest* Foundation. (USA)

■232–234 Black-and-white pages from a series to promote The Episcopal Church, in which the illustrations act as a foil to the copy. (USA)

■230 Inserat gegen Kokainkonsum. Die weisse Fläche steht für die 30 Minuten des Rausches, die schwarze für den Tod. (USA)

■231 «Bevor ich mich von einem Betrunkenen fahren lasse, fahre ich lieber selbst.» Inserat mit Porträt von Stevie Wonder gegen Alkohol am Steuer. (USA)

■232–234 Für die Episkopalkirche: Die Kraft des Kreuzes erkennt man nicht durch Horrorfilme; gegen Einsamkeit hilft nur der Glaube; nicht der Tod soll Anlass für die Rückkehr sein. (USA)

■230 Double page pour une campagne de l'organisation *Citizens Against Cocaine Abuse* contre le cocaïnisme. (USA)

■231 Portrait de Stevie Wonder: «plutôt que de monter dans la voiture d'un ivrogne, je conduis moi-même.» Pour la Fondation *Reader's Digest* (USA)

■232–234 D'une série publicitaire pour l'Eglise épiscopalienne: la puissance de la Croix ne ressort pas des films d'horreur; la foi vainc la solitude; revenir à Dieu avant la mort, durant la vie. (USA)

"Before I'll ride with a drunk, I'll drive myself." —Stevie Wonder

Driving after drinking, or riding with a driver who's been drinking, is a big mistake. Anyone can see that.
This message courtesy of *College Outlook* in conjunction with Reader's Digest Foundation and Fallon McElligott Advertising.

ART DIRECTOR:
Bob Barrie

DESIGNER:
Bob Barrie

PHOTOGRAPHER:
Bobby Holland

COPYWRITER:
Mike Lescarbeau

AGENCY:
Fallon McElligott

CLIENT:
Reader's Digest

■231

Are your kids learning about the power of the cross on the late, late show?

With all due regard to Hollywood, there's more to Christianity than stopping vampires. Come with your children to the Episcopal Church this Sunday as we celebrate the resurrection of Jesus Christ in love and fellowship.
The Episcopal Church

You can't meet God's gift to women in a singles' bar.

If the singles life sometimes leaves you feeling alone and empty, remember that God's gift to all women and men is Jesus Christ. Come join us in worship this Sunday in the Episcopal Church.
The Episcopal Church

Will it take six strong men to bring you back into the church?

The Episcopal Church welcomes you no matter what condition you're in, but we'd really prefer to see you breathing. Come join us in the love, worship and fellowship of Jesus Christ this Sunday.
The Episcopal Church

"The Great Train Robbery." Monday night at 7:30. **32** WFLD TV

OUR NEW DESIGNS ARE SO EXCITING, THEY MADE OUR STORE LOOK OLD.

So we've just redesigned Storehouse at Lenox Square from top to bottom! Our new look is post-modern, bold and colorful. And in addition to the classic contemporary home furnishings that have made us one of the fastest growing retailers in the country, you'll find some brilliant new collections of accessories. Come see unique and wondrous items from international designers like Richard Meier and Ettore Sottsass. And elegant objects from innovative manufacturers like Swid Powell, Alessi and Hall China. Come in soon and see the beautiful change in Lenox Square.

storehouse at lenox square

261-3482 Open Monday through Saturday 10:00-9:30. Sunday 12:30-5:30.

ART DIRECTOR:
Houman Pirdavari
ILLUSTRATOR:
Dan Craig
COPYWRITER:
Mike Lescarbeau
AGENCY:
Fallon McElligott
CLIENT:
WFLD TV
■235

ART DIRECTOR:
Jerry Sullivan
PHOTOGRAPHER:
Dan Fitz Randolph
COPYWRITER:
Liz Severance
AGENCY:
Sullivan Haas Coyle
CLIENT:
Storehouse
■236

■**235** Black-and-white ad from a series to promote various programs on US television Channel 32 WFLD, this time for a popular film. (USA)

■**236** Post-modern, bold and colorful household articles on this full-page ad to announce the redesigning of the *Storehouse* at Lenox Square, Atlanta. (USA)

■**237–240** Series of double-spread ads to sell advertising space in *Rolling Stone* magazine. Shown here: scooters, fragrances (with a "scratch n' sniff" inset), groceries and sporting goods. (USA)

■**235** Schwarzweiss-Inserat aus einer Kampagne für einen amerikanischen TV-Sender, hier mit Ankündigung eines Films (Eisenbahnraub). (USA)

■**236** «Neben dem aufregenden Design unserer Artikel sah unser Laden plötzlich alt aus.» Inserat für die Bekanntgabe der Renovierung eines Geschäftes für Haushaltartikel. (USA)

■**237–240** Doppelseitige Anzeigen als Inserentenwerbung der Zeitschrift *Rolling Stone* Hier geht es um falsche Vorstellungen über die Leser und die tatsächlichen Ausgaben für Konsumgüter. (USA)

■**235** Annonce noir et blanc figurant dans une série promotionnelle pour divers programmes de la chaîne de télévision américaine 32 WFLD. (USA)

■**236** Annonce pleine page, illustrée d'articles ménagers postmodernes dont le design audacieux, haut en couleur est assorti à la rénovation du *Storehouse* sur Lenox Square à Atlanta. (USA)

■**237–240** Série d'annonces double page destinées aux annonceurs du magazine *Rolling Stone*. Ces scooters, parfums (déposés sur la page), articles d'épicerie et équipements de sport représentent les goûts des lecteurs. (USA)

Perception.

Reality.

If you think Rolling Stone readers are still cruising down the highway with the American flag between their knees, put this in your gas tank: Last year, Rolling Stone readers helped set the trend for a whole new way to get around. Selling scooters? Your product might be an alternative. But running your ad in Rolling Stone is not.

Rolling Stone

Perception.

(Scratch and sniff.)

Reality.

(Scratch and sniff.)

If your olfactory impression of Rolling Stone readers smells like something far out or far east, take a whiff of this: Last week alone, Rolling Stone readers used the world's most fashionable fragrances 34 million times. If you've got fragrances to sell, Rolling Stone can hit your target right on the nose.

Rolling Stone

Perception.

Reality.

If you think a plate of homemade brownies can satisfy the munchies of a Rolling Stone reader, here's the scoop on what else it takes. Last week, Rolling Stone readers spent 290 million dollars in grocery stores, drank 40 million glasses of soda, ate 6 million cups of yogurt and polished off 4 million candy bars. And they're still hungry.

Rolling Stone

Perception.

Reality.

If you still think Rolling Stone readers are trying to get a grip on what life is all about, check their score on what life after five is all about. Last year, Rolling Stone readers served up $50 million dollars worth of recreational purchases. If you've got sporting goods to sell, you just hit the sweet spot.

Rolling Stone

ART DIRECTOR:
HOUMAN PIRDAVARI
DESIGNER:
HOUMAN PIRDAVARI
PHOTOGRAPHER:
RICK DUBLIN
COPYWRITER:
BILL MILLER
AGENCY:
FALLON MCELLIGOTT
CLIENT:
ROLLING STONE MAGAZINE
■237-240

BOYCOTTEN OF BEMIDDELEN?

SLEGS NIE-BLANKES
NON-WHITES ONLY...

Alle pluriformiteit ten spijt, is vrijwel elke regering ter wereld tegen de apartheidspolitiek in Zuid-Afrika. Over de bestrijding van dit verschijnsel lopen de meningen echter nogal uiteen.

Wordt het verzet om Reagan en Thatcher tegen bepaalde sancties gedreven door eigenbelang, dan wel gebaseerd op vrees voor de nadelige gevolgen bij de zwarte bevolking?

Of heeft de anti-apartheidsbeweging gelijk als zij stelt dat een totale boycot het lijden van de zwarte bevolking zal bekorten?

Waarschijnlijk bent u inmiddels al zo vaak met deze materie geconfronteerd dat u een persoonlijke mening op bovenstaande vragen kunt geven.

Vindt u dat de krant die u leest die mening moet bevestigen? Of prefereert u een krant die de nuance laat zien alle partijen, zodat u een overzicht licht op de zaak u wel eens zo klaarten verdacht tot standpunt te bepalen?

In dat geval is u het objectieve karakter van NRC Handelsblad wel eens een intensievere uitdaging voor u kunnen zijn.

NRC Handelsblad is een krant die niet dicht in zwart wit termen Reagan, Thatcher, Gorbatsjov, of welke andere politieke leider dan ook, zijn met het voorkeur voor het een artikel.

Vooropgezet een inslag is het mogelijk de waargave van de feiten. Informatie die uit veel gevallen afkomstig is uit eigen redacteuren.

NRC Handelsblad heeft namelijk de meeste buitenlandse correspondenten van alle Nederlandse kranten. Behalve het bondig geschreven nieuws bevat de krant ook veel deskundige commentaar.

Maar wel altijd strikt gescheiden van de feiten. Dit in tegenstelling tot veel andere kranten. NRC Handelsblad is een serieuze krant. Wat willen we geen massa verstand over laten bestaan. Er wordt ruim aandacht geschonken aan politieke, sociale, economische en culturele onderwerpen.

Wat niet wegneemt dat u wel degelijk ook minder ernstige zaken een plaats in de krant vindt.

Wij noemen u bij voorbeeld de achterpagina met de Bommelsaga, het Soepprogramma, het Hollands Dagboek en niet te vergeten de vele columns. Waar uit u rustig kunt concluderen dat NRC Handelsblad een veelzijdige krant is. De veelzijdigheid gaat echter nooit zover dat de nieuwe vriendin van een oude scheepsmagnaat een plaats in onze kolommen waardig wordt geacht.

Als Nederlander verkeert u in de aangename omstandigheid dat u kunt kiezen uit tientallen kranten. Vanzelfsprekend hopen wij dat de objectieve berichtgeving van NRC Handelsblad, de strikte scheiding van nieuws en commentaar, de vele culturele rubrieken van ruim, de evenwichtige opmaak en de vier bijlagen van NRC Handelsblad voor u aanleiding zijn om niet één van de andere kranten te nemen, maar NRC Handelsblad.

Wie gaat is het zulke genoeg om te verteieien dat u niet af zult gaan op vroeger af dan niet maar is op de woorden alleen. Vandaar de mogelijkheid van een proefabonnement.

Als u ons – kosteloos vanuit het hele land – belt (tel. 06-0555 tot 20.30 uur), krijgt u de krant vier weken voor de prijs van twee weken. Daarna is de conclusie aan u.

NRC HANDELSBLAD
ONONTKOOMBAAR VOOR WIE
DE NUANCE ZOEKT.

BESCHERMD OF VOGELVRIJ?

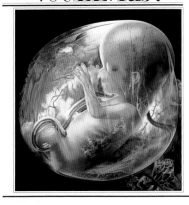

Genetisch onderzoek, reageerbuisbevruchtingen, draagmoederschap, homofiele ouderparen. Misschien verdacht u van uw dagblad dat het dergelijke verschijnselen met de nodige reserves beoordeelt.

Wellicht prefereert u juist een krant die voornoemde ontwikkelingen ondubbelzinnig onder de noemer "vooruitgang" plaatst.

Mogelijk, tenslotte, stelt u de voorkeur aan een krant die op een eerste plaats een objectieve weergave van de feiten nastreeft.

En de meningen die in het spel zijn strikt scheidt van de feiten. Daarbij alle partijen de nuance laten. Zodat u zelf kunt bepalen wat waarschijnlijk is. Zullen wat we nu embryo's noemen straks blije kinderen van de 21e eeuw of cliënten voor de psychiater zijn?

Voelt u zich aangetrokken tot het laatste type krant, dan zou NRC Handelsblad wel eens interessant voor u kunnen zijn. En is het de moeite waard om eens wat meer over deze krant te vernemen.

NRC Handelsblad is een krant die u niet vertelt wat u moet denken, maar wat u moet weten. Het is dan ook niet meer dan logisch, dat de krant een uitgebreide berichtgeving voorstaat.

En niet alleen waar het binnenlands nieuws betreft. Want al zijn we een landelijke krant en daartoe vanzelfsprekend met vertegenwoordigd in Den Haag, onze blik reikt natuurlijk ook tot ver over de landsgrenzen.

De achterliggende gedachte is, dat Nederland, politiek en economisch gezien, sterk van het buitenland afhankelijk is.

Waarbij we aantekenen dat we Frau Antje verkiezingen minder relevant vinden dan de ontwikkelingen in het Midden-Oosten.

Overlaatstgenoemde en andere zaken van internationaal belang wordt u royaal geïnformeerd. Niet in de laatste plaats door een klein legertje buitenland-correspondenten.

Onder uitgebreide verstaan we ook diepgaande berichtgeving. Menig nieuwsteller leert zich immers voor meer beschouwing. Kan vaak beter geïnterpreteerd worden als het in een brede maatschappelijke context geplaatst wordt.

Hopelijk is u in dit korte bestek het een ander duidelijk geworden over de intentie waarmee NRC Handelsblad gemaakt wordt.

En sinds dit beeld met uw opvatting over de manier waarop journalistiek bedreven dient te worden.

Mogen we u dan wijzen op de mogelijkheid een proefabonnement? Als u ons – kosteloos vanuit het hele land – belt (tel. 06-0555 tot 20.30 uur), krijgt u de krant vier weken voor de prijs en twee weken. De ideale manier om de filosofie van NRC Handelsblad aan de werkelijkheid te toetsen.

NRC HANDELSBLAD
ONONTKOOMBAAR VOOR WIE
DE NUANCE ZOEKT.

WETENSCHAP OF WAANZIN?

De opiniepagina's van NRC Handelsblad vormden onlangs het podium voor een gepeperde discussie rond dierproeven.

Aanleiding was een ingezonden artikel waarin sprake was van "genadeloze wreedheid" jegens proefdieren en "concentratiekampen" als typering voor laboratoria.

Bedoeld artikel oogstte een regen aan ingezonden brieven. In sommige werd de emotionele lading van het schrijven geroemd. In andere het tendentieuze karakter van het stuk gelaakt.

Argumenten van ethische, medische, politieke en filosofische aard werden aangevoerd.

Of het nut voor mens én dier het nemen van dierproeven nu wel of niet rechtvaardigt, in ons land blijken daarover tal van opinies te leven.

NRC Handelsblad laat u onbekrompen kennismaken met die opvattingen. Omdat de krant zich niet gebonden weet aan welke politieke, sociale, religieuze of andere groepering dan ook.

Geen krant voor mensen die menen te weten hoe alles in elkaar steekt en wat de oplossing voor elk probleem is.

Maar des te meer een krant voor mensen die een voorkeur hebben voor de open discussie.

En daar bij voorkeur zelf een genuanceerde conclusie aan verbinden.

Hoewel NRC Handelsblad een sterke afkeer van manipulatie en indoctrinatie heeft en derhalve streeft naar objectiviteit, zal een volledig objectieve weergave van de werkelijkheid altijd een fictie blijven. Want zowel bij de nieuwsgaring als de berichtgeving moet gekozen worden.

Komt een bericht op pagina één of vier? Moet er een grote of juist een bescheiden kopregel boven? Wordt het een uitvoerig dan wel een zeer beknopt artikel? Vragen waarop per definitie slechts een subjectief antwoord mogelijk is.

Daar komt nog bij dat NRC Handelsblad soms heel bewust alle objectiviteit overboord zet.

Als bijvoorbeeld de parlementaire democratie of de vrijheid van meningsuiting in het geding is, schromen we niet onze ongezouten mening daarover kenbaar te maken.

Onlosmakelijk onderdeel van NRC Handelsblad zijn de vier bijlagen.

Een logisch gevolg van ons streven om de werkelijkheid zo goed mogelijk weer te geven. En die werkelijkheid laat zich vaak niet vangen in een eenvoudig, kort artikeltje.

De bijlagen bieden NRC Handelsblad journalisten de gelegenheid om u nog meer achtergrondgegevens te verschaffen. Waar nodig alle feiten op een rijtje te zetten. Een uitvoerige analyse te maken.

Is een onderwerp erg veelomvattend, dan sluiten we zeker niet de mogelijkheid uit er een complete bijlage aan te wijden.

Voor de lezers die niet graag aan de buitenkant van het nieuws blijven steken moet dat een waar genoegen zijn.

NRC Handelsblad is niet de krant met de grootste oplage. Daarentegen is het wel een krant die zich als een van de weinige mag verheugen in een nog steeds stijgende oplage.

Naar de reden valt slechts te gissen. Wellicht heeft u in de voorgaande alinea's een paar aanknopingspunten kunnen ontdekken.

Mochten u die aanspreken dan verdient het zeker aanbeveling ons even te bellen voor een proefabonnement. Vanuit het hele land kosteloos: 06-0555 (tot 20.30 uur).

Wij zorgen dan dat u vier weken lang NRC Handelsblad elke avond in de bus krijgt. U betaalt ons dan slechts twee weken.

NRC HANDELSBLAD
ONONTKOOMBAAR VOOR WIE
DE NUANCE ZOEKT.

ART DIRECTOR:
William McCaffery

COPYWRITER:
Jay Cheek

AGENCY:
McCaffery & Ratner, Inc.

CLIENT:
National Geographic

■ 241–243

ART DIRECTOR:
Pieter van Velsen

DESIGNER:
Pieter van Velsen

COPYWRITER:
Celine van Gent

AGENCY:
GGK Amsterdam

CLIENT:
NRC Handelsblad

■ 244–246

XEROX

Winning takes more than fancy footwork. The most advanced equipment

Success takes more than just using your head, whether you play

can only complement a strong team behind you. The same is true of

in the sports or corporate arena. Which is why at Xerox, we don't

success in business. Which is why we've created Team Xerox

just make some of the smartest office equipment in the world, we

also offer the finest service and support organization in the industry.

to provide you with the most fitting combination of Xerox products and

support. It's our way of keeping you a step ahead of the game.

That's how we help you stay on top of things.

XEROX is a trademark of XEROX CORPORATION.

XEROX is a trademark of XEROX CORPORATION.

ART DIRECTOR:
ANNE CHUTE
DESIGNER:
ANNE CHUTE/JAMES TUGHAN
ILLUSTRATOR:
JAMES TUGHAN
COPYWRITER:
LISA MAYER
AGENCY:
NEEDHAM DDB WORLDWIDE
CLIENT:
XEROX CORP.
■**247, 248**

■**247, 248** Advertisements for *Xerox* with emphasis on their customer service. (CAN)

■**249** Black-and-white double spread, one of a series for ITT Life Insurance Corp., here with the "paperwork" deleted. (USA)

■**247, 248** »Der Kopf allein bringt keinen Erfolg«, »Fussarbeit allein bringt keinen Sieg«. Inserate für *Xerox* (CAN)

■**249** Inserat einer Versicherungsgesellschaft, die den Papierkrieg vermeidet – wie hier am Wort demonstriert. (USA)

■**247, 248** Annonces pour *Xerox* »le succès ne s'obtient pas qu'avec la tête«; »gagner, pas seulement faire avec ses pieds.« (CAN)

■**249** Double page d'une série de l'ITT Life Insurance Corp.: »nous avons coupé court à la (paperasserie).« (USA)

ART DIRECTOR:
DEAN HANSON
AGENCY:
FALLON MCELLIGOTT
CLIENT:
ITT LIFE INSURANCE CORP.
■249

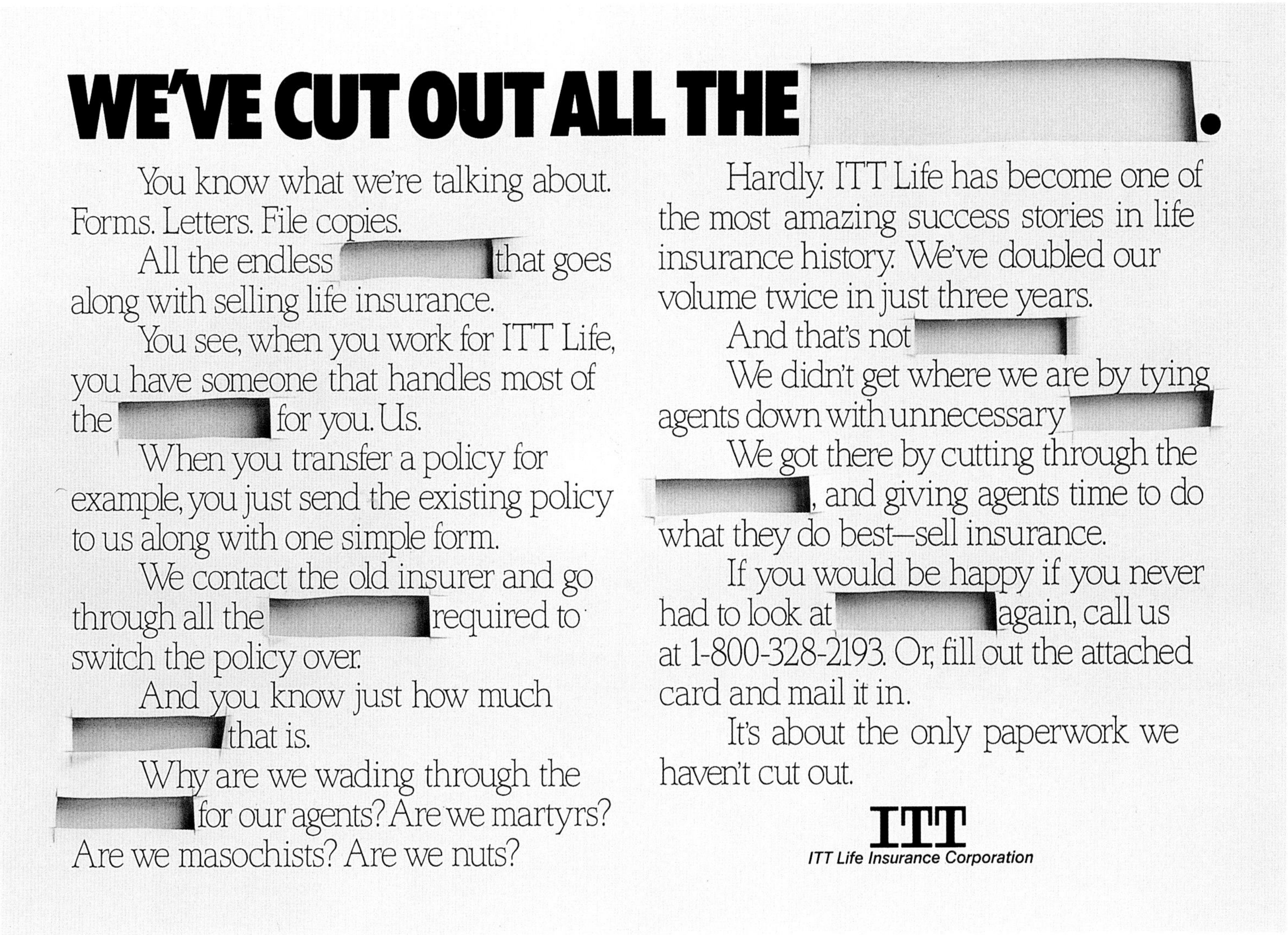

WE'VE CUT OUT ALL THE   .

You know what we're talking about. Forms. Letters. File copies.

All the endless   that goes along with selling life insurance.

You see, when you work for ITT Life, you have someone that handles most of the   for you. Us.

When you transfer a policy for example, you just send the existing policy to us along with one simple form.

We contact the old insurer and go through all the   required to switch the policy over.

And you know just how much   that is.

Why are we wading through the   for our agents? Are we martyrs? Are we masochists? Are we nuts?

Hardly. ITT Life has become one of the most amazing success stories in life insurance history. We've doubled our volume twice in just three years.

And that's not

We didn't get where we are by tying agents down with unnecessary

We got there by cutting through the   , and giving agents time to do what they do best—sell insurance.

If you would be happy if you never had to look at   again, call us at 1-800-328-2193. Or, fill out the attached card and mail it in.

It's about the only paperwork we haven't cut out.

ITT
ITT Life Insurance Corporation

DESIGN : KAZUMASA NAGAI
こもん
株式会社 竹尾

DESIGN BY KAZUMASA NAGAI
サーブル
株式会社 竹尾

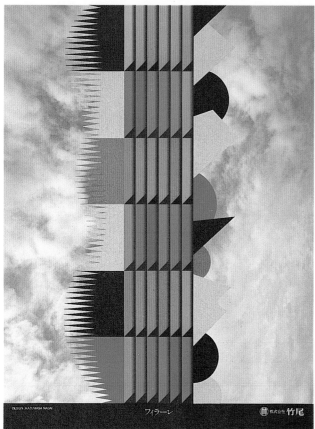

DESIGN : KAZUMASA NAGAI
フィラーレ
株式会社 竹尾

DESIGN BY KAZUMASA NAGAI
ダイヤホワイト
株式会社 竹尾

ART DIRECTOR:
Kazumasa Nagai
DESIGNER:
Kazumasa Nagai
AGENCY:
Nippon Design Center
CLIENT:
Takeo Co., Ltd.
■ 250–254

■**250–254** Magazine ads for Takeo Co. Ltd. (paper whole-saler). Each ad. is printed on one of the company's paper qualities, i.e. Komon, Sable, Filare, Dia-White, NT Rasha. (JPN)

■**250–254** Zeitschriftenanzeigen für Takeo Ltd. (Papier-Grossist). Jede Anzeige ist auf eine der angebotenen Papierquali-täten gedruckt. (JPN)

■**250–254** Annonces pour la Takeo Co. Ltd., un grossiste en papier, chacune imprimée sur une qualité de papier différente: Komon, Sable, Filare, Dia-White, NT Rasha. (JPN)

255 Magazine advertisement for Dotmar Fine Paper Merchants – here with emphasis on *Zanders* paper qualities. (CAN)

256 Illustration side of a double-sided magazine ad for *S.D.Warren.* The bottom line reads: If an idea is worth the paper it's printed on – it's worth *Warren.* (USA)

257 *Siegwerk Druckfarben* (printing inks) has commissioned works by renowned US artists dedicated to «the rainbow of printing art.» Shown is Brad Holland's interpretation. (GER)

258 Magazine ad for Knapp Colour Graphics. (USA)

255 Zeitschrifteninserat für einen Papier-Grossisten, der hier speziell für *Zanders*-Papierqualitäten wirbt. (CAN)

256 Vorderseite einer Anzeige für eine Papierqualität. «Wenn die Idee das Papier wert ist, auf dem sie gedruckt wird – dann ist sie *Warren*-Papier wert.» (USA)

257 Anzeige für die «Regenbogen»-Druckfarben von *Siegwerk*, aus einer Seite, die bei namhaften Künstlern in Auftrag gegeben wurde. Hier eine Interpretation von Brad Holland. (GER)

258 Inserat mit Wortspiel für einen Lithographen. (USA)

255 Pour Dotmar Fine Paper Merchants: «pensez *Zanders* si vous désirez une qualité d'impression parfaite.» (CAN)

256 Côté illustration d'une annonce de magazine double page pour *S.D. Warren:* «si une idée vaut le papier où elle figure, elle vaut un papier *Warren.*» (USA)

257 Le fabricant d'encres d'imprimerie *Siegwerk Druckfarben* a commandé à divers artistes américains réputés une interprétation de «l'arch-en-ciel de l'art de l'imprimeur». (GER)

258 Annonce pour Knapp Colour Graphics. (USA)

ART DIRECTOR:
GOTTSCHALK + ASH INT'L
DESIGNER:
JOANNE LEE/STUART ASH
ILLUSTRATOR:
YOSH INOUYE
AGENCY:
GOTTSCHALK + ASH INT'L
CLIENT:
DOTMAR FINE PAPER
255

ART DIRECTOR:
CHERYL HELLER
DESIGNER:
CHERYL HELLER
PHOTOGRAPHER:
JEFFREY MEYERS
AGENCY:
HBM/CREAMER DESIGN GROUP
CLIENT:
S.D. WARREN CO.
256

Chromolux

Ikonorex

Ikonolux

Think Zanders for perfect printability*

*Applied Arts did!

Ikonofix

Halls-Canada Paper
Buntin Reid Paper
McFarlane Son & Hodgson
Schoffield Paper
Buntin Gillies

GLOSS

is a slicker coating surface. And when you have a high gloss surface going for you, there's nothing that can rain on your parade. Excellent gloss helps give you depth, detail, and brilliant color reproduction. And proof positive is Warren Lustro Gloss, the paper upon which this is printed.

ART DIRECTOR:
Robert Pütz

ILLUSTRATOR:
Brad Holland

AGENCY:
Robert Pütz GmbH

CLIENT:
Siegwerk Druckfarben

■ **257**

R E G E N B O G E N

Dem Regenbogen der
Druckkunst gewidmet sind
die Arbeiten, die Siegwerk
bei namhaften Künstlern
in Auftrag gegeben hat.
  Was Brad Holland, einen
der bedeutendsten ameri-
kanischen Illustratoren,
zu seiner metaphysischen
Regenbogen-Auffassung
gebracht hat, könnte man
real so nachvollziehen:
  Die Regenbogenfarben
sind ein Geschenk des
Himmels – und der
Regenbogen-Service
schenkt das Spektrum an
Leistungen, das man als
Drucker für die Druck-
kunst braucht.

Dem Künstler im Drucker
gewidmet sind Siegwerks
Regenbogenfarben:
  Ihre Qualität gewähr-
leistet eine Druckwieder-
gabe, die der Qualität des
Originals entspricht.
  Der Siegwerk-Service
rund um die Regenbogen-
farben tut ein übriges,
damit Sie sich voll auf die
Kunst des Druckens
konzentrieren können.

D E R   D R U C K K U N S T

ART DIRECTOR:
John Vitro

PHOTOGRAPHER:
David Kramer

AGENCY:
Phillips-Ramsey

CLIENT:
Knapp Colour Graphics

■ **258**

See Sharp.

If you're singing the blues because your color
separations are looking flat and off-key, tune in to
Knapp Colour. We'll sharpen up your image.

Knapp Colour Graphics
San Diego / Irvine / San Francisco

KODACOLOR GOLD FILM. DAS FARBWUNDER.

Jetzt ist das Rot roter, das Gelb gelber, das Blau blauer und das Grün grüner. Der neue KODACOLOR GOLD Film sieht die bunte Welt in ihren schönsten Farben.

KODACOLOR GOLD FILM. DAS FARBWUNDER.

KODACOLOR GOLD Filme sehen die bunte Welt in ihren schönsten Farben besonders scharf. Und der KODACOLOR GOLD 200 Film läßt Ihnen noch mehr Freiheit beim Belichten.

ART DIRECTOR:
Karl Heinz Daniel/
Heribert Burkert
PHOTOGRAPHER:
Jeanloup Sieff/
Christian von Alvensleben
COPYWRITER:
Gerd Anlauf/
Susanne Hessing
AGENCY:
Young & Rubicam GmbH
CLIENT:
Kodak AG
■259, 260

BOB LAMBERT · RETOUCHING · 835-2166

**HE KILLED THEM IN UKRAINE.
THEN KNOCKED THEM DEAD IN CANNES.**

Between 1932 and 1933, Joseph Stalin caused an "artificial" famine, taking the
lives of at least 7 million Ukrainians.
In 1985, Slavko Nowytski made an award winning film about it.
Come see HARVEST OF DESPAIR at Titsworth Lecture Hall, on Wednesday,
December 3rd. Lights go off at 7:00 p.m. sharp.

ART DIRECTOR:
Tom Lichtenheld
AGENCY:
Fallon McElligott
CLIENT:
Lambert Retouching
■**261**

ART DIRECTOR:
Kirk Souder
DESIGNER:
Kirk Souder
COPYWRITER:
Martin Canellakis
AGENCY:
Homer & Durham Advertising
CLIENT:
Sarah Lawrence College
■**262**

■**259, 260** Spreads from the *Kodak* advertising campaign
for *Kodacolor Gold* film - "the color miracle." Top, a tuareg
motif, bottom, a mulatto. (USA)

■**261** Hitler minus moustache. One of a series of black-and-
white "retouched" magazine ads for Lambert Retouching. (USA)

■**262** Stalin's portrait (black-and-white) on an ad issued by
Columbia University to publicize the film "The Harvest of
Despair", about the Ukrainian famine of 1933. (USA)

■**259, 260** Doppelseiten aus einer Inseratenkampagne für
Kodacolor-Gold-Filme von *Kodak.* Oben eine Tuareg, Angehö-
rige eines berberischen Volksstammes, unten eine Mulattin. (GER)

■**261** Hitler ohne Schnurrbart. Aus einer Serie von »retuschier-
ten« Anzeigen in Schwarzweiss, für einen Retuscheur. (USA)

■**262** Anzeige mit Stalins Porträt für die Vorführung eines
Films über die von Stalin 1933 künstlich verursachte Hungersnot
in der Ukraine. Der Film wurde in Cannes ausgezeichnet. (USA)

■**259, 260** «Le miracle de la couleur»: doubles pages de la
campagne *Kodak* en faveur du film *Kodacolor Gold.* En haut,
un motif targui; en bas, une mulâtresse. (GER)

■**261** Hitler sans sa moustache. Elément d'une série d'annonces
noir et blanc «retouchées», pour Lambert Retouching. (USA)

■**262** Portrait de Staline, en noir et blanc, sur une annonce
publiée par l'Université Columbia pour le film «La Récolte du
désespoir» sur la grande famine de 1933 en Ukraine. (USA)

Would you like your Swiss summer

on the rocks,

or straight,

or with some water?

More precisely: Would you like to go hiking, or swimming, or cycling, surfing, or mountain climbing? How about riding, playing tennis or golf? Or would you prefer to go to a concert, tour the country or simply relax in a comfortable hotel? Our brochure "Switzerland and the Alpine World. Summer 1986" might help you to make up your mind. By the way, the prices are as accommodating as the people who will do everything to spoil you during your Swiss vacation.

swissair

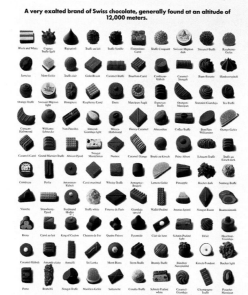

A very exalted brand of Swiss chocolate, generally found at an altitude of 12,000 meters.

We're not exaggerating: our *chocolatiers* make a hundred different chocolates for our First Class passengers – even if you think that's overdoing things and if there's unlikely to be anyone who'll try them all at one go. But there is one conclusion you can draw from this: an airline which takes so much trouble does a little bit more for all its guests than it needs to. At an altitude of 12,000 meters as well as on the ground. From inflight service to aircraft maintenance. Something which even those people who don't like chocolate won't regard as an exaggeration.

swissair

27

Why not spend your next vacation in a work of art?

Detail from the painting "New Snow in the Engadine" (private collection) by the Swiss painter Ferdinand Hodler (1853–1918).

It's nice that Ferdinand Hodler's work of art is also a work of art in reality. And in fact a very pleasant one to live in. Because over the years hospitality and diligence have made the winter Alps into a holiday paradise in which you get pampered like nobody's (not even the artist's) business. And you don't need to be an artist to find out about a large number of reasonably priced arrangements in this glittering white fairyland. Just ask Swissair or your travel agent for our brochure "Switzerland and the Alpine World. Winter 1985/86".

swissair

ART DIRECTOR:
P. Leuenberger
COPYWRITER:
J. Jost
AGENCY:
GGK Basel Werbeagentur
CLIENT:
Swissair
■263

ART DIRECTOR:
A. Burkard
PHOTOGRAPHER:
N. Monkewitz
COPYWRITER:
J. Jost
AGENCY:
GGK Basel Werbeagentur
CLIENT:
Swissair
■264

ART DIRECTOR:
A. Burkard
ARTIST:
Ferdinand Hodler
COPYWRITER:
J. Jost
AGENCY:
GGK Basel Werbeagentur
CLIENT:
Swissair
■265

■**263–265** Series of full-page magazine ads issued by *Swissair*: The variety of summer activities in Switzerland; the airline that "does a little bit more than it needs to" (100 different chocolates for First Class passengers); and "Switzerland and the Alpine World in Winter." (SWI)

■**266** Magazine ad for Wild Dunes, an island resort on the US East Coast where "the game (golf) is as it should be". (USA)

■**267** Double-spread ad for *British Airways* who claim they fly more people to more places than any other airline. (GBR)

■**263–265** «Möchen Sie Ihren Schweizer Sommer mit Eis, pur (gerade) oder mit etwas Wasser?» «Eine sehr gehobene Schokoladenmarke, meistens in einer Höhe von 12000 m anzutreffen.» «Warum verbringen Sie Ihre nächsten Ferien nicht in einem Kunstwerk?» Anzeigenserie für *Swissair*. (SWI)

■**266** «Das Spiel (Golf), wie es sein sollte.» Zeitschrifteninserat für Wild Dunes, eine Insel an der Ostküste der USA. (USA)

■**267** «Was immer Sie am liebsten mögen, wir fliegen Sie hin.» Doppelseitige Anzeige für *British Airways*. (GBR)

■**263–265** Série d'annonces de magazines double page de la *Swissair*. «Vous le voulez comment, votre été suisse, avec de la glace, tel quel, avec de l'eau?»; «une marque de chocolat suisse portée aux nues – en général à 12 000 m»; «pourquoi pas des vacances dans une œuvre d'art?» (SWI)

■**266** Annonce de magazine pour Wild Dunes, une île sur la côte est des E.-U. où «le jeu (le golf) est comme il se doit.» (USA)

■**267** Pour *British Airways* qui se fait fort de transporter plus de passagers en un nombre inégalé d'endroits. (GBR)

THE GAME AS IT SHOULD BE.

Golf began in just such a place. Where Atlantic winds sweep in over towering natural dunes. Where finishing holes are right on the ocean. Where water, marsh, and sand combine for some of the most breathtaking challenges the game can offer.

Come to our island and play two spectacular courses, one ranked 34th in the world, and another that soon will be. Enjoy the luxury and privacy of one of the East Coast's most exclusive island resort communities. 2½ miles of secluded beach. A Racquet Club that's in the nation's Top 50. A full service yacht harbor. Superb dining. On the island, or in Charleston, just minutes away. Stay in a lush private villa. No crowds. No traffic. No waiting. Only you and some of the best golf on this side of the Atlantic.

Wild Dunes

ART DIRECTOR:
Nancy Rovabaugh
DESIGNER:
Nancy Rovabaugh
PHOTOGRAPHER:
Paul Barton
AGENCY:
Pringle Dixon Pringle
CLIENT:
Wild Dunes
■266

PHOTOGRAPHER:
Onofrio Paccione
AGENCY:
Paccione Photography
CLIENT:
British Airways
■267

Whatever your cup of tea, we'll fly you to it.

Rose Hip Tea
Copenhagen, Denmark

Black Sea Tea
Istanbul, Turkey

Darjeeling Tea
New Delhi, India

Eyelashes of the Swan Tea
Singapore

Earl Grey
London, England

Green Tea
Osaka, Japan

Russian Caravan Tea
Moscow, Soviet Union

Tippy Tea
Dublin, Ireland

Tea Cider
Stuttgart, West Germany

Camomile Tea
Paris, France

Pearl Tea
Beijing, China

We fly to 148 cities in 71 countries on six continents. And while preferences in tea may change from destination to destination, the preference in airlines seems to be universal.

It's certain that travelers prefer British Airways, because we fly more people to more places than any other airline.

BRITISH AIRWAYS
The world's favourite airline.®

ART DIRECTOR:
Uli Weber

DESIGNER:
Uli Weber/Ursel Koch

ILLUSTRATOR:
Seymour Chwast

COPYWRITER:
Brigitte Fussnegger

AGENCY:
Leonhardt & Kern

CLIENT:
Hapag-Lloyd

■268

ART DIRECTOR:
Uli Weber

DESIGNER:
Uli Weber/Ursel Koch

ILLUSTRATOR:
Willi Rieser

COPYWRITER:
Brigitte Fussnegger

AGENCY:
Leonhardt & Kern

CLIENT:
Hapag-Lloyd

■269

Der Sonne auf den Fersen.

Europa hat rund *345 Sonnentage* im Jahr! Weil wir mit unserem Kreuzfahrtschiff Europa immer hinter der Sonne her sind. Wenn in unseren Breiten noch Minus auf den Straßen liegt, schippern wir mit der Europa in Richtung Südsee. Statt »Matschsehen Sie »much«.

Die allererste Sehenswürdigkeit ist *das Schiff* selbst. Auf den 13 Decks ist alles untergebracht und los, was eine Kreuzfahrt auf der Europa so unvergeßlich macht: *Riesige Foyers* zum Flanieren, *elegante Gesellschaftsräume* wie in einem Grand-Hotel, komfortable Kabinen, die eigentlich Appartements sind. Für Leseratten gibt es eine *Bibliothek,* wo man hochgeistige Kulturgeschichten oder tiefschürfende Kriminalstories leihen kann. Für Wasserratten haben wir *drei Schwimmbäder:* ein Meerwasserschwimmbad mit 28 Grad und Schiebedach, ein großes Freibad und ein Hallenbad mit Gegenstromanlage. Es gibt ein perfekt ausgestattetes Fitness-Center, wo Sie Ihren Body builden können.

An Bord ist sogar eine *Druckerei,* die jeden Morgen frische Menukarten, Bordprogramme und Weltnachrichten druckt. Und eine *Wäscherei,* die täglich 3,6 Tonnen Tisch- und Bettwäsche wäscht. Und eine *Bäckerei,* die paarmal am Tag sieben verschiedene Sorten Brötchen bäckt. Und ein *Weinkeller* mit 3450 Flaschen herrlicher Jahrgänge. Und ein eigenes Fernsehstudio. Und einiges mehr.

Während wir Sie zu den westindischen oder echt indischen Inseln bringen, können Sie bei uns alle Walzer linksrum *tanzen,* elf Gänge oder Diät *essen,* farbfernsehen oder in die Ferne *sehen,* mit Zwiefaltendorf via Satellit *telefonieren* oder Tontauben vom Himmel *holen,* auf unserem versteckten FKK-Plätzchen *sonnen* oder beim Shuffleboard *schummeln*... oder was halten rein gar nix tun.

Wollen Sie mit der Europa dorthin, wo die Welt wohltemperiert und dabei weltbewegend schön ist? Dann *kreuzen* Sie mal bei Ihrem Reisebüro auf. Oder *schreiben* Sie uns.
Hapag-Lloyd Kreuzfahrten, Postfach 10 79 47, D-2800 Bremen 1.

Wir bringen Sie mit Sicherheit in die Wildnis.

Der Mensch, das unbekannte Wesen, möchte im Urlaub einerseits viel Abenteuer, aber andererseits viel Sicherheit. Beides zusammen geht nicht und geht doch: Machen Sie mit uns eine Kreuzfahrt auf der Europa!

Wir zeigen Ihnen die verwegensten Flüsse, die verrücktesten Städte, die verschwiegensten Tempel, die verträumtesten Strände, die verwirrendsten Basars, die verlassensten Inseln und die verborgensten Fjorde.

Wir bringen Sie über den Äquator, über die Datumsgrenze bis hin zur Packeisgrenze. Wir schippern mit Ihnen den Amazonas lang bis hin zum weltberühmten Urwaldopernhaus, wo schon Caruso sang. Wir bringen Sie in die Wildnis von Alaska, wo Sie auf Braunbären und Blaubeeren, Totempfähle und Goldminen stoßen.

Alles wird herrlich aufregend sein, ohne daß Sie sich aufregen. Denn Sie brauchen sich um nichts zu kümmern. Wir organisieren das so perfekt und unmerklich, daß Sie jedes Abenteuer mit Sicherheit in Ruhe genießen werden.

Und das Schöne: Wenn Sie von einem Landausflug zurück an Bord der Europa kommen, erwartet Sie ein Drink oder eine Massage oder ein Swimmingpool oder ein Liegestuhl oder ein Tanztee oder ein elfgängiges Menu oder ein Klavierkonzert – oder Ihre riesige, komfortable, klimatisierte, mucksmäuschenstille Kabine.

Ein Abenteuerurlaub auf der Europa dauert zwischen 7 Tagen und 7 Wochen und kostet zwischen DM 2780,– und DM 54060,–. Wenn Sie der Kapitän auf eine unserer 28 Reisen mitnehmen soll, dann kreuzen Sie einfach mal bei Ihrem Reisebüro auf. Oder schreiben Sie uns: Hapag-Lloyd Kreuzfahrten, Postfach 10 79 47, D-2800 Bremen 1.

Sind Sie abenteuerlustig, Madame?

Wenn man sich die schönsten Ansichtskarten der Welt an Ort und Stelle persönlich abholen will, dann tut man das mit Sicherheit mit einem noblen Kreuzfahrtenschiff, wie's beispielsweise die Europa ist. Das gilt auch, wenn man als Frau alleine reist. Denn nun werden Sie bestens betreut und aufmerksam verwöhnt.

Bevor wir Ihnen jedoch die Welt zeigen, zeigen wir Ihnen unser Traum-Schiff, das auch ein wahres Raum-Schiff ist: mit riesigen Foyers, eleganten Gesellschaftsräumen, Restaurant, Bars, Theater, Boutique, Juwelier, Frisiersalon, Wäscherei, Konditorei, Fernsehstudio etc. Nicht zu vergessen die 21 qm großen komfortablen Kabinen.

Gleich am Willkommenstag lernen Sie die Mit-Passagiere und die Besatzung kennen, »Ihren« Tischsteward, »Ihren« Getränkesteward, »Ihren« Kabinensteward...oder »Ihre« stewardeß.

Beim Blick in unsere täglich wechselnden Menukarten denken Sie bestimmt an Ihre Kreuzfahrtlinie. Aber dafür bzw. dagegen gibt's entweder unser ausgetüfteltes Diät-Programm oder viel Sport an Bord: z. B. drei Swimmingpools oder das Fitness-Center oder Shuffleboard oder Tischtennis oder Frühgymnastik oder Jogging oder ein Boogie-Woogie-Kurs oder ganz wie sie wünschen. Wenn Sie lieber abnehmen, ohne sich groß zu bewegen, kommen Sie einfach in die Sauna oder unter die Hände unserer Massagemeister.

Wenn es Nacht wird, holen wir für Sie die Sterne vom Himmel: Stars von Film, Funk, Fernsehen und von der Bühne zeigen ihre Künste. Und wenn Sie dann immer noch munter sind, können Sie im Nachtclub »Kajüte« cheek to cheek tanzen.

Während Sie all dies tun (oder lassen), bringt Sie die Europa von Rio nach Shanghai, über Java nach Bombay...

Haben Sie Lust mitzukommen, Madame? Monsieur? Dann gehen Sie zu Ihrem Reisebüro vorbei. Oder schreiben Sie uns kurz: Hapag-Lloyd Kreuzfahrten, Postfach 10 79 47, D-2800 Bremen 1.

Land-Ausflug in Sicht.

Das kann doch einen Seemann schön erschüttern, wenn ein Zipfelchen Land in Sicht ist. Das war früher so, das ist heut noch so. Darum freut man sich auf einer See-Fahrt so, wenn noch so. auf einen Land-Ausflug. Und umgekehrt.

Wenn Sie mit uns auf Reisen gehen, können Sie beides voll genießen. Denn die Europa kreuzt nicht nur auf allen Weltmeeren auf, sondern macht auch an den interessantesten Plätzen halt: Wir zeigen Ihnen z.B. Sana'a, die geheimnisvolle Hauptstadt des Jemen. Oder die in rosa Stein gehauenen Tempel von Petra. Oder die Indianersiedlungen in Alaska. Oder den Panama-Kanal. Oder die Elephanta-Insel bei Bombay. Oder den Amazonas. Oder das Haus von Edvard Grieg bei Bergen. Oder die St. Patricks Kathedrale von Dublin. Oder den Sultanspalast von Casablanca. Oder die Katakomben von Syrakus. Oder die Dschunken von Hongkong. Oder bei Montego Bay ein dreistöckiges Haus mit 365 Fenstern. Oder Disneyland. Oder die Packeisgrenze. Oder die Blaue Moschee von Istanbul. Oder den Papageien-Dschungel von Miami. Oder die Geysire von Island. Oder ein Opernhaus im Urwald. Oder den Schlangentempel von Penang. Oder zwei Tage Peking. Oder Tulum, wo die Mayas lebten. Oder die Alaska-Pipeline. Oder Suakin, die verlassene Stadt am Roten Meer. Oder die Affenfelsen von Gibraltar. Oder die Golden-Gate-Bridge von San Francisco. Oder eine Jade-Fabrik in Shanghai. Oder das Theater von Ephesus. Oder die Eremitage in Leningrad. Oder die Große Mauer in China. Oder eine Taverne in der Altstadt von Lissabon. Oder das Katharinenkloster von Sinai. Oder Singapore bei Nacht. Oder die Inseln in der Karibik. Oder Carcross, wo einst die Goldgräber schürften. Oder die Pyramiden am Nil. Oder ein Tempeltanz auf Java. Oder den Markusplatz von Venedig. Oder ganz was anderes.

Alle unsere Landausflüge sind schon lange im voraus organisiert; Sie brauchen sich also nur darauf zu freuen.

Die Seh- und Seetage haben wir so aufgeteilt, daß Sie einerseits bei interessanten Ausflügen mitmachen können, aber andererseits ruhige, erholsame Tage an Bord verbringen, um nur die Wolken, die wunderbaren Wolken anzusehen.

Wenn Sie jetzt die Welt kennenlernen und dabei nur einmal den Koffer packen wollen, dann kreuzen Sie mal bei Ihrem Reisebüro auf. Oder schreiben Sie uns.
Hapag-Lloyd Kreuzfahrten, Postfach 10 79 47, D-2800 Bremen 1.

ART DIRECTOR:
Uli Weber

DESIGNER:
Uli Weber/Ursel Koch

ILLUSTRATOR:
Marlis Weber-Raudenbusch

COPYWRITER:
Brigitte Fussnegger

AGENCY:
Leonhardt & Kern

CLIENT:
Hapag-Lloyd

■270

ART DIRECTOR:
Uli Weber

DESIGNER:
Uli Weber/Ursel Koch

ILLUSTRATOR:
Heseler & Heseler

COPYWRITER:
Brigitte Fussnegger

AGENCY:
Leonhardt & Kern

CLIENT:
Hapag-Lloyd

■271

Glückliches Europa.

Vor vier Jahren ging die neue Europa von Hapag-Lloyd

Die Reederei hat in 130 Jahren 1300 Schiffe auf die 7 Weltmeere geschickt.

auf Jungfernfahrt, und seither

waren rund fünfzigtausend Passagiere mit auf Reisen, die sich einig sind, daß

Der Kapitän nimmt jedesmal 600 Gäste mit auf die Reise.

dieses Schiff ein Traum-Schiff und ein Raum-Schiff und

33 819 BRT, 29 000 PS, 13 Decks, 200 m lang, 21 Knoten schnell.

Auch die Kabinen sind riesig: 21 qm, komfortabel ausgestattet. 85% haben große Fenster.

ein Sport-Schiff und ein Spiel-Schiff und ein Lern-Schiff und

3 Swimmingpools, Fitness-Center, Tischtennis, Gymnastik, Tontauben-schießen, Jogging.

Bingo, Deckschach, Shuffleboard, Skat, Bridge, Klavier.

Malen, Boogie-Woogie ohne Überschlag, Kultur-vorträge, fremde Länder, ferne Inseln.

Abenteuer-Schiff und ein Freundschafts-Schiff und ein

Wir bringen Sie mit Sicherheit in die Wildnis.

Ob Mann oder Frau, ob Großfamilie oder solo, ob jung oder alt ... alle funken auf derselben Wellenlänge.

Sonnen-Schiff und ein Unterhaltungs-Schiff und ein Erholungs-Schiff ist, das überall

Die Europa hat rund 345 Sonnentage im Jahr, weil wir stets der Sonne auf den Fersen sind.

Jeden Abend holen wir für Sie die Sterne vom Himmel: d.h. Stars von Film, Funk, Fernsehen werden Sie unterhalten.

Wir haben über 600 Liegestühle, damit Sie sich vom Sporteln, Essen, Trinken etc. ausruhen können.

dort aufkreuzt, wo die Welt am allerschönsten aussieht, weshalb

Wir bringen Sie über die Datumsgrenze bis zur Packeisgrenze ... und von Rio nach Shanghai, über Java nach Bombay.

aus obigen Gründen viele Europa-Passagiere immer wieder und immer

wieder kommen. Wenn Sie auch ein glücklicher Europäer

Viele machen die Europa quasi zu ihrem Zweitwohnsitz, wie das Ehepaar, das in dreieinhalb Jahren ganze 365 Tage an Bord war.

werden wollen, dann fragen Sie bei Ihrem Reisebüro nach den

Dort führt man 21 Europa-Reisen zwischen 7 Tagen und 7 Wochen.

entsprechenden grenzüberschreitenden Papieren. Oder schreiben Sie uns.

Hapag-Lloyd Kreuzfahrten, Postfach 10 79 47, D-2800 Bremen 1.

ms **Europa**   Hapag-Lloyd Kreuzfahrten

ART DIRECTOR:
ULI WEBER

DESIGNER:
ULI WEBER/URSEL KOCH

ILLUSTRATOR:
SEYMOUR CHWAST

COPYWRITER:
BRIGITTE FUSSNEGGER

AGENCY:
LEONHARDT & KERN

CLIENT:
HAPAG-LLOYD

■272

■**268–272** Double-spread advertisements placed in various issues of FAZ *magazine* to promote *Hapag-Lloyd* cruises in *ms Europa*. "The sun hard on the heels"; "We take you safely into the jungle"; "Do you long for adventure, Madame?"; "Land excursion in sight»; "Happy Europe". (GER)

■**268–272** In verschiedenen Ausgaben des *F.A.Z.-Magazins* erschienene Anzeigen für *Hapag-Lloyd*-Kreuzfahrten mit der *MS Europa*. Das Schwergewicht der Werbebotschaft liegt in der Kombination Komfort/Abenteuer, ermöglicht durch die Ausstattung des Schiffes und Organisation der Landausflüge. (GER)

■**268–272** Annonces double page dans divers numéros du *FAZ Magazine* pour les croisières du paquebot *Europa* de la *Hapag-Lloyd*: «sur les talons du soleil»; «avec nous, vous serez en sécurité dans la jungle»; «un peu d'aventure, Madame?»; «excursion à terre en vue»; «Bienheureuse Europe.» (GER)

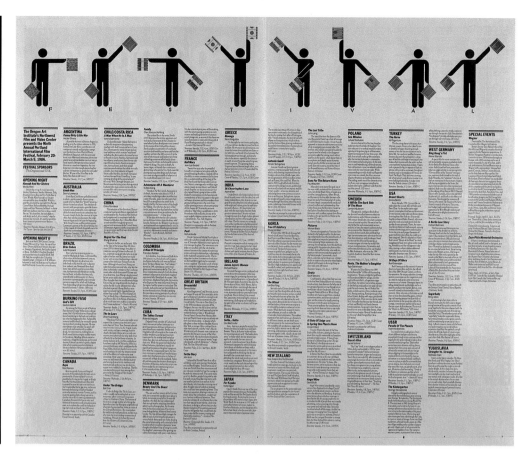

Sometimes the most enlightening place you can be is in the dark.

ART DIRECTOR:
Warren Eakins

DESIGNER:
Warren Eakins

COPYWRITER:
Pamela Sullivan

AGENCY:
Borders, Perrin & Norrander, Inc.

CLIENT:
Northwest Film & Video Center

■ 273, 274

■ **273, 274** Introductory page and spread of a newspaper insert issued by the Oregon Art Institute's Northwest Film and Video Center to mark the occasion of the 9th annual Portland International Film Festival. (USA)

■ **275, 276** Newspaper ads for *Swissair.* "Can a country 13 000 km from Switzerland still be reached in extreme comfort?" and "Holiday pleasure begins right at the money-exchange desk," (reductions in tarifs for senior citizens). (SWI)

■ **273, 274** Einleitende Seite und Doppelseite aus einer Zeitungsbeilage als Anzeige eines internationalen Film-Festivals in Portland: «Manchmal ist nichts so «erleuchtend» wie der Platz im Dunkeln.» (USA)

■ **275, 276** Zeitungsanzeigen für die Swissair. Hier geht es um die Ankündigung einer neuen Polarroute nach Tokio und um Spezialtarife für Senioren: «Manchmal merkt man schon beim Geldwechseln, wie schön Ferien mit der *Swissair* sind.» (SWI)

■ **273, 274** Page initiale et double page d'un encart de presse de l'Oregon Art Institute's Northwest Film and Video Center pour le 9e Festival du cinéma à Portland: «parfois, l'endroit le plus éclairant qui soit peut être une salle sombre.» (USA)

■ **275, 276** Annonces pour la *Swissair.* «Est-ce qu'on peut se rendre très confortablement dans un pays situé à 13 000 km de la Suisse?»; et le slogan sur le plaisir qui commence dès le guichet de change, pour les passagers du 3e âge. (SWI)

ART DIRECTOR:
A. Burkard
COPYWRITER:
J. Jost
AGENCY:
GGK Basel Werbeagentur
CLIENT:
Swissair
■275

ART DIRECTOR:
L. Fischer
COPYWRITER:
W. Ropele
AGENCY:
GGK Basel Werbeagentur
CLIENT:
Swissair
■276

Kann ein Land rund 13 000 km von der Schweiz entfernt und trotzdem besonders bequem erreichbar sein?

JA**PAN**

Zu Recht steht die Antwort in so grossen Lettern da. Denn unsere neue Polarroute nach Tokio (mit Zwischenlandung in Anchorage) bringt Ihnen im Vergleich zu unserer Südroute einen erfreulichen Zeitgewinn. Was natürlich nicht heisst, dass die Zeit in unseren modernen Langstreckenflugzeugen verlorene Zeit sein muss. Das werden Sie zum Beispiel merken, wenn Sie in der ruhigen Atmosphäre unserer Business Class viel konzentrierter arbeiten können als im Büro. Oder wenn Sie viel besser essen als in manchem Restaurant. Dass wir nicht übertreiben, lässt sich übrigens nicht nur auf unserer neuen Polarroute nachprüfen, sondern zum Beispiel auch auf einem Flug nach unserer neuen Destination Seoul, der Olympia-Stadt im Sommer 1988. Oder auf dem Weg nach Beijing, das wir jetzt zweimal pro Woche anfliegen.   swissair✈

Die Swissair oder Ihr IATA-Reisebüro gibt Ihnen gerne alle weiteren Auskünfte.

Pour certains, le plaisir des vacances commence déjà au guichet de change.

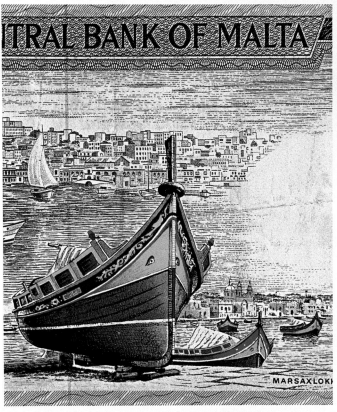

C'est notamment le cas des dames qui ont atteint 62 ans et des messieurs de 65 ans et plus. En accordant une forte réduction de tarif aux seniors, Swissair leur permet d'économiser autant de pesetas, de drachmes, de lires, de livres, de dirhams, d'escudos et de dinars qui seront fort appréciés sous le soleil méditerranéen. En Espagne, en Grèce, en Italie, à Malte, au Maroc, au Portugal ou en Yougoslavie. A moins qu'ils ne préfèrent économiser des francs belges, des forints hongrois, des florins hollandais, des zlotys polonais ou des couronnes tchécoslovaques ou encore une poignée de dollars grâce au tarif Seniors pour Anchorage, Boston, Chicago ou New York.   swissair✈

Swissair ou votre agence de voyages IATA vous dira volontiers combien on peut économiser tout en s'offrant un changement d'air bénéfique.

ART DIRECTOR:
Muneaki Andoh

DESIGNER:
Muneaki Andoh/
Mitsuru Inagaki

ILLUSTRATOR:
Takeo Ohno/
Muneaki Andoh

COPYWRITER:
Shioko Kishimoto/
Yukari Hasegawa

AGENCY:
Dentsu Inc.

CLIENT:
Kirin Brewery Co., Ltd.
■ **277,278**

■ **277, 278** Advertisements for *Kirin* beer. Left, a caricature of Norianga, philosopher/historian who loved the sound of windbells. The message runs, "ring the bell and drink *Kirin* beer." Right, Jingoro, a dragon sculptor who today would drink *Kirin* beer while producing his masterwork. (JPN)

■ **279–283** Advertisements for the Rokin bank in the town of Aichi. The top three concern loans for education and studying; the bottom two refer to a couple's deposit account. (JPN)

■ **277, 278** Für *Kirin*-Bier. Links eine Karikatur von Norianga, Arzt/Philosoph/Historiker, der den Ton von Glocken im Wind liebte. Rechts Jingoro, ein Drachenschnitzer. Das Schönste für sie wäre heute, gemäss Anzeigen, der Ton der Glocken bzw. die Anfertigung eines Meisterwerks und *Kirin*-Bier. (JPN)

■ **279–283** Für die Rokin-Bank in Aichi. In der oberen Reihe geht es um Darlehen für Grundausbildung und Studium, die unteren Anzeigen betreffen die Vorteile eines Sparkontos. (JPN)

■ **277,278** Annonces pour la bière *Kirin*. A gauche, caricature du philosophe et historien Norianga qui aimait le son des clochettes au vent: «faites retentir la clochette en buvant votre bière *Kirin*.» A droite, le sculpteur de dragons Jingoro qui opterait joyeusement pour la bière *Kirin*. (JPN)

■ **279–283** Annonces pour la banque Rokin à Aichi. La série du haut concerne les prêts pour les études. Les deux annonces du bas expliquent les avantages du carnet d'épargne «couples». (JPN)

そんなもん子供が心配しないで勉強しなさ〜い！

学資が心配で落ち付かない。工学部だから？それに東京の生活費？

●限度額10万円〜300万円●期間10年以内（うち最長4年間元金据置可）■会員以外の方でもどなたでもご利用できます。

こんなに低利　年**7.60**%

と、言うための**教育ローン**

合格本命はこれからだけど

でも入学金だけはブッ両方とも受かったらどうしよう。

合**格**だ。

よけいなこと考えないで勉強しなさい！

●限度額10万円〜300万円●期間10年以内（うち最長4年間元金据置可）

こんなに低利　年**7.60**%

どなたでもご利用できます。

と、言うための**教育ローン**

合格したか！でかした。

うれしい。でも、困った。

●限度額10万円〜300万円●期間10年以内（うち最長4年間元金据置可）

こんなに低利　年**7.60**%

どなたでもご利用できます。

と、おっしゃるご両親のために

ろうきん　教育ローン

最近、やたらと金融問題にめざめた女房曰く……

いざというとき借りられるほうがいい。

だから、融資も魅力な

ろうきん　㊲　期日指定定期

ワイド定期　●お利息は1年ごとの複利計算●預入期間は最長3年●最高300万円のワクを活用●残高を10倍に活かすローンの利用を

私、テニスクラブの会員権を……エアコンをもう一台。チビちゃんの教育資金も。

ボーナス俺の分はどうなる。

そこで、融資も魅力な

ろうきん　㊲　期日指定定期

ワイド定期　●お利息は1年ごとの複利計算●預入期間は最長3年●最高300万円のワクを活用●残高を10倍に活かすローンの利用を

ART DIRECTOR:
Tsutomu So/Hiroyasu Itoh
DESIGNER:
Tsutomu So
ILLUSTRATOR:
Tsutomu So
AGENCY:
Koh Koku-Sha Co. Ltd.
CLIENT:
Roh-doh Bank
■279–283

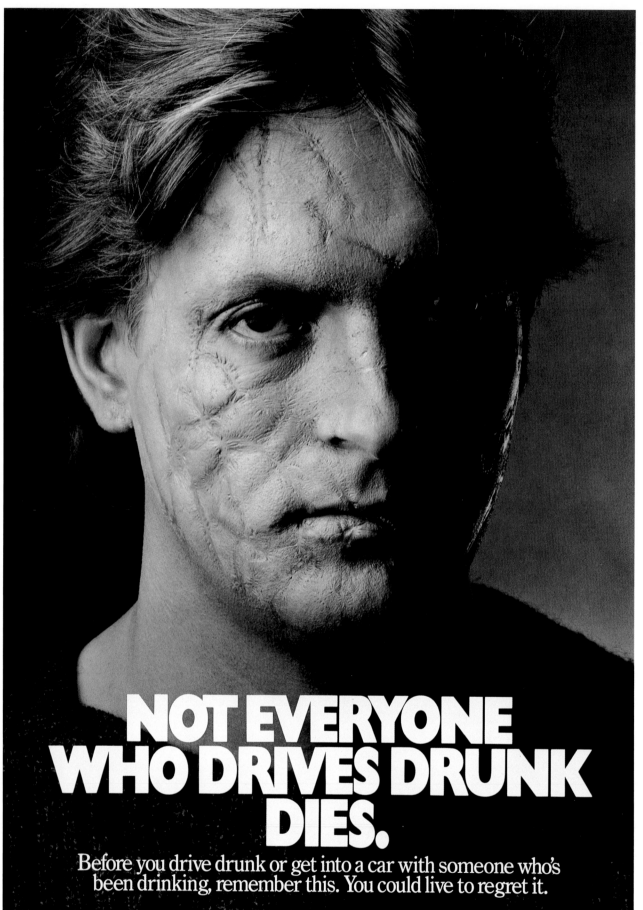

NOT EVERYONE WHO DRIVES DRUNK DIES.

Before you drive drunk or get into a car with someone who's been drinking, remember this. You could live to regret it.

ART DIRECTOR:
Sal DeVito
DESIGNER:
Sal DeVito
PHOTOGRAPHER:
Cailor/Resnick
AGENCY:
Chiat/Day
CLIENT:
Reader's Digest
■284

Thanks for putting us on top.

Season's Greetings to you and our New York, New Jersey and Connecticut Volkswagen dealers.
You've made Volkswagen the best-selling European import in the tri-state area.
World-Wide Volkswagen Corp.

ART DIRECTOR:
Bob Dion

DESIGNER:
Bob Dion

AGENCY:
Chiat/Day

CLIENT:
Drexel Burnham Lambert

■285

ART DIRECTOR:
Shony Rivnay

DESIGNER:
Shony Rivnay

COPYWRITER:
Lisa Mayer

AGENCY:
DDB Needham Worldwide

CLIENT:
World-Wide Volkswagen

■286

■**284** Black-and-white advertisement in the *Reader's Digest* in an effort to remind readers of the dangers of drinking and driving. (USA)

■**285** Full-page black-and-white ad for Drexel Burnham Lambert Incorporated (investment brokerage). (USA)

■**286** Full-page ad carrying seasonal greetings from the World-Wide Volkswagen Corporation and which appeared in the *New York Times* on December 23. (USA)

■**284** «Nicht jeder, der trinkt, stirbt.» In *Reader's Digest* veröffentlichte Schwarzweiss-Anzeige als Warnung vor den Folgen von Trunkenheit am Steuer, für Fahrer und Mitfahrer. (USA)

■**285** «Ich dachte, ich sei zu klein für *Drexel Burnham*.» Ganzseitiges Inserat in Schwarzweiss für Börsenmakler. (USA)

■**286** «Vielen Dank, dass Sie uns an die Spitze gebracht haben.» Inserat der Worldwide Volkswagen Corporation mit Weihnachtsglückwünschen, erschienen am 23. Dezember. (USA)

■**284** Annonce noir et blanc publiée dans le *Reader's Digest*. Campagne contre l'alcool au volant: «tous ceux qui conduisent en état d'ivresse ne meurent pas.» (USA)

■**285** Annonce pleine page, noir et blanc, pour les courtiers en investissements Drexel Burnham Lambert Inc. (USA)

■**286** «Merci de nous avoir placés en tête»: annonce de vœux pleine page de la Worldwide Volkswagen Corporation dans le *New York Times* du 23 décembre. (USA)

ART DIRECTOR:
Tom Kelly
DESIGNER:
Tom Kelly
ILLUSTRATOR:
George Cheney
COPYWRITER:
Greg Eiden
AGENCY:
Borders Perrin & Norrander
CLIENT:
Lilly/Miller
■ **287**

ART DIRECTOR:
Ann Lemon
PHOTOGRAPHER:
Jimmy Williams
AGENCY:
Jim Johnston Advertising
CLIENT:
The Wall Street Journal
■ **288**

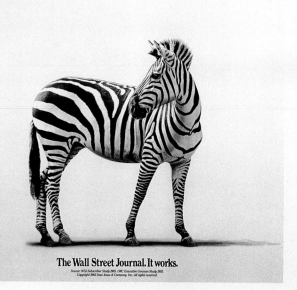

We'd like to poke holes in some gas lines.

The gas company has been handing out some real lines about heat pumps lately. The truth is, most of their lines are already full of holes—we're just pointing them out. It's what they're *not* telling you (or *the way* they're telling you) that can hurt you. The Professional Heat Pump Society of Greater Indianapolis would like you to see through the holes.

Comfort. "Gas sends out a much warmer heat—so most people find it a lot more comfortable." That's true if you spend all your time sitting on a register, but you don't. The reality is a room warmed to 70° is a room at 70° regardless of the heating system. And a constant flow of lower temperature air from a heat pump provides more even heat than high temperature air which creates hot spots (and leaves other cold spots).

Single heating system. "Because unlike a heat pump, a natural gas furnace does a full time heating job, down to the coldest temperature." Very true. A heat pump system does a full time heating job when you need it—the rest of the year it can cool your house less expensively than central air. A gas furnace will *never* cool your

home. If you have a gas furnace, keep it. Add a heat pump or replace your air conditioner with one. The price difference between a complete heat pump system and an air conditioning unit is probably less than you'd expect. And you'll have a choice of heating source. But you'll probably want to use the heat pump year-round for its efficient, even, and clean environment control.

Cost. "Best of all, a high-efficiency gas furnace costs much less to operate." The hole in this line is that nothing is more efficient with energy than a heat pump. Nothing.

The purchase price of a high efficiency gas furnace and central air conditioning is much higher than the cost of a heat pump for the same results. In final analysis, a heat pump is the least expensive way to heat *and cool* your home. The payback period to replace your existing gas furnace with a high efficiency gas furnace can run into decades. But a heat pump saves you money year-round, and the payback is surprisingly short.

Our installation is the key. Proper installation of a heat pump is crucial. This is why the Professional Heat Pump Society of

Greater Indianapolis was created. To be a member of the society, contractors must follow a strict code of ethics, including the assurance of a satisfactory installation. All members have extensive training programs for their technicians. They evaluate the comfort requirements of a home then engineer and design the right system. The Society provides quality assurance for customers.

Talk to the experts. Call us, and you will be put in contact with one of our approved contractors. They will assure you of an excellent system. Be sure to give your contractor the coupon for a $100 rebate from the Professional Heat Pump Society. 298-8842.

> Redeem this $100 coupon on the installation of a heat pump in your home by Sept. 1, 1986. Contact the:
> **PROFESSIONAL HEAT PUMP SOCIETY OF INDIANAPOLIS,**
>
> NAME
>
> ADDRESS

Aaron York's Quality Air Conditioning & Heating • Broad Ripple Heating & Air Conditioning, Inc. • Bryant-Allen, Inc. • Godby Brothers Heating & Air Conditioning • Koehring & Sons, Inc. • Love Heating & Air Conditioning, Inc. • Modern Heating & Cooling, Inc. • Mr. Build/Phelps Heating & Air Conditioning, Inc. • Smith & Son, Inc. Heating & Air Conditioning • Williams Comfort Air, Inc.

A summer music festival that really swings.

See Northcoast in concert Saturday, May 24 at 4 p.m. This special exhibit brought to you with the help of Cities 97 FM.

Jazz at The Minnesota Zoo.

ART DIRECTOR:
Young & Laramore

DESIGNER:
Young & Laramore

COPYWRITER:
David Jemerson Young/ John Young

AGENCY:
Young & Laramore

CLIENT:
Heat Pump Society of Indianapolis

■ 289

ART DIRECTOR:
Bob Barrie

DESIGNER:
Bob Barrie

ILLUSTRATOR:
Bob Bluett

COPYWRITER:
Phil Hanft

AGENCY:
Fallon McElligott

CLIENT:
Minnesota Zoo

■ 290

WE'LL SHOOT YOUR BOSS FOR FREE!

Yes, it's true! We'll shoot a top quality black and white, 8x10 executive portrait of your boss (or you) absolutely free if you'll give *us* a shot at your next advertising, industrial or publication photo assignment.

J. Gerard Smith Photography offers you the finest in studio and location photography *and* an extensive stock photo library. We'll treat you and your job with the utmost care and consideration. Each assignment will receive special, personal attention from the owner/photographer, J. Gerard Smith.

We're new in this area and we're hungry. So take advantage of our *free* offer and fill out the coupon or call anytime for an appointment to meet us and view our studio.

> I'm interested in your offer of a FREE black and white, 8x10 executive portrait with any photo assignment received by October 31, 1986. I understand that this coupon must be mailed by September 30, 1986 to validate this offer.
>
> NAME/TITLE
>
> COMPANY
>
> ADDRESS
>
> TOWN   ZIP CODE
>
> PHONE

SM**⊙**TH
J. GERARD SMITH PHOTOGRAPHY
300 WOODBURY ROAD, WOODBURY, NEW YORK 11797
516/692-6640

ART DIRECTOR:
Anthony Taibi

DESIGNER:
Constance Kovar

COPYWRITER:
Constance Kovar/ Anthony Taibi

AGENCY:
Constance Kovar & Co.

CLIENT:
J. Gerard Smith Photography

■ 291

ART DIRECTOR:
Houman Pirdavari
AGENCY:
Fallon McElligott
CLIENT:
Bloomingdale's
■ 293–295

Ed Koch, 1940

When I was 17, I wanted to look like a preppy, even though I wasn't attending a preppy school. And, I also had hair when I was 17. Today, I still like to dress informally, although my hairline has changed.

Ed Koch

For one hundred years, Bloomingdale's sportswear has been pulled over many a changing hairline.

bloomingdale's
It wouldn't be the same without you.

ART DIRECTOR:
John Green
DESIGNER:
John Green
PHOTOGRAPHER:
Lee Crum
AGENCY:
Bauerlein, Inc.
CLIENT:
New Orleans Dental Society
■ 296, 297

Don't forget to brush

A public service of the New Orleans Dental Society

Don't forget to brush

A public service of the New Orleans Dental Society

Zubin Mehta, 1940

1940 — The world's turmoil is far from this vacation in Bangalore, India — So are the dreams that later became the Philharmonics of New York & Israel! 1986 — Bangalore seems so far away!

For one hundred years, Bloomingdale's has witnessed the dreams of extraordinary people in an extraordinary city. And they have all been music to our ears.

bloomingdale's
It wouldn't be the same without you.

Isaac Stern, 1927

Mom — do you really think that if I practice very hard I can really get to Carnegie Hall?

For one hundred years, Bloomingdale's has seen the shadows of great men lengthen along with their pants.

bloomingdale's
It wouldn't be the same without you.

■ **293–295** Series of ads for *Bloomingdale's* featuring famous personalities in their youth and a signed "handwritten" quotation from each. Left to right – Ed Koch in 1940, Zubin Mehta in 1940, and Isaac Stern in 1927. (USA)

■ **296, 297** Newspaper advertisements in a public service campaign for the New Orleans Dental Society. (USA)

■ **293–295** Zeitungsinserate für *Bloomingdale's* mit handschriftlichen Jugenderinnerungen und -Photos berühmter Persönlichkeiten: der New Yorker Bürgermeister Ed Koch, der Dirigent Zubin Mehta und der Violinist Isaac Stern. (USA)

■ **296, 297** «Zähneputzen nicht vergessen.» Zwei Zeitungsanzeigen einer zahnärztlichen Gesellschaft. (USA)

■ **293–295** Série d'annonces pour *Bloomingdale's*, avec des photos de jeunesse et des textes manuscrits de personnalités en vue. De gauche à droite: Ed Koch en 1940, Zubin Mehta en 1940, Isaac Stern en 1927. (USA)

■ **296, 297** Annonces de journaux tirée d'une campagne d'hygiène buccale: «n'oubliez pas de vous les brosser.» (USA)

ART DIRECTOR:
Bernie Hogya/
Maureen O'Brien
COPYWRITER:
Ronald Wachino
AGENCY:
USAdvertising
CLIENT:
New Jersey Division of
Vocational Rehabilitation
■ **298, 299**

ART DIRECTOR:
Bernie Hogya/Maureen O'Brien
COPYWRITER:
Leland Rosemond
AGENCY:
USAdvertising
CLIENT:
New Jersey Division of
Vocational Rehabilitation
■ **300**

■ **298–300** Series of newspaper ads for the New Jersey Division of Vocational Rehabilitation Services. Each features a handicap put to good use: Porky Pig's stutter, Edison's partial deafness since youth, Beethoven's total deafness. (USA)

■ **301, 302** Double-spread advertisements to promote the financing services to car dealers offered by Marine Midland Automotive Financial. (USA)

■ **298–300** Für einen Arbeitsvermittlungsdienst für Behinderte. Texte und Illustrationen beziehen sich auf Porky Pig, den Warner Bros. trotz Stotterns unter Vertrag nahm, den in seiner Jugend schwerhörigen Edison und den tauben Beethoven. (USA)

■ **301, 302** «Die aufregendste Neuheit an diesem Auto ist das Darlehen.» «Wir sind in diesem Geschäft tätig, seit es hässlich zu werden begann.» Für eine Autofinanzierungsgesellschaft. (USA)

■ **298–300** Série d'annonces de journaux: aucun handicap n'a jamais empêché le succès: Warner Bros. offrant sa chance au bègue Porky Pig, Edison se débrouillant malgré sa surdité partielle, Beethoven malgré sa surdité totale. (USA)

■ **301, 302** Annonces pour le financement d'automobiles: «l'option la plus novatrice sur cette voiture, c'est le prêt»; «nous sommes dans la branche depuis que ça va mal.» (USA)

The most innovative option on this car is the loan.

Today's cars do just about everything but drive themselves.

Unfortunately, high technology leads to high prices. Which makes it harder for cars to sell themselves.

At Marine Midland Automotive Financial, we believe you have to be just as creative in selling today's cars as the factories were in designing them.

So while engineers work to develop the latest in technology, we work to develop the latest in financing.

You see, automotive financing is all we do. So we can see needs and design programs other financial sources never dream of.

Like our Reduced Auto Payment Plan. A unique method for making monthly payments more affordable.

Plus other creative packages that let a dealer offer as many options when financing a car as when ordering one.

Call 800-448-3400, ext. 334, for the name and number of your local representative.

We'd be glad to show you how a little innovation can help cars move faster.

AUTOMOTIVE FINANCIAL
A MARINE MIDLAND COMPANY

We've been in this business since it started getting ugly.

Some 40 years ago in the car business, something happened.

It started getting fiercely competitive. With imports. And comparative advertising. Something else happened, too. A new financial source from Marine Midland Bank started helping dealers play the new game.

Today, the competition is uglier than ever. Which makes Automotive Financial look better than ever.

We're now a national company. With the experience to understand the kinds of problems car dealers face.

Unlike many financial sources, the automotive business is our only business. So you get quick response. Plus some of the industry's most innovative financing options.

And we can finance virtually any need a dealership has. Covering everything from sales, to leasing, to construction.

Call 800-448-3400, ext. 329, for the name and number of your local representative.

We'd be glad to discuss any need you might have.

We know your business. Because it's our business. And we can help you get the bugs out.

AUTOMOTIVE FINANCIAL
A MARINE MIDLAND COMPANY

ART DIRECTOR:
A. Burkhard

PHOTOGRAPHER:
William K. Everson

COPYWRITER:
J. Jost

AGENCY:
GGK Basel Werbeagentur

CLIENT:
Publicitas Basel

■303

■303–307 Series of spreads for the *Basler Zeitung* (newspaper) targeted at potential "fastidious" advertisers in the agglomeration. Each bears witty captions relating to the generosity of, inclination towards luxury and the demand for "the best of the best" by the Basle readers. (SWI)

■303–307 Aus einer Serie doppelseitiger Anzeigen der *Basler Zeitung*, die sich auf witzige Art auf typische Basler Eigenschaften beziehen: die Grosszügigkeit (in bezug auf das gepflegte Äussere), die Sicherheit, das Understatement, den Anspruch auf das Beste vom Besten, den Wohlstand. (SWI)

■303–307 Série de double pages pour les annonceurs potentiels du journal *Basler Zeitung*. Les légendes amusantes renvoient à des qualités typiquement bâloises: la générosité, le goût du luxe et le désir de s'offrir ce que la vie offre de meilleur - une publicité qui doit flatter les patriotes locaux. (SWI)

ART DIRECTOR:
A. BURKHARD

PHOTOGRAPHER:
WILLIAM K. EVERSON

COPYWRITER:
J. JOST

AGENCY:
GGK BASEL WERBEAGENTUR

CLIENT:
PUBLICITAS BASEL

■ 304

ART DIRECTOR:
A. BURKHARD

PHOTOGRAPHER:
BRASSAI

COPYWRITER:
W. ROPELE

AGENCY:
GGK BASEL WERBEAGENTUR

CLIENT:
PUBLICITAS BASEL

■ 305

ART DIRECTOR:
A. BURKHARD

PHOTOGRAPHER:
THOMAS HÖPKER

COPYWRITER:
W. ROPELE

AGENCY:
GGK BASEL WERBEAGENTUR

CLIENT:
PUBLICITAS BASEL

■ 306

ART DIRECTOR:
A. BURKHARD

PHOTOGRAPHER:
FRANZ HUBMANN

COPYWRITER:
W. ROPELE

AGENCY:
GGK BASEL WERBEAGENTUR

CLIENT:
PUBLICITAS BASEL

■ 307

ART DIRECTOR:
Dean Hanson

DESIGNER:
Dean Hanson

PHOTOGRAPHER:
Majorie Nugent

COPYWRITER:
Jarl Olsen

AGENCY:
Fallon McElligott

CLIENT:
First Tennessee

■308

See The Great Oils At The Memphis Brooks Museum.◆

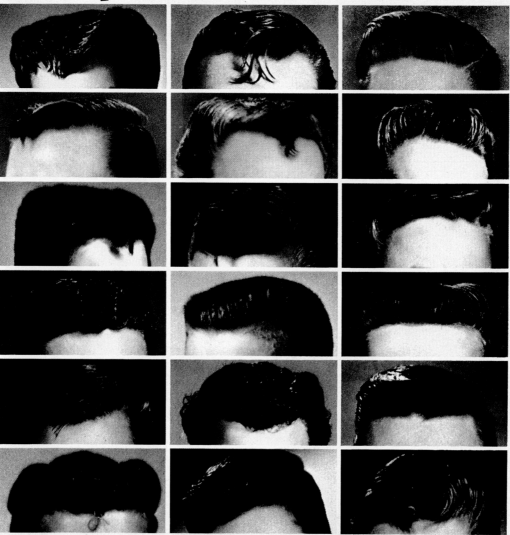

Return to a time when artists worked in Brylcreem. See Memphis 1948-1958, an exhibition of postwar photography, art, and popular culture at Memphis Brooks until January 11. Museum hours are Monday through Friday 10-5, and Sunday from 1-5. Open an IRA, CD, Premier Visa or All-in-One Account at First Tennessee and get two free tickets to the show or a commemorative poster when you bring in this ad. **FIRST TENNESSEE**

■**308** As promotion for the First Tennessee Bank, an advertisement for an art/photography/pop culture exhibition entitled "Memphis 1948-1958" sponsored by this bank. (USA)

■**308** «Seht Euch die wunderbaren Ölbilder an» – für «Memphis 1948-1958», eine von der First Tennessee Bank unterstützte Ausstellung von Photographie, Kunst und Pop-Kultur. (USA)

■**308** «Regardez ces huiles superbes» – annonce de la First Tennessee Bank pour l'exposition «Memphis 1948-1958» (art, photo, culture pop) qu'elle patronne. (USA)

EDITORIAL DESIGN

Consumer Magazines

Trade Magazines

Company Magazines

ANNUAL REPORTS

REDAKTIONELLES DESIGN

Publikumszeitschriften

Fachzeitschriften

Firmenpublikationen

JAHRESBERICHTE

DESIGN DE PÉRIODIQUES

Périodiques

Revues professionnelles

Magazines de sociétés

RAPPORTS ANNUELS

ART DIRECTOR:
Ron Albrecht

PHOTOGRAPHER:
Gilles Bensimon

PUBLISHER:
Elle

■**309**

ART DIRECTOR:
Phyllis Schefer

PHOTOGRAPHER:
Gilles Bensimon

PUBLISHER:
Elle

■**310**

ART DIRECTOR:
Ron Albrecht

PHOTOGRAPHER:
Toscani

PUBLISHER:
Elle

■**311**

ART DIRECTOR:
Phyllis Schefer

PHOTOGRAPHER:
Gilles Bensimon

PUBLISHER:
Elle

■**312**

■**309, 310** Two covers of the women's magazine *Elle* Far left for an issue devoted to modern classics, left, a December issue with emphasis on party fashions. (USA)

■**311, 312** Two double spreads from *Elle* Top: foam-rubber wet suit, foam-rubber sunglasses case and other accessories. Bottom: introductory spread to an article on skin-care. (USA)

■**309, 310** Zwei Umschläge der amerikanischen Ausgabe der Frauenzeitschrift *Elle* In den Ausgaben geht es um neue klassische Mode und, im Dezember, um Party-Mode. (USA)

■**311, 312** Doppelseiten aus der amerikanischen *Elle*. Die Themen: farbenfrohe Badekleidung und Zubehör aus Kunststoff (*311*) und die Pflege der Haut, von Kopf bis Fuss (*312*). (USA)

■**309, 310** Deux couvertures de l'édition américaine d'*Elle*. à l'extrême-gauche, pour un numéro de nouveautés classiques; à gauche, pour un no de décembre (modes de soirées). (USA)

■**311, 312** Deux doubles pages de l'édition américaine d'*Elle* En haut: maillot de bain, divers accessoires en caoutchouc mousse. En bas: début d'un article de cosmétologie. (USA)

REVVED UP SUMMER GEAR

COLOR POP

Wet suits on a whim — the "authentic" base rubber becomes part of the tropical scheme. Shocking pinks, outrageous reds, tremendous the suit in color black brights. All the bare necessities you head to the beach

Dive footie pincherz, $55 at Patricia Field, NYC. *St. suit* Bodyglove Sunkissed Palm Scuba. Mtask $22, Alain Mikli vintage shown with leather gloves. Pointed $18. For *Sunkissed Palm* fins $80. *Lac* footies shades, $22 for rubber eyeglass holder. Body Glove rubber shoes $16. For Shopping *St. Yellow* team, Francesca Mattei rubber sunglass

ANATOMY OF MODERN SKIN CARE

THE LATEST NEWS, THE BEST CARE FOR YOUR SKIN FROM THE NECK DOWN: WHAT WORKS, WHAT DOESN'T.

BODY BEAUTIFUL

It's your body's largest organ. Between you and the environment, a resilient barrier that can be invaded by a scratch or a pinprick. What, quite literally, holds you together. It is, of course, your skin—and the majority of it, on your body, often ends up a poor cousin to treatment-pampered facial skin. We ignore our bodies unless we have a problem: cold-weather chapping or post-tan peeling. But regular body care can be preventive, keeping skin supple and moisturized, toned and texturized so that it looks firmer and is less likely to require emergency treatments.

The dermal difference. Is the skin on your body different from that on your face? Yes and no. As Mitchell Wortzman, Ph.D., director of scientific affairs for Neutrogena, explains, "Body skin is about the same as facial skin. The face has thinner local areas and has a higher concentration of sensory nerves, so it is more sensitive. But the real difference stems from the fact that the face is usually exposed, while the body isn't."

Body skin does age at a different rate, says Dr. Wortzman, but that's primarily because it's shielded from the sun. It also has a different concentration of cells affecting moisturization, and hair, which offers a little natural protection, is more prevalent. But this doesn't make body skin "damage-proof." If you expose a previously covered area to the sun—say, you're in the South of France and want to experience topless sunbathing for the first time—the skin may be even more delicate than that on your face. It's wise to use an SPF 15 sunscreen on such areas.

Overall, body skin also has fewer sebaceous glands, and so less oil. "This can cause problems because the body is soaked longer in hot, soapy water—something most people would never dream of doing to their faces—and so is easily dehydrated," points out A. John Penicnak, Ph.D., senior vice-president/corporate scientific department for Cosmair, Inc. And when skin is dry, lines become more visible.

The body also is subjected more to stretching from weight gain and loss;

think of how much weight you gain in your face as opposed to the weight gain to your body during pregnancy. While you can't help gaining weight during pregnancy, up-and-down dieting has the same effect on body skin, and is the worst thing you can do to your body, according to skin-care expert Aida Grey: "As we get older, skin loses some of its elasticity—its ability to bounce back. Think of a rubber band that's lost its snap. Instead of conforming to your new contours after weight loss, it will sag." For this reason it is better to take off any significant overweight before age 30—and "significant" can be as little as 15 pounds, depending on your particular size and bone structure.

Body basics. The basics of body care are the same as those of facial care—to

BOTTOM LINES

It's no secret: A sleek-looking derrière and thighs take work. Diet and exercise help the underlying muscle and fat, while exfoliation and moisturizing smooth and retexturize skin.

ART DIRECTOR:
Alberto Nodolini

PHOTOGRAPHER:
Chiba

PUBLISHER:
Conde Nast S.p.A.

■313

SOTTO LA LUNA

Sotto la luna a tirar tardi per il placere di tirar tardi si diceva una volta. O per portare avanti una «occasione sentimentale», come invece direbbe un ragazzo di oggi. Per provare un brivido lungo la schiena mentre i passi risuonano sull'acciottolato, come scriverebbero Fruttero & Lucentini. Per schiarirsi finalmente le idee all'aria fresca della notte se i pensieri non fanno dormire, come penserebbe una malata di stress. Per andare a una cena all'aperto con gli amici, «un abito dalla scollatura a tuffo dietro, un velo per coprire le spalle» come trovereste nella didascalia di una foto di Vogue. Noi aggiungiamo «... e per sentirsi magicamente belle». La luna che passa attraverso i capelli li fa brillare e, se per caso poche ore prima li avrete trattati con quell'Azurée Hair Program di Estée Lauder che è un metodo modernissimo per il fai da te dei capelli, ecco che sembreranno an che una massa incredibilmente folta...

ESTÉE LAUDER Azurée Hair Care Program si compone di otto prodotti, tutti a base di alghe marine e vitamine che lavorano in sinergia. Ci sono tre shampoo fra cui scegliere il proprio, un conditioner nutriente, due spray, una mousse e un impacco per dare lussentezza e corposità.

270

bellezza

ART DIRECTOR:
Alberto Nodolini

PHOTOGRAPHER:
Piero Gemelli

PUBLISHER:
Conde Nast S.p.A.

■314

Per un'estate colorata. Di MONTORFANO il secchiello plastificato verde con riporti in cuoio naturale traforato. Di PANCALDI il sandalo in pelle multicolore stampata a fiori, con piccola zeppa. DI MARIA CALDERARA le collane folk variopinte.

accessori ultimissime

■**313, 314** "Under the moon", and the beauty of *Estée Lauder Azurée* Hair Care Program in a spread from *Vogue Italia*, and a bag, sandals and necklace - accessories for a colorful summer - in a double spread, also for *Vogue Italia* (ITA)

■**315, 316** Two spreads from the German *Vogue* fall fashions and "the new symbols" from Paris, and a 7-day diet. (GER)

■**313, 314** Doppelseiten aus *Vogue Italia*. *313* gehört zu einem Schönheitsbeitrag, hier speziell für Haarpflegeprodukte von *Estée Lauder* ("Unter dem Mond"), *314* zu einem Modebeitrag mit Accessoires für einen farbenfrohen Sommer. (ITA)

■**315, 316** Herbstmode aus Paris und eine Erfolgsdiät sind die Themen dieser Doppelseiten aus der deutschen *Vogue* (GER)

■**313, 314** Doubles pages de *Vogue Italia* «Sous la lune» où s'affirme la beauté du programme de capilliculture *Estée Lauder Azurée*, sac, sandales et collier composant les accessoires idéaux pour un été haut en couleur. (ITA)

■**315, 316** Pages de l'édition allemande de *Vogue*, les modes automnales parisiennes; une semaine de régime. (GER)

ART DIRECTOR:
Angelica Blechschmidt
PHOTOGRAPHER:
Eric Boman
PUBLISHER:
Conde Nast Verlag GmbH
■315

F R A N K R E I C H

DIE
NEUEN
SYMBOLE

eleganz aus Paris: Die neue Herbstmode spiegelt die Kreativität der französischen Top-Designer — und Symbole bestimmen
ihre wirkungsvolle Optik. Das sind die Kennzeichen der kom-
menden Saison: ein „disziplinierter", doch nicht strenger Look,
mit klaren Konturen. Mit Silhouetten, die den Körper modellie-
ren, und Effekten, die ihn verführerisch in Szene setzen.

EMANUEL
UNGARO
PARALLÈLE

Paris liebt Eleganz mit Dramatik,
wie Samtkappen, Stulpenhand-
schuhe, Super-Schmuck. Zur
Wolljacke mit Samtbesatz gehört
ein Glencheck-Rock mit Taft-
Plissée (Stoffe: Corisia/Ideaco-
mo-Gruppe). Accessoires von
Emanuel Ungaro. Auf allen zwölf
Seiten Frisuren: Kim für Mod's
Hair, Make-up von Kevyn Aucoin.

Eric Boman

ART DIRECTOR:
Angelica Blechschmidt
PHOTOGRAPHER:
Neil Kirk
PUBLISHER:
Conde Nast Verlag GmbH
■316

ERFOLGS-
DIÄT

**Delikat essen – und da-
bei abnehmen! Gäste
bewirten und dabei
konsequent Diät halten:
Die neue VOGUE-Diät
bietet alles, was Erfolg
verspricht: Genuß für
Feinschmecker, eine
optimale Versorgung
mit Vitaminen und Mi-
neralstoffen, zeitspa-
rende und effektive
Kochanleitungen. Mit
unserer Erfolgs-Diät
nehmen Sie in sieben
Tagen problemlos drei
Kilo ab. Sie läßt sich gut
um eine Woche verlän-
gern und eignet sich
auch für ein Wochen-
end-Kursprogramm.**

Schlank & schön in sieben Tagen

VON MARTINA MEUTH

**So funktioniert
die VOGUE-Diät:**

Pro Tag gibt es höchstens 1000 Kalorien.
Fest verplant sind davon 200 fürs Frühstück, je etwa 300 bis 350 für zwei Mahlzeiten: Ein kleineres, oft kaltes Essen, das
nicht viel Arbeit macht, und ein etwas auf-
wendigeres Mahl, zu dem man getrost auch
Gäste laden kann (in diesem Fall die im
Rezept angegebenen Mengen einfach
entsprechend der Anzahl von Mit-Essern
vervielfachen). Es bleibt also ein tägli-
ches Guthaben von knapp 200 Kalorien
für Extras, falls die Lust auf etwas
zum Knabbern zwischendurch oder auf ein
Glas Wein doch unüberwindbar wird (sie-
he Kasten auf Seite 241).

Nach einer Woche zeigt die Waage ga-
rantiert fünf bis sechs Pfund weniger. Wer
auf die Extra-Kalorien verzichtet, nimmt
zur Belohnung schneller und noch mehr ab.
Auf gar keinen Fall sollte man aber das
Guthaben aufsparen und dann am letzten
Tag gesammelt essen.

Die Versorgung mit Vitaminen, Mineral-
und Ballaststoffen ist so ausgewogen, daß
man die Diät unbesorgt auf zwei, drei Wochen ausdehnen kann. Aber: anschließend
nur schrittweise und behutsam wieder zu
großzügigeren Mahlzeiten zurückkehren,
vor allem beim Alkohol maßvoll bleiben,
sonst sitzen die endlich verschwundenen
Pfunde nur zu schnell wieder auf den Hüf-
ten. Beschleunigen läßt sich der Erfolg,
wenn man die Diätwoche mit folgendem
Kur-Drink beginnt: 40 Gramm Glaubersalz
(Apotheke) in 3/4 l lauwarmem Wasser auf-
lösen und in kleinen Schlucken trinken
(schmeckt leicht bitter und salzig). Das Ab-
führmittel wirkt schnell, deshalb lieber zu
Hause bleiben – die Kur am besten also an
einem Wochenende beginnen. Der Körper
wird so gründlich entschlackt und aufge-
räumt, stellt sich leichter auf die neue Er-
nährung um und greift freiwilliger und
nachhaltiger die eigenen Reserven an.

Wer abnehmen will, muß frühstücken!
Auch, wer sonst am Morgen nicht gern
etwas zu sich nimmt. Der Magen muß Arbeit bekommen, damit er Sättigung signalisiert. Nur so ist man leistungsfähig und vor
der Versuchung gefeit, zu naschen. Man
kommt bei einem Frühstück mit nur 200
Kalorien aus. Drei Vorschläge zum Aussu-
chen und Abwechseln (Seite 241).

**Damit der
Busen
straff bleibt**

Während einer Diät ist eine besonders
intensive Busenpflege unumgänglich.
Der Busen kann durch die Reduzierung
des Fettgewebes den „Unterbau" und dadurch auch an Spannkraft verlieren. Mit
der neuen „Bust Firming Lotion" von SHI-
SEIDO erzielt man eine Festigung des
Hautgewebes. Sie wird täglich nach einer
speziellen Methode auf den Busen und
auch auf das Dekolleté einmassiert. (Eine
bebilderte Massage-Anleitung liegt der
Packung bei.) Eine gerade, aufrechte
Haltung und Gymnastik kräftigt außer-
dem den Brustmuskel. Das Kleid auf
diesem Foto stammt von John Galliano.

Neil Kirk

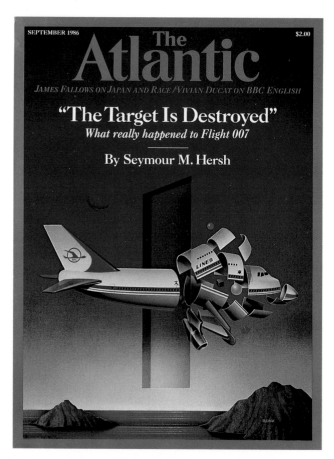

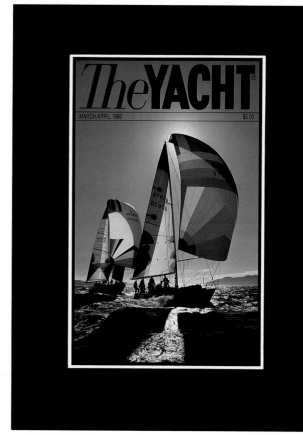

ART DIRECTOR:
Judy Garlan

DESIGNER:
Judy Garlan

ILLUSTRATOR:
Theo Rudnak

PUBLISHER:
The Atlantic Monthly

■317

ART DIRECTOR:
Judy Garlan

DESIGNER:
Judy Garlan

ILLUSTRATOR:
Milton Glaser

PUBLISHER:
The Atlantic Monthly

■318

ART DIRECTOR:
Stephen Doyle

DESIGNER:
Rosemarie Sohmer

PHOTOGRAPHER:
Chris Callis

AGENCY:
Drenttel Doyle Partners

PUBLISHER:
Spy Publishing Partners

■319

ART DIRECTOR:
Paul N. Williams

PHOTOGRAPHER:
Chuck Place

PUBLISHER:
The Yacht Magazine

■320

317, 318 Covers of *The Atlantic* magazine. Far left, to illustrate a non-fiction article. Left, relating to an article on the history, brand variety and cooking methods of pasta. (USA)

319 Cover of the October issue of *Spy* magazine. (USA)

320 Cover of *The Yacht* magazine relating to the Big Boat series in San Francisco. (USA)

321 *inside Chicago* – cover of the premier issue of this magazine appealing to the young, professional readership. (USA)

317, 318 Umschläge der Zeitschrift *The Atlantic* Hier geht es um Beiträge über das abgeschossene koreanische Passagierflugzeug und über Rezepte und Geschichte der Teigwaren. (USA)

319 Umschlag einer Ausgabe des Magazins *Spy*. (USA)

320 Umschlag der Zeitschrift *The Yacht*, im Zusammenhang mit einer Serie über Segelregatten in San Francisco. (USA)

321 Umschlag der ersten Ausgabe des Magazins *inside Chicago* mit Details der Illustrationen zu den Artikeln. (USA)

317, 318 Couvertures du magazine *The Atlantic* A l'extrême-gauche, l'avion coréen abattu par la chasse soviétique. A g., l'histoire et la préparation des pâtes alimentaires. (USA)

319 Couverture d'octobre du magazine *Spy*. (USA)

320 Couverture du magazine *Yacht*, avec référence aux régates de grands voiliers dans la baie de San Francisco. (USA)

321 Couverture du premier numéro du magazine *inside Chicago* qui s'adresse aux jeunes cadres. (USA)

DESIGN DIRECTOR:
Steven Bagby
DESIGNER:
Michael Borchew/
Sandi Weindling
PHOTOGRAPHER:
James Caulfield
AGENCY:
Bagby Design Inc.
PUBLISHER:
Signature Publishing, Inc.
■ **321**

GIANNI BARBATO. È ispirata alle calzature dei Navajo la scarpa stringata in camoscio con nappine usate come motivo ornamentale.

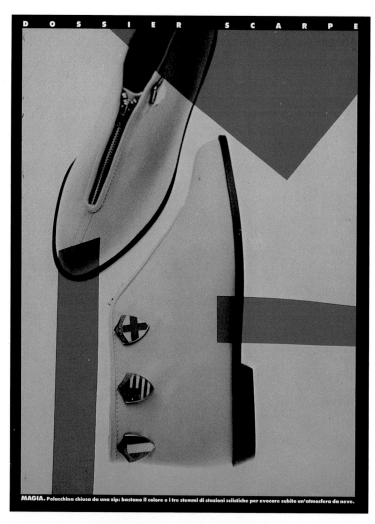

MAGIA. Polacchina chiusa da una zip: bastano il colore e i tre stemmi di stazioni sciistiche per evocare subito un'atmosfera da neve.

PANCALDI. La décolletée di camoscio nero gioca coi colori del tacco e della 'figurina' imbottita che sembra posata quasi per caso.

ARMANDO POLLINI DESIGN. Modernissima ma con una grazia settecentesca: scarpa in camoscio stampato con effetto marmo.

ROM IST EINE FRAU

Ich liebe mein Rom, weil es eine weibliche Stadt ist. Rom gleicht der Frau, die sie am schönsten verkörpert hat: der unvergleichlichen Anna Magnani.

In jedem Land, ganz besonders in Italien, gibt es weibliche und männliche Städte. Palermo und Turin zum Beispiel sind männlich. Meine Heimatstadt Parma dagegen oder Florenz und Venedig sind weiblich. Rom hat alle Eigenschaften einer Schauspielerin wie Anna Magnani – Rom liebt es, sich wie auf einer Bühne darzustellen, genießt aber genausosehr die Intrigen hinter den Kulissen. Rom ist ungestüm und triebhaft, aber die Stadt weiß auch um die Süße und die Nuancen der Sinnlichkeit: sie ist hinreißend, wenn sie lacht, aber oft scheint sie so schmerzlich zu seufzen wie Anna Magnani, als sie in Roberto Rossellinis Film *Rom – offene Stadt* ihrem verhafteten Mann nachläuft.

Die Lieblingslegende der Römer heißt „la Carità del seno femminile", was etwa so viel bedeutet wie „die Wohltätigkeit der weiblichen Brust". In dieser Legende geht es um einen alten Mann, der in einem Kerker zum Hungertod verurteilt ist, aber von seiner Tochter, die ihn mit der Milch aus ihren Brüsten nährt, am Leben gehalten wird. Welche dieser beiden Figuren symbolisiert nun eigentlich Rom? Die Tochter oder der Vater? Vielleicht erkennen sich die Römer in dem Band zwischen ihrem historischen Alter und den Legenden um ihre Herkunft, wie jene von der Wölfin, die Romulus und Remus säugte.

Bis vor drei Jahren wirkte Rom wie ausgestorben. Aus Angst vor dem Terrorismus wagte sich damals kein Mensch mehr auf die Straße. Schlimm für eine Stadt, deren wahres Leben erst nach Sonnenuntergang beginnt. Heute sind die römischen Nächte wieder die von einst. Besonders im Sommer ist es herrlich, vor den Restaurants in Trastevere im Freien zu essen oder über die Via Veneto zu schlendern, auf der heute wieder etwas vom „Dolce vita" der sechziger Jahre zu spüren ist. Es ist ein Irrtum zu glauben, Federico Fellini habe das Phänomen des süßen Lebens lediglich für einen Film geschaffen. Dieses „Dolce vita" ist auch kein besonderes, ja keineswegs exclusiver Lebensstil berühmter Schauspielerinnen und Schauspieler und sie umschwirrenden Fotografen, der „Paparazzi". Nein, das wahre „Dolce vita" ist das aller Römer, die jeder Art von Star-Rummel schon von jeher gleichgültig gegenüberstanden.

Die wirkliche Neigung, ja die Verehrung der Römer gilt dem „pranzo", dem Mittagsmahl, bevorzugt auf dem Hügel, wo es den besten Frascati gibt, dem gilt dem „gelato", dem Eis in den Bars auf der Piazza Navona oder bei Giolitti, einer berühmten Eisdiele im Zentrum der Stadt.

Aber die wahre Süße des Lebens besteht darin, über die Via del Corso, die Via dei Condotti, die Via Fratini zu spazieren, ohne einen besonderen Grund und ohne ein festes Ziel.

Die Mädchen, die einen dort begegnen, sind wohlgeformt und dunkel, und sie erinnern ein

176

Sie ist hinreißend und ungestüm, mütterlich und kapriziös, rätselhaft und geheimnisvoll; sie genießt das „Dolce vita", steckt voller Lebensfreude und liebt es, sich zur Schau zu stellen. Die Ewige Stadt ist mit allen typisch weiblichen Eigenschaften gesegnet. Rom ist eine Frau – zu diesem Schluß kam Alberto Bevilacqua, Autor des Erfolgsromans „Frau der Wunder", der exclusiv für VOGUE „sein" Rom einmal wieder durchwanderte und beschrieb.

wenig an die „Fornarina", die Raffael gemalt hat.

Ihren vollkommenen Ausdruck findet die Weiblichkeit Roms nämlich in dieser Margherita Luti. Raffael verliebte sich auf den ersten Blick in sie, als er Margherita dabei beobachtete, wie sie im Tiber ihre Füße wusch. „Eine Frau", so die Römer über Margherita Luti, „die Sinnlichkeit und Ironie in sich vereint."

Wenn Sie das Bild der Fornarina in der Galleria Nazionale aufmerksam betrachten, werden Sie vielleicht mehr von Rom begreifen. In ihren schwarzen, mandelförmigen Augen, die so rätselhaft wie die Augen einer Schlange blicken, liegt römischer Sarkasmus; dieser kritisch-spöttische Zug spielt auch um ihre Lippen, die in der rosigen und noch jugendlichen Rundung ihres Gesichtes deutliche sexuelle Akzente setzen; diesen römischen Sarkasmus signalisiert auch der Schwung ihrer Nase und der kräftige Hals. Der elastischen Straffheit der Brüste ist anzumerken, daß sie Berührung gewohnt sind.

Die wirkliche Bedeutung des „Dolce vita"

drückt sich bei ihr in einer Geste aus. Die rechte Hand hält den Schleier zwischen ihren Brüsten, so daß er nichts mehr verbirgt. Die Körpersprache der Fornarina – und ganz Rom – scheint zu sagen: „Das ist die Scham, sie verhüllt, aber sie kennt nicht das rechte Maß, weil sie nicht sehen kann, denn sie ist nur kurzsichtige Heuchelei."

Die Fornarina – und mit ihr ganz Rom – scheint einzuladen: „Ich gehöre euch, ihr seid alle meine Liebhaber."

Das Rom, das ich liebe, mein Rom, das sind all jene Straßen, die von ihren Bewohnern einer historischen Geliebten gewidmet sind. In Campo de' Fiori, an einem der eindrucksvollsten Plätze der Stadt, lebte Vannozza Cattanei, Geliebte von Papst Alexander VI. Der Bronze-Engel auf der Spitze der Engelsburg soll von Beatrice La Ferrarese gestiftet worden sein, die über die Jahrhunderte hinweg als „Geliebte aller" galt. Die Straßen längs des Tiber und selbst die Piazza del Popolo sind zum größten Teil mit Mitteln aus Liebesdiensten der „freien Frauen" gepflastert worden.

Ich wandere gern durch Rom und entdecke diese lächelnden Geheimnisse, die jeder Ort birgt.

Dazu ein persönliches Erlebnis. Cineasten fragen sich noch heute, wo der niemals aufgeführte Film gelandet ist, den Orson Welles über „Don Quijote" gedreht hat. Dieses unvollendete Meisterwerk ist aber keine Fiktion, es existiert tatsächlich. Und der überraschendste Aspekt daran ist wohl, daß zahlreiche Sequenzen im Rom von heute spielen: so zum Beispiel in EUR, jenem Stahl- und Beton-Babylon der Banken und Büros; nach seiner Rückkehr vom Mond wird Don Quijote dort von den Augen der Fernsehkameras belauert. Vieles ist auch in Bracciano gedreht worden. Und ich war es, der Orson Welles auf der Suche nach Drehorten durch Rom geführt hat. Ich fragte ihn: „Warum willst du das große Werk von Cervantes gerade in dieser Stadt verfilmen?" Orson Welles antwortete: „Weil Gott Rom als vollkommene Hauptstadt der Mysterien geschaffen hat. Der römische Zynismus nährt sich in Wirklichkeit von Dämonen und Gespenstern. Hier habe ich einmal eine sehr sublime Erkenntnis gehört: Nichts ist unmöglich außer dem Möglichen."

Auf den Spuren unserer Dulcinea wanderten wir weiter. Ich führte Orson in die Kirche von Santa Sabina und zeigte ihm den Basaltblock, auf dem der Teufel den Abdruck seiner Hand hinterlassen hat. Welles streckte seine rechte Hand aus und legte die Finger in die schwarzen Konturen im Stein. Ich erzähle ihm, daß nach einer anderen Legende der Dämon den Basaltblock dem Heiligen Dominikus an den Kopf geschleudert hatte, weil dieser auf dem Fußboden liegend für seinen Geschmack mit viel zu monotoner Stimme betete. Welles, der große Schauspieler und Regisseur, lachte, daß das Gewölbe dröhnte: „Mir gefällt so ein Teufel, der in Zorn gerät und Heiligen Steine an den Kopf

Fortsetzung auf Seite 238

Fortsetzung auf Seite 238

Brunnen-Schönheit auf der Piazza Barbarini (unten) und ein Blick hinauf zum Capitol (oben).

Fotos: Tobias Heldt, Thomas Höpker/A. Hamann

ART DIRECTOR:
Gianni Brancaccio

PHOTOGRAPHER:
Paulo Greuel

PUBLISHER:
Edizioni Edimoda S.p.A.

■ 322–325

ART DIRECTOR:
Angelica Blechschmidt

PHOTOGRAPHER:
Tobias Heldt/
Thomas Höpker/
A. Hamann

PUBLISHER:
Conde Nast Verlag GmbH

■ 326

■ **322–325** From the editorial pages of the women's magazine *Donna* (Italian edition) under the title "Shoe File" and presenting laced chamois-leather shoes by *Gianni Barbato*, zipped bootees by *Magia*, pumps by *Pancaldi* and marble-effect court shoes by *Armando Pollini Design*. (ITA)

■ **326** From *Vogue* Germany, dedicated to Italy. "Rome is a Women" is the title and the Eternal City is attributed with feminine characteristics. (GER)

■ **322–325** Beispiele aus dem Inhalt der Frauenzeitschrift *Donna* (italienische Ausgabe) unter dem Titel «Dossier Schuhe». Hier Wildlederschuhe von *Gianni Barbato*, Stiefeletten mit Reissverschluss von *Magia*, Pumps von *Pancaldi* und Wildlederschuhe mit Marmoreffekt von *Armando Pollini Design*. (ITA)

■ **326** Doppelseite aus der deutschen Ausgabe von *Vogue* für einen Beitrag über die Ewige Stadt von dem Autor Alberto Bevilacqua, der zu dem Schluss kam: «Rom ist eine Frau.» (GER)

■ **322–325** Pages rédactionnelles de l'édition italienne du magazine féminin *Donna*, au chapitre «Dossier chaussures»: en chamois à lacets de *Gianni Barbato*, bottines à fermeture Eclair de *Magia*, escarpins de *Pancaldi* et d'*Armando Pollini Design*, ces derniers au dessin marbré. (ITA)

■ **326** Double page de l'édition allemande de *Vogue* consacrée à l'Italie. L'écrivain Alberto Bevilacqua identifie la Ville éternelle: «Rome est une femme.» (ITA)

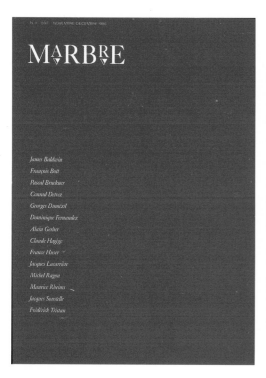

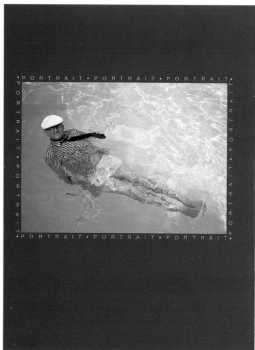

ART DIRECTOR:
Jim Waters

DESIGNER:
Debbie Tiso/Jo Walton

PHOTOGRAPHER:
Julio Donoso

AGENCY:
Orchestra

PUBLISHER:
Marbre Sarl

■ 327, 328

ART DIRECTOR:
Jim Waters

DESIGNER:
Debbie Tiso/Jo Walton

PHOTOGRAPHER:
Yves Gellie

AGENCY:
Orchestra

PUBLISHER:
Marbre Sarl

■ 329

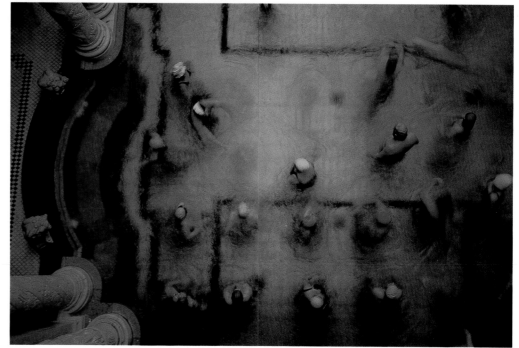

ART DIRECTOR:
Erika Schmied

PHOTOGRAPHER:
Werner Gartung

PUBLISHER:
Hoffmann & Campe

■ **330**

ART DIRECTOR:
Erika Schmied

PHOTOGRAPHER:
Timm Rautert

PUBLISHER:
Hoffmann & Campe

■ **331**

■ **327–329** Cover and spreads from of the magazine *Marbre*. Top: from a feature entitled "Portrait of David Hockney". Bottom: from an article "The Waters of Budapest". (FRA)

■ **330, 331** Covers of the magazine *Merian*. Left: a Saharan nomad well protected from sun, sand and wind. Right: Frankfurt's latest landmark, the 117 m high "Torhaus". (GER)

■ **327–329** Umschlag der ersten Ausgaben der Zeitschrift *Marbre* und Doppelseiten daraus, die zu Beiträgen über David Hockney bzw. über die Bäder von Budapest gehören. (FRA)

■ **330, 331** Ein Nomade, dessen kunstvoll geschlungenes Tuch Kopf und Gesicht schützt, und Frankfurts neues Wahrzeichen, das 117 m hohe Torhaus, auf den Umschlägen von *Merian*. (GER)

■ **327–329** Couverture et pages doubles du premier numéro du magazine bimestriel *Marbre*, ces dernières consacrées à David Hockney (en haut), aux bains de Budapest (en bas). (FRA)

■ **330, 331** Couvertures du magazine de voyages *Merian*. A. g., un nomade saharien se protégeant du sable et du soleil. A. dr., le Torhaus (117 m), nouvel emblème de Francfort. (GER)

ART DIRECTOR:
Hans-Georg Pospischil
DESIGNER:
Bernadette Gotthardt
PHOTOGRAPHER:
Anthony Crickmay
PUBLISHER:
Frankfurter Allgemeine
■332

ART DIRECTOR:
Hans-Georg Pospischil
DESIGNER:
Bernadette Gotthardt
PHOTOGRAPHER:
Abe Frajndlich
PUBLISHER:
Frankfurter Allgemeine
■333

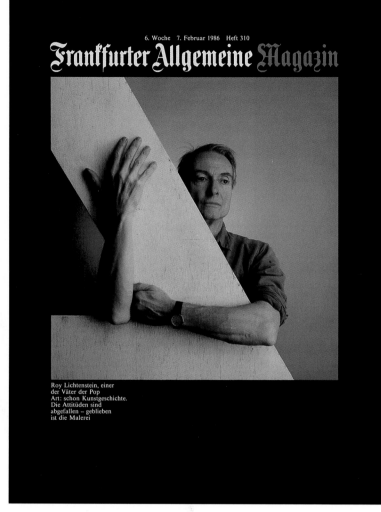

ART DIRECTOR:
Hans-Georg Pospischil
DESIGNER:
Bernadette Gotthardt
PHOTOGRAPHER:
Abe Frajndlich
PUBLISHER:
Frankfurter Allgemeine
■334

ART DIRECTOR:
Hans-Georg Pospischil
DESIGNER:
Bernadette Gotthardt
ILLUSTRATOR:
Jose Cruz
PUBLISHER:
Frankfurter Allgemeine
■335

8. Woche 21. Februar 1986 Heft 312

Frankfurter Allgemeine Magazin

Ein Vulkan, der
jederzeit ausbrechen
kann: Celia Cruz,
kubanische Sängerin
unbekannten
Alters und ungeahnter
Ausstrahlung

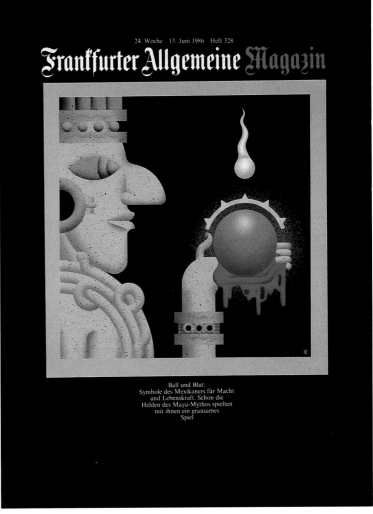

24. Woche 13. Juni 1986 Heft 328

Frankfurter Allgemeine Magazin

Ball und Blut:
Symbole des Mexikaners für Macht
und Lebenskraft. Schon die
Helden des Maya-Mythos spielten
mit ihnen ein grausames
Spiel

■ **332–335** Covers of the *Frankfurter Allgemeine Magazin.*
Opposite far left: "Men, don't be afraid of flying, in the new
dance the women are awfully strong!" – relating to an article on
British ballet. Left: portrait of Roy Lichtenstein, a pioneer of pop
art. Above left: the vibrant Cuban singer Celia Cruz. Right: Ball
and blood are symbols of power and vitality to the Mexicans
(relates to Mexican ritual sports and their meaning today). (GER)

■ **332–335** Umschläge verschiedener Ausgaben des *Frankfurter Allgemeine Magazins.* Sie gehören (von links nach
rechts) zu Beiträgen über das Contemporary Dance Theatre,
London; den amerikanischen Maler Roy Lichtenstein, einen Pio-
nier der Pop Art; über die kubanische Sängerin Celia Cruz und
über die Tradition von ritualisierten Kampfspielen in Mexiko und
ihre heutige Bedeutung. (GER)

■ **332–335** Couvertures du *Frankfurter Allgemeine Magazin* Ci-contre, à l'extrême-g.: «N'ayez pas peur de voler, messieurs, les nouvelles danseuses ont de la poigne!», pour un article
sur le ballet anglais. A g.: Roy Lichtenstein, pionnier du pop art.
Ci-dessus, à g.: la Pasionaria de la chanson cubaine, Celia Cruz. A
dr.: les sports rituels sanglants du Mexique symbolisent toujours
la puissance et la vitalité. (GER)

ART DIRECTOR:
Hans-Georg Pospischil

DESIGNER:
Bernadette Gotthardt

ILLUSTRATOR:
Heinz Edelmann

PUBLISHER:
Frankfurter Allgemeine

■336

ART DIRECTOR:
Hans-Georg Pospischil

DESIGNER:
Bernadette Gotthardt

PHOTOGRAPHER:
Heiner Blum

PUBLISHER:
Frankfurter Allgemeine

■337

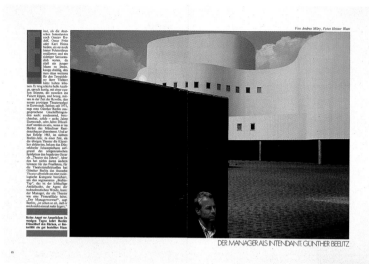

ART DIRECTOR:
Hans-Georg Pospischil

DESIGNER:
Bernadette Gotthardt

ILLUSTRATOR:
Jose Cruz

PUBLISHER:
Frankfurter Allgemeine

■338, 339

ART DIRECTOR:
Hans-Georg Pospischil
DESIGNER:
Bernadette Gotthardt
PHOTOGRAPHER:
Abe Frajndlich
PUBLISHER:
Frankfurter Allgemeine
■340

ART DIRECTOR:
Hans-Georg Pospischil
DESIGNER:
Bernadette Gotthardt
PHOTOGRAPHER:
Serge Cohen
PUBLISHER:
Frankfurter Allgemeine
■341

ART DIRECTOR:
Hans-Georg Pospischil
DESIGNER:
Bernadette Gotthardt
ILLUSTRATOR:
Heinz Edelmann
PUBLISHER:
Frankfurter Allgemeine
■342, 343

■336–343 From the *Frankfurter Allgemeine Magazin* Top left: introductory spread to an article entitled "Pain"; top right: spread from an article "The Manager as Theater Director". Bottom: both spreads from a story "A Banquet for Hot Tongues, a Mexican Wedding". Opposite, top left: introductory spread for a feature "The Voice of the Blues – Joe Cocker"; right: from an article about artist Jasper Johns. Bottom: Two spreads from an article on the dangers of flying. (GER)

■336–343 Aus dem *Frankfurter Allgemeine Magazin* Oben v.l.n.r.: Einleitende Doppelseiten aus einem Artikel über den Schmerz, für einen Beitrag über Günther Beelitz, der Düsseldorf verlässt und als Intendant ans Münchner Residenz-Theater geht, und zwei Doppelseiten aus «Ein Fest für scharfe Zungen: mexikanische Hochzeit»; rechte Seite v.l.n.r.: einleitende Doppelseiten für Berichte über Joe Cocker, den amerikanischen Maler Jasper Johns und über Flugkatastrophen, die nicht stattfanden. (GER)

■336–343 Doubles pages du *Frankfurter Allgemeine Magazin* En haut: à g., début d'un article sur la douleur; à dr., «le magnager devenu directeur de théâtre». En bas, deux doubles pages du récit «Banquet pour langues chaudes, une noce mexicaine». Ci-contre: en haut, à g., début de l'article «La Voix du blues – Joe Cocker»; à dr., article consacré à l'artiste américain Jasper Johns. En bas: deux doubles pages sur les dangers du déplacement en avion. (GER)

ART DIRECTOR:
Hans-Georg Pospischil
DESIGNER:
Bernadette Gotthardt
PHOTOGRAPHER:
Susan Lamèr
PUBLISHER:
Frankfurter Allgemeine
■344

Der amerikanische Milliardär Benjamin Guggenheim soll einen Smoking angelegt haben, um beim Untergang der Titanic angemessen gekleidet zu sein. Jeder der Herren der ersten Klasse dürfte einen Smoking mit sich im Schrankkoffer geführt haben. Denn wie in den Hotels der ersten Kategorie legte man in den geselligen Salons, beim Diner und bei den kleinen Tanzvergnügen an Bord Wert auf dieses informelle, doch elegante Kleidungsstück, das allerdings den Frack nicht ersetzte.
"Der Smoking ist die Abendkleidung des Herrn", heißt es lapidar in einem konservativen Brevier für den eleganten Herrn. "Regel ist allerdings, daß man vor sieben Uhr abends nirgends im Smoking erscheinen kann.". Liberale Instanzen dulden ihn schon in späten Nachmittag. Doch früher wollten die Regeln des schwarz-weißen Eleganz mit absoluter Strenge eingehalten werden. Nicht nur, was die Smoking-Gelegenheiten betraf. Auch bei den Details. Einreihig oder zweireihig, mehr war nicht zu entscheiden. Schon ein mitternachtsblauer Smoking galt als ein wenig exzentrisch. Die Zeitschrift "Die Dame", die in Deutschland jahrzehntelang, bis 1943, tonangebend war, warnte vor jeglicher Phantasie in der Herrenmode. Denn sie könnte als feminin ausgelegt werden.
Heute gehören zu jeder Herrenkollektion phantasievolle Smoking-Varianten. "Wir verkaufen sie viel", sagt Patrick La-

DER SMOKING MACHT DEN MANN

Von Martin Kazmaier
Fotos Susan Lamèr

Überlegener Verführer: Vor einer langen Nacht wirft sich der Mann in Schale

---

ART DIRECTOR:
Hans-Georg Pospischil
DESIGNER:
Bernadette Gotthardt
PHOTOGRAPHER:
Abe Frajndlich
PUBLISHER:
Frankfurter Allgemeine
■345

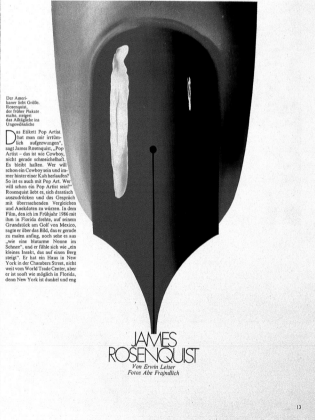

Der Amerikaner liebt Größe. Rosenquist, der früher Plakate malte, steigert das Alltägliche ins Ungewöhnliche

Das Etikett Pop Artist hat man mir irrtümlich aufgezwungen", sagt James Rosenquist, "Pop Artist – das ist wie Cowboy, nicht gerade schmeichelhaft. Es bleibt haften. Wer will schon ein Cowboy sein und immer hinter einer Kuh herlaufen? So ist es wie mit Pop Art. Wer will schon ein Pop Artist sein?" Rosenquist liebt es, sich drastisch auszudrücken und das Gespräch mit überraschenden Vergleichen und Anekdoten zu würzen. In dem Film, den ich im Frühjahr 1986 mit ihm in Florida drehte, auf seinem Grundstück am Golf von Mexico, sagte er über das Bild, das er gerade zu malen anfing, noch sehe er es aus "wie eine blutarme Nonne im Schnee", und er fühle sich wie "ein kleines Insekt, das auf einen Berg steigt". Er hat ein Haus in New York in der Chambers Street, nicht weit vom World Trade Center, aber er ist sooft wie möglich in Florida, denn New York ist dunkel und eng

JAMES ROSENQUIST

Von Erwin Leiser
Fotos Abe Frajndlich

13

■344–347 Double spreads from the *Frankfurter Allgemeine Magazin* This page, top: to introduce a feature on the tuxedo; bottom: portrait of artist James Rosenquist (born N. Dakota, 1933) in front of one of his paintings. Opposite, top: belonging to a feature about variety artistes (here Duo Wlades and the Schwenks, all Hansa-Theater); bottom: from "On the Way to the Unconscious" – an article about dreams. (GER)

■344–347 Doppelseiten aus dem *Frankfurter Allgemeine Magazin* 344 gehört zu einem Bericht über den Smoking. 345 zu einem Artikel über den Künstler James Rosenquist. 346 zeigt die einleitende Doppelseite zu einem Beitrag über Artisten (hier links das Duo Wlades und rechts die Geschwister Schwenk, alle Hansa-Theater), 347 ist die Einleitung für einen Artikel über den Traum. (GER)

■344–347 Doubles pages du *Frankfurter Allgemeine Magazin* Ci-dessus: en haut, début d'un article sur le smoking; en bas, James Rosenquist (né au Dakota du Nord en 1933) devant l'une de ses peintures. Ci-contre: en haut, article consacré aux artistes de variétés (ici Duo Wlades et les Schwenks, tous du Hansa-Theater); en bas, article d'onirologie intitulé «Sur les chemins de l'inconscient». (GER)

ART DIRECTOR:
Hans-Georg Pospischil

DESIGNER:
Bernadette Gotthardt

PHOTOGRAPHER:
Burkhard von Harder

PUBLISHER:
Frankfurter Allgemeine

■ 346

Sie ist stark – er fühlt zart

Sie ist schwer – er hat Begehr

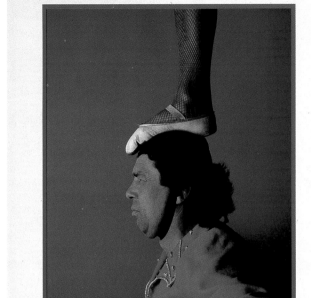

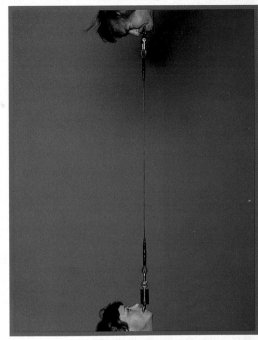

ennen Sie den? Im Varieté ist ein Equilibrist angesagt. Höhepunkt seiner Darbietung ist eine musikalische Pyramide. Auf einer Billardkugel steht schräg, mit einem Fuß, ein Stuhl. Auf dessen Lehne balanciert, wiederum schräg, mit einem Fuß, ein Tisch. Auf dessen Kante halten sich zwei Billardkugeln übereinander im Gleichgewicht. Auf den Kugeln steht senkrecht ein Queue – darauf thront ein Teller, gepolstert durch ein Kissen, denn ganz oben balanciert der Akrobat im Kopfstand. Dabei spielt er die Violine. Fritz Kreislers „Liebesleid" zieht halbwegs virtuos durch den Saal. Und dort, in der ersten Reihe, sagt einer zu seiner Frau: „Na ja, Heifetz is' er nich'." Hat man Töne für solche geflüsterte Ungerechtigkeit?

ARTISTENLEBEN
Von Michael Freitag
Fotos Burkhard von Harder

43

ART DIRECTOR:
Hans-Georg Pospischil

DESIGNER:
Bernadette Gotthardt

ILLUSTRATOR:
Heinz Edelmann

PUBLISHER:
Frankfurter Allgemeine

■ 347

ZUM UNBE-WUSSTEN UNTER-WEGS

enk dir: Auf riesenhaften dunklen Schiffen / segeln sie auf das Meer des Schlafs hinaus / bis zu den heimlichen Korallenriffen, / dort werfen sie die langen Netze aus." – Oneiromantie, Traumdeutung, beschäftigt die Menschen seit frühester Zeit. Als „Traumfischer", so der Titel des auszugsweise zitierten Gedichtes von Michael Ende, war man schon im Morgengrauen der Geschichte unterwegs. Das Gilgamesch-Epos (um 2500 v. Chr.) eröffnet die Liste der uns erhalten gebliebenen Träume mit einem Nachtmahr. Der Träumer wird von einem Adler in die Lüfte gehoben und bleibt schließlich zerschmettert am Boden liegen.

Die wissenschaftliche Betrachtungsweise des Traums wird in ihren Anfängen bis zu Platon und Aristoteles zurückdatiert. Im zweiten Jahrtausend vor Christus hatten die Ägypter schon ein Traumbuch zusammengestellt, das Anleitungen zur Deutung der flüchtigen Gebilde enthält. Indes: Ehrwürdiges Alter schützt nicht vor heftigen Attacken. Noch 1964 entspann sich anläßlich des Erscheinens von Arthur Koestlers „The Act of Creation" ein öffentlicher Disput. Der Autor hatte den Traum in den Rang eines Psycho-Fossils aus paradiesischer Urzeit versetzt; der Zoologe J. P. Medawar entgegnete ihm, daß der Traum viel eher als Phantasmagorie ohne jegliche Bedeutung einzuordnen sei.

Andernorts schritt man derweil zum Festakt für den vermeintlichen Taugenichts aus dem Schattenreich. Am 6. Mai 1977 wurde aus gegebenem Anlaß auf dem Kahlenberg bei Wien eine Gedenktafel angebracht: „Hier enthüllte sich am 24. Juli 1895 dem Dr. Sigm. Freud das Geheimnis des Traumes."

Von Hubertus Schneider
Illustrationen Heinz Edelmann

Wer schläft, ist nicht untätig, denn er baut im Traum eine eigene Welt

The New York Times Magazine

PART 2 / SEPTEMBER 21, 1986

HOME DESIGN

PARING DOWN

A SENSE OF ORDER

Amid stark white walls and highly polished oak floors, four Jacob chairs, an Egyptian Revival chaise and a large white cube appear like vignettes in a still life. These objects, though few in number, have been arranged with utmost precision.

"My last apartment was even sparer," recalls Robert L. Turner, creative director of In Fashion, a television production company. "It was a studio on the 29th floor with black lacquered walls, 28 feet of glass and only a bed in the middle of the room. I felt as though I were living in a jewel box in the sky." This apartment has something of a jewel-like quality, too. Unlike the modernists of 20 years ago, Turner has used minimalist ideas in a romantic fashion.

So has Suzie Frankfurt, a longtime friend of Turner's and the New York-based decorator who collaborated with him on the renovation of this two-bedroom apartment. "We worked hand in hand," says Turner. "The apartment hadn't been touched for over 30 years. With mustard-green walls and antiquated kitchen appliances, the place looked like a set from 'The Honeymooners.'"

Turner's penchant for simplicity, he says, is a reaction to his parents' cluttered home in Baton Rouge, La. Frankfurt's vision stems from an effort to find some relief from the oppressive, often trivial-minded designs that are a result of the recent craze among decorators for re-creating the Belle Epoque. While Frankfurt herself lives in a Regency Revival town house resplendent with ornate Bieder-

meier furniture, she feels design is on the brink of change. "Things have just become too claustrophobic," the designer says. "That doesn't mean I'm going to put modern furniture in a modern environment. But if you study the great homes of 18th-century Europe, they have an orderliness about them that's much to be admired."

Here, orderliness was achieved by removing a wall to combine the living and dining rooms, off of which is the all-white newly renovated kitchen. And while the walls are devoid of such details as moldings or baseboards, the designer created an octagonal entrance hall that features a pair of black glass columns punctuated by century-old Corinthian capitals and bases.

By studying the original floor plans, the designer discovered a chimney flue that had been blocked. She had it opened up and had a Louis XVI marble mantel installed, now the central focus of the bedroom. For proximity to the fireplace, the bed floats in the middle of the space. Beside it is a méridienne, an Empire love seat with one arm higher than the other, one of a matched pair found at auction.

The second méridienne, draped in a paisley shawl, can be found in the library, originally the second bedroom. This room, with its purple glazed walls, marbleized bookshelves and Audubon prints, is a departure from the rooms in the rest of the apartment. "Everything I'm not sure what to do with always ends up here," Turner says. But still a sense of order pervades.

A white cube, a Louis XVI Jacob chair and a painting by the Italian artist Carlo Maria Mariani are arranged like a still life.

LIZZIE HIMMEL

24   HOME DESIGN

ART DIRECTOR:
Susan Slover

DESIGNER:
Mario Pulice/Susan Slover

PHOTOGRAPHER:
Lizzie Himmel

AGENCY:
Susan Slover Design

PUBLISHER:
The New York Times

■ **348, 349**

■ **348, 349** Cover and spread from the *New York Times* special section *Home Design*. Subtitled "Paring Down", this issue is devoted to the minimalist look – as shown in these views of the designer's living/dining room. (USA)

■ **348, 349** Umschlag und Doppelseite aus einer Sonderbeilage der *New York Times* über Inneneinrichtungen mit dem Untertitel «auf ein Minimum beschränken» – wie hier anhand einer Wohnungseinrichtung demonstriert. (USA)

■ **348, 349** Couverture et double page de la section spéciale du *New York Times* consacré à la décoration intérieure. Ce numéro intitulé «Eliminer le superflu» présente le nouveau look minimaliste par l'exemple d'un salon-salle à manger. (USA)

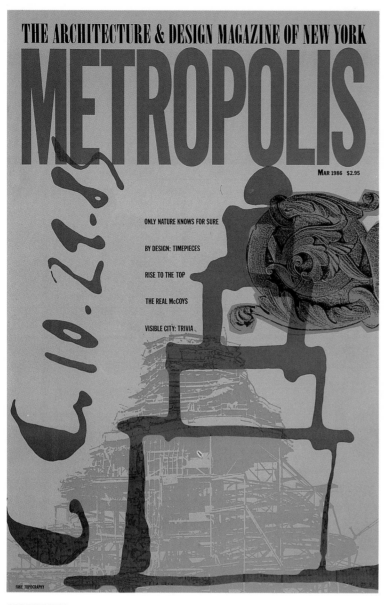

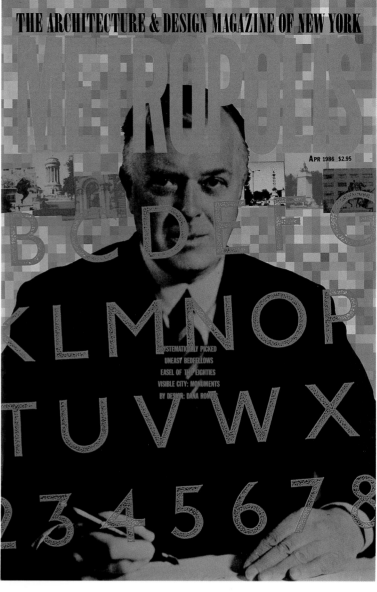

ART DIRECTOR:
Helene Silverman
DESIGNER:
Helene Silverman
PUBLISHER:
Metropolis Magazine
■ **350**

ART DIRECTOR:
Helene Silverman
DESIGNER:
Helene Silverman
PUBLISHER:
Metropolis Magazine
■ **351**

■ **350–353** Four covers of *Metropolis*, a New York monthly magazine devoted to architecture and design. (USA)

■ **350–353** Umschläge von vier Ausgaben der New Yorker Monatszeitschrift *Metropolis* über Architektur und Design. (USA)

■ **350–353** Quatre couvertures de *Metropolis*, magazine mensuel d'architecture et de design publié à New York. (USA)

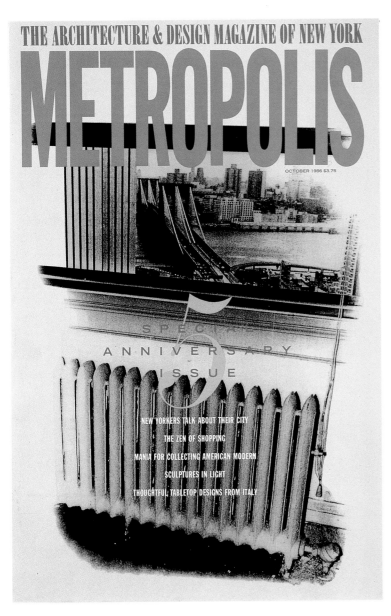

ART DIRECTOR:
Helene Silverman

DESIGNER:
Helene Silverman

PHOTOGRAPHER:
Elaine Ellman

PUBLISHER:
Metropolis Magazine

■ 352

ART DIRECTOR:
Helene Silverman

DESIGNER:
Helene Silverman

PUBLISHER:
Metropolis Magazine

■ 353

The New York Times Magazine

JULY 20, 1986 / SECTION 6

THE HARVARD FACTOR
The University Celebrates Its 350th Anniversary
BY COLIN CAMPBELL

Teresa Fasolino

354 Cover of *The New York Times Magazine* portraying some of Harvard University's most illustrious sons, on the occasion of its 350th anniversary. (USA)

355, 356 Covers of *West*, the Sunday supplement published by the *San Jose Mercury News*. Left, concerning the FM stations' endeavour to win the youngsters over with rock'n'roll music. Right: relating to the cover story about the young "save the whale campaigner" Rodney Coronado. (USA)

354 Umschlag des *New York Times Magazine* mit Porträts einiger der berühmtesten Söhne der Harvard University, anlässlich des 350. Jahrestages der Universität. (USA)

355, 356 Umschläge von *West*, der Sonntagsbeilage der *San José Mercury News*. In *355* geht es um die Bemühungen der FM-Radiostationen, die Jugend mit Rock'n'Roll-Musik für sich zu gewinnen, *356* betrifft einen Artikel über einen jungen Mann, der gegen den Walfang kämpft. (USA)

354 Couverture du *New York Times Magazine* avec plusieurs personnalités de premier plan issues de l'Université Harvard, pour les cérémonies du 350e anniversaire de Harvard. (USA)

355, 356 Couvertures de *West*, le supplément dominical des *San José Mercury News*. A g., rappel des efforts qu'entreprennent les stations de radio FM pour s'attirer des auditeurs jeunes via le rock. A dr., la vedette de la Une, le jeune défenseur des baleines Rodney Coronado. (USA)

ART DIRECTOR:
Ken Kendrick
ILLUSTRATOR:
Teresa Fasolino
PUBLISHER:
The New York Times Magazine
■ **354**

ART DIRECTOR:
Bambi Nicklen
DESIGNER:
Bambi Nicklen
ILLUSTRATOR:
Andrzej Dudzinski
PUBLISHER:
San Jose Mercury News
■ **355**

ART DIRECTOR:
Bambi Nicklen
DESIGNER:
Bambi Nicklen
ILLUSTRATOR:
Greg Spalenka
PUBLISHER:
San Jose Mercury News
■ **356**

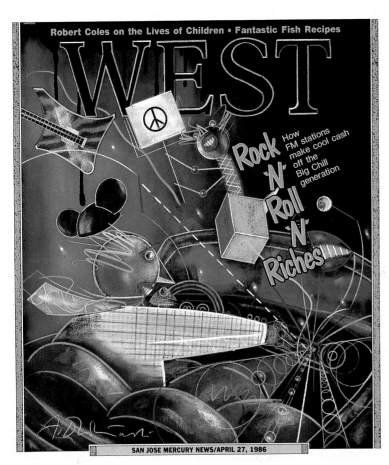

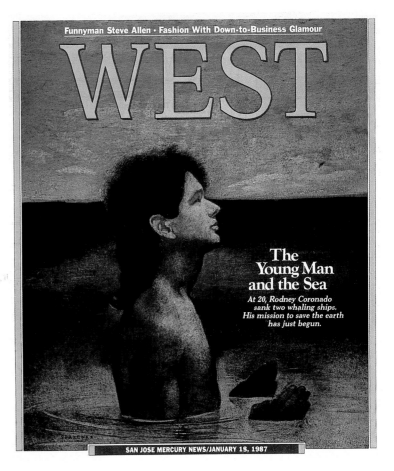

Industrial
Launderer
November
1986
The Industrial
Laundry
Industry
And Its
Markets

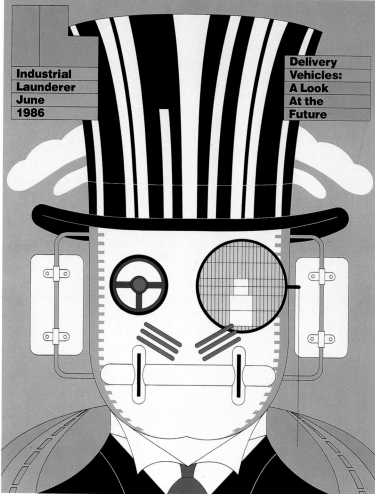

Industrial
Launderer
June
1986

Delivery
Vehicles:
A Look
At the
Future

ART DIRECTOR:
Jack Lefkowitz

DESIGNER:
Jack Lefkowitz

ILLUSTRATOR:
Virginia Strnad

AGENCY:
Jack Lefkowitz Inc.

PUBLISHER:
Industrial Launderer

■ **357, 358**

ART DIRECTOR:
Jack Lefkowitz

DESIGNER:
Jack Lefkowitz

ILLUSTRATOR:
Virginia Strnad

AGENCY:
Jack Lefkowitz Inc.

PUBLISHER:
Industrial Launderer

■ **359, 360, 362** ▶

ART DIRECTOR:
Jack Lefkowitz

DESIGNER:
Jack Lefkowitz

ILLUSTRATOR:
Tim Flatt

AGENCY:
Jack Lefkowitz Inc.

PUBLISHER:
Industrial Launderer

■ **361**

■ **357–362** Cover of the trade magazine *Industrial Launderer.* Left to right: Statistics on Potential Industry Growth; The New Face of Delivery Vehicles to Come; The First Fruits of a New Market go to Those who Take the Risk; Special issue on Selling Walk-off Mats; New Tax Reform means More Work for Accountants; and ID Labels with Bar Codes. (USA)

■ **357–362** Umschläge der Wäscherei-Fachzeitschrift *Industrial Launderer.* Die Themen v.l.n.r.: Statistik über das potentielle Wachstum; die Lieferwagen der Zukunft; die ersten Früchte eines neues Marktes ernten jene, die den ersten Schritt riskieren; Spezialausgabe über Fussmatten; die neue Steuerreform und Wäscheetiketten mit Computer Codes. (USA)

■ **357–362** Couvertures de la revue de blanchisserie industrielle *Industrial Launderer.* De g. à dr.: statistiques de croissance potentielle; les camionnettes de livraison de l'avenir; les premiers fruits d'un nouveau marché sont cueillis par ceux qui ont le goût du risque; les paillassons; la réforme fiscale et les comptables; le code barres dans la gestion moderne. (USA)

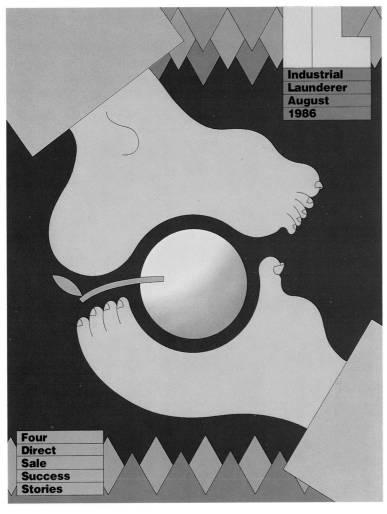

Industrial
Launderer
August
1986

Four
Direct
Sale
Success
Stories

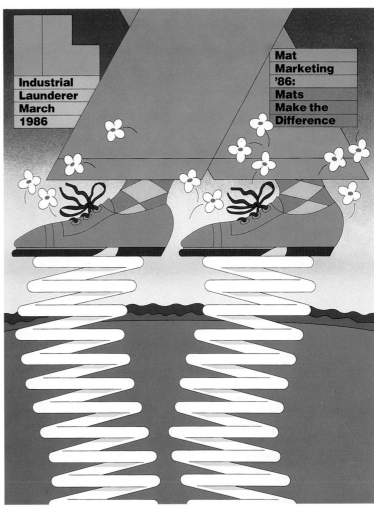

Industrial
Launderer
March
1986

Mat
Marketing
'86:
Mats
Make the
Difference

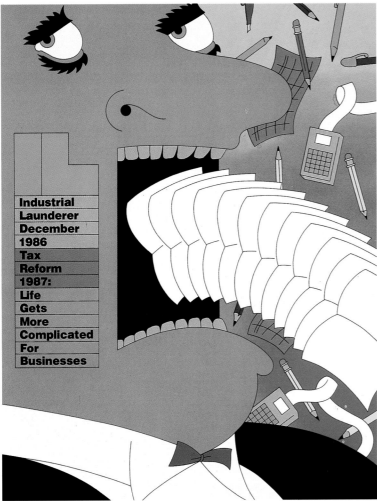

Industrial
Launderer
December
1986
Tax
Reform
1987:
Life
Gets
More
Complicated
For
Businesses

Industrial
Launderer
July
1986

Garment
Identification:
Computerized
Label
Printing

ART DIRECTOR:
Andrew Kner

DESIGNER:
Andrew Kner

PHOTOGRAPHER:
Jon Oertner

PUBLISHER:
RC Publications

■363

ART DIRECTOR:
Andrew Kner

DESIGNER:
Bob Conge

ILLUSTRATOR:
Bob Conge

AGENCY:
Conge Design

PUBLISHER:
RC Publications

■364

■363, 364 Two covers of the American graphic-art magazine *Print* Left: New York's famous Empire State Building, Right: illustrating "The Designer's Flash of Inspiration". (USA)

■365, 366 Two covers of *Photo Metro* a trade magazine published in San Francisco. Left, to publicize the *Photo Metro* Benefit Auction; right, "Humphrey and Tabby" by Lonnie Graham. (USA)

■363, 364 Umschläge des amerikanischen Graphik-Magazins *Print* 363zeigt das Empire State Building, das alte Wahrzeichen New Yorks; 364«Die Blitzidee des Designers». (USA)

■365, 366 Zwei Umschläge der Zeitschrift *Photo Metro* eine Photo-Fachzeitschrift. 365betrifft eine Auktion von *Photo Metro* 366«Humphrey and Tabby, 1978, Kenya» aufgenommen von Lonnie Graham. (USA)

■363, 364 Deux couvertures du magazine américain d'art graphique *Print* A g.: le fameux Empire State Building à New York; A dr.: le flash de l'inspiration chez le designer. (USA)

■365, 366 Deux couvertures de *Photo Metro* revue professionnelle publiée à San Francisco. A g., une vente aux enchères *Photo Metro* à dr., photo de «Humphrey and Tabby», par Lonnie Graham. (USA)

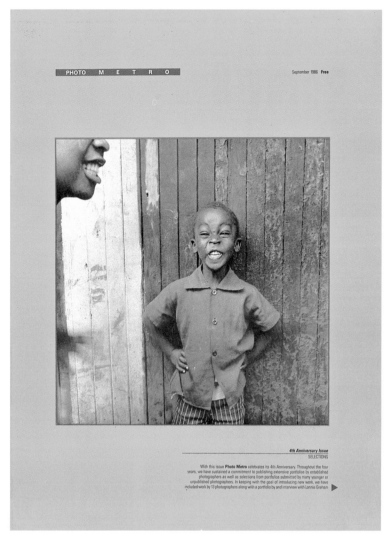

ART DIRECTOR:
Henry Brimmer

DESIGNER:
Brimmer, Mejia & Randall

PHOTOGRAPHER:
Steve Winter

AGENCY:
Henry Brimmer Design

PUBLISHER:
Photo Metro

■365

ART DIRECTOR:
Henry Brimmer

DESIGNER:
Brimmer, Mejia & Randall

PHOTOGRAPHER:
Lonnie Graham

AGENCY:
Henry Brimmer Design

PUBLISHER:
Photo Metro

■366

367–369 Cover and spreads from issues of *Skald, Royal Viking Line's* company magazine. Cover shows a Japanese boy wearing the traditional "happy coat" and headband; double spread shows Ayers Rock (Australia) and the gatefold spread presents treasures found on a round-the-world cruise. (USA)

370 Cover of the *American Ceramics* magazine. (USA)

371 For the Brazilian graphic-design magazine *Gràfica* (BRA)

367–369 Aus der *Skald*-Clubzeitschrift der *Royal Viking Line* Der Umschlag zeigt einen japanischen Jungen mit traditionellen Kleidungsstücken, die Doppelseite den Ayers Rock (Australien) und die Doppelseite mit Auslegern all die Schätze, die man bei einer Schiffsreise um die Welt entdecken kann. (USA)

370 Umschlag des Magazins *American Ceramics*. (USA)

371 Umschlag des brasilianischen Magazins *Gràfica* (BRA)

367–369 Couverture et doubles pages de *Skald* le magazine de *Royal Viking Line* La couverture montre un garçon japonais coiffé selon la coutume, la double page Ayers Rock en Australie, la double page dépliante les trésors qu'une croisière autour du monde permet de découvrir. (USA)

370 Couverture du magazine *American Ceramics*. (USA)

371 Couverture du magazine d'art graphique *Gràfica* (BRA)

ART DIRECTOR:
KIT HINRICHS
DESIGNER:
KIT HINRICHS/KAREN BERNDT
ILLUSTRATOR:
ROSEMARY WOODFORD GANF
PHOTOGRAPHER:
MICHELLE CLEMENT (COVER)
PETE TURNER/IMAGE BANK
AGENCY:
PENTAGRAM DESIGN, INC.
PUBLISHER:
ROYAL VIKING LINES
367–369

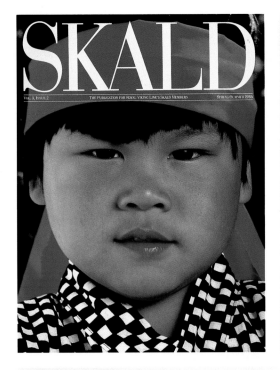

BY TOM KENEALLY

The country is as big as a continent. Its origins as a penal station for British criminals—and later as a destination for immigrants—shaped a national character of old-fashioned egalitarianism, or "mateship," and a tradition of service inspired in part by proving yourself to be a "good bloke."

AUSTRALIA

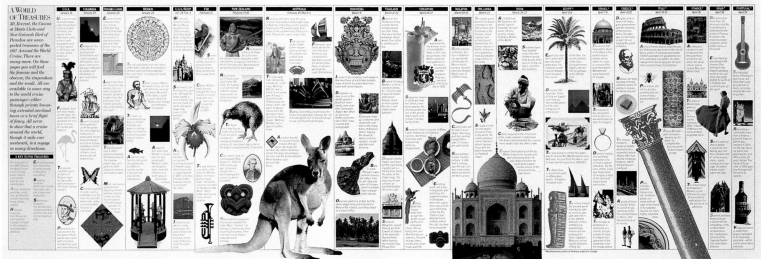

A WORLD OF TREASURES

ART DIRECTOR:
Douglas Frueh
DESIGNER:
Massimo Vignelli
PHOTOGRAPHER:
Brad Guice
AGENCY:
Vignelli Associates
PUBLISHER:
American Ceramics
■ **370**

ART DIRECTOR:
Oswaldo Miranda
DESIGNER:
Oswaldo Miranda
ILLUSTRATOR:
Marshal Arisman
AGENCY:
Miran Studio
PUBLISHER:
Grafica Magazine
■ **371**

ART DIRECTOR:
ROLF MÜLLER
DESIGNER:
ROMAN LORENZ/
BARBARA MIEDANER
PUBLISHER:
HEIDELBERGER DRUCKMASCH.
■ **372**

ART DIRECTOR:
ROLF MÜLLER
DESIGNER:
ROMAN LORENZ/
BARBARA MIEDANER
PHOTOGRAPHER:
ROLF MÜLLER
■ **373**

ART DIRECTOR:
ROLF MÜLLER
DESIGNER:
ROMAN LORENZ/
BARBARA MIEDANER
PHOTOGRAPHER:
MANFRED RIEKER
■ **374**

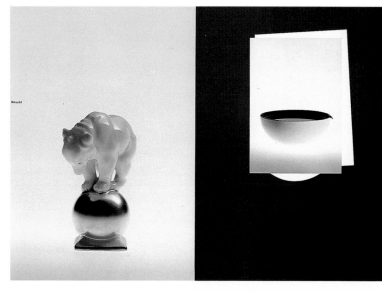

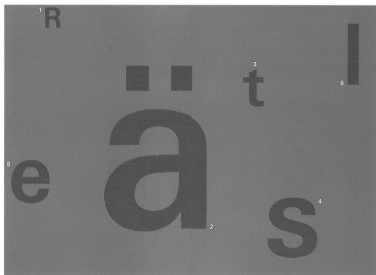

ART DIRECTOR:
ROLF MÜLLER
DESIGNER:
ROMAN LORENZ/BARBARA MIEDANER
PHOTOGRAPHER:
MANFRED RIEKER
AGENCY:
BÜRO ROLF MÜLLER
PUBLISHER:
HEIDELBERGER DRUCKMASCHINEN
■ **375**

ART DIRECTOR:
ROLF MÜLLER
DESIGNER:
ROMAN LORENZ/BARBARA MIEDANER
AGENCY:
BÜRO ROLF MÜLLER
PUBLISHER:
HEIDELBERGER DRUCKMASCHINEN
■ **376**

■ **372–380** Covers and spreads from issues of *HQ* (High Quality/Heidelberg Quality), a trade magazine to show the connection between good design and good printing. Published three times a year by Heidelberg Printing Machines AG, it features works by international contributors. Subject to the issue shown in *372* is "Puzzles and Puzzling" (see spreads *376–380*). The cover of an issue about bounderies is shown in *373*. Manfred Rieker photographed a visible boundary between kitsch and good design (see spreads *374, 375*). (GER)

■ **372–380** Umschläge und Doppelseiten von zwei Ausgaben der Zeitschrift *HQ* (High Quality/Heidelberg Qualität), welche die Verbindung von gutem Design und Druck zeigen will und von der Heidelberger Druckmaschinen AG herausgegeben wird. Hier der Umschlag zum Thema »Rätsel und Rätselhaftes« (*372*) und Doppelseiten der Ausgabe (*376-380*) sowie der Umschlag der Ausgabe »Grenzen« (*373*) und zwei Doppelseiten daraus (*374, 375*), die den Versuch einer sichtbaren Abgrenzung von Kitsch und gutem Design zeigen. (GER)

■ **372–380** Couvertures et doubles pages de *HQ* (High Quality/Heidelberg Quality), revue professionnelle d'un constructeur des machines à imprimer. Trois fois par an, la revue associe le design et l'impression de qualité dans des numéros bénéficiant d'une collaboration internationale. Ici un numéro sur le thème »Enigmes et choses insolites« (la couverture *372* et doubles pages *376-380*) ainsi qu'une couverture et deux pages doubles (*373-375*) d'un numéro sur les »frontières« visibles entre le kitsch et le design de qualité. (GER)

ART DIRECTOR:
ROLF MÜLLER
DESIGNER:
ROMAN LORENZ/
BARBARA MIEDANER
ILLUSTRATOR:
SEYMOUR CHWAST
■ 377

ART DIRECTOR:
ROLF MÜLLER
DESIGNER:
ROLF MÜLLER/
ROMAN LORENZ/BARBARA MIEDANER
PUBLISHER:
HEIDELBERGER DRUCKMASCHINEN
■ 378

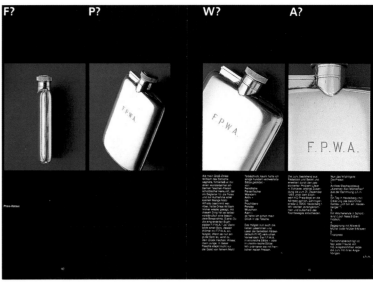

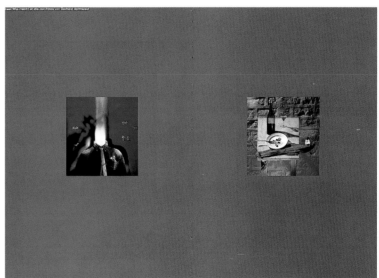

ART DIRECTOR:
ROLF MÜLLER
DESIGNER:
ROMAN LORENZ/BARBARA MIEDANER
AGENCY:
BÜRO ROLF MÜLLER
PUBLISHER:
HEIDELBERGER DRUCKMASCHINEN
■ 379

ART DIRECTOR:
ROLF MÜLLER
DESIGNER:
ROMAN LORENZ/BARBARA MIEDANER
PHOTOGRAPHER:
GERHARD VORMWALD
AGENCY:
BÜRO ROLF MÜLLER
PUBLISHER:
HEIDELBERGER DRUCKMASCHINEN
■ 380

I N N O V A

N E W S

1985 INNOVA Gala a success

Formica Product Design competition winners
(see inside)

VOKO (U.S.), Inc. signs lease at INNOVA

INNOVA announces AIA Library/Bookshop

Mike Vance at INNOVA

Names in the news

Product Profile

INNOVA's "Office" Update

C A L E N D A R

ICF becomes independent

First annual IBD masquerade a success!

ART DIRECTOR:
Craig Minor

DESIGNER:
Kenny Kane

STUDIO:
Creel Morell, Inc.

PUBLISHER:
Innova

■381, 382

ART DIRECTOR:
Peter Davenport/
Brian Griffin

DESIGNER:
Peter Davenport

PHOTOGRAPHER:
Brian Griffin

AGENCY:
Davenport Associates

PUBLISHER:
Rosehaugh Stanhope
Developments PLC

■383, 384

■**381, 382** Cover and spread from a newsletter issued by *Innova* (lessors of manufacturers' showroom facilities). (USA)

■**383, 384** Cover and spread from *Broadgate* magazine, a photographic newsletter showing progression of phases and specifications of a giant business complex in the City of London (Phases 1 and 2 of the total 9 phases built in 365 days.) (GBR)

■**381, 382** Vorderseite und Doppelseite eines Mitteilungsblattes von *Innova*, Vermieterin von Ausstellungsraum. (USA)

■**383, 384** Umschlag und Doppelseite des *Broadgate*-Magazins, das anhand von Aufnahmen über die Fortschritte der Bauphasen (hier 1 und 2 von 9 in 365 Tagen) und Einzelheiten eines Geschäftskomplexes in der City von London informiert. (GBR)

■**381, 382** Couverture et double page d'un bulletin d'information publié par *Innova*, qui loue des locaux d'exposition. (USA)

■**383, 384** Couverture et double page du magazine *Broadgate*. Ce bulletin illustré renseigne sur l'avancement des travaux d'un complexe d'affaires dans la City de Londres: ici, les étapes 1 et 2, sur 9 au total à exécuter en 365 jours. (GBR)

2 BROADGATE MAGAZINE

BROADGATE MAGAZINE 3

BUILT

PHASES 1 AND 2
Inaugurated by

The Rt. Hon.
Margaret Thatcher
Prime Minister
11 July 1986

ART DIRECTOR:
Richard Hess/Lyle Metzdorf

DESIGNER:
Richard Hess

ILLUSTRATOR:
John Alcorn

AGENCY:
Jonson Pirtle Pedersen
Alcorn Metzdorf & Hess

PUBLISHER:
Chase Manhattan Bank

■385

ART DIRECTOR:
Richard Hess
Lyle Metzdorf

DESIGNER:
Richard Hess

PHOTOGRAPHER:
Tom Hollyman
Lyle Metzdorf

AGENCY:
Jonson Pirtle Pedersen
Alcorn Metzdorf & Hess

PUBLISHER:
Edward S. Gordon

■386, 389

Vol. I, No. 3

September/October 1986

THE INDIVIDUAL BANKER

STEPPING OUT ACROSS THE U.S.A.

PERSONAL
FINANCIAL
SERVICES'
GROWTH
IS
ONE
EXAMPLE
OF
INDIVIDUAL
BANKING'S
NATIONWIDE
PUSH.

STORY
ON PAGE
FOUR

■**385** Cover of *The Individual Banker,* the house organ of the Chase Manhattan Bank. The illustration relates to an article on the Corporation's plan of nationwide development. (USA)

■**386–389** Cover (aerial view of footbridge linking Manhattan with Ward's Island) and spreads from *Gordon's New York,* a construction company's magazine. Spreads top to bottom: postmodern architecture in Midtown West; rising costs of N.Y. constructions; Javits Convention Center. (USA)

■**385** Umschlag der Hauszeitschrift der Chase Manhattan Bank. Die Illustration bezieht sich auf einen Beitrag über die landesweiten Expansionsbestrebungen der Bank. (USA)

■**386–389** Umschlag (Luftaufnahme einer Fussgängerbrücke zwischen Manhattan und Ward's Island) und Doppelseiten aus *Gordon's New York* Magazin eines Bauunternehmens. Die Doppelseiten v.o.n.u.: Postmoderne Architektur; steigende Baukosten in New York; das Javits Convention Center. (USA)

■**385** Couverture de l'*Individual Banker,* revue d'entreprise de la Chase Manhattan Bank. L'illustration se rapporte au projet d'implantation nationale de la Chase Manhattan. (USA)

■**386–389** Couverture (vue aérienne d'une passerelle entre Manhattan et Ward's Island) et doubles pages de *Gordon's New York* magazine d'un entrepreneur. De haut en bas, ces doubles pages représentent le postmodernisme à Manhattan, le coût croissant de la construction, le palais des congrès Javits. (USA)

The long awaited rebirth of Midtown West is finally underway. The legal stimulants for the shift of office construction to Midtown West — tax and zoning advantages — are potent economic medicine. One way or another, the city has tinkered with the designs for a quarter century. The effort to fine-tune the controls continues, but one thing is now certain: the "old apple" is in for a brand new shine.

The New West Side Story.

After years of studies, plans, debates, lawsuits, politics, pressure, and compromise, the stage has begun to clear over the redevelopment of Manhattan's west side. When all is said and done, the result will be nothing less than a stunning transformation of Midtown West. In the next five to ten years New York's commercial, tourist, and entertainment life will have a vital new center.

Leading the charge in this remarkable metamorphosis are two gigantic redevelopment projects which are proceeding almost simultaneously: the $2 billion face lift for Times Square, (including both renovated and new theaters), and the $1 billion reconstruction of the New York Coliseum site on Columbus Circle.

Not far behind these mega-projects are the 15 to 20 million square feet of new office space — enough to accommodate 85,000 employees — slated for construction on the west side of Midtown in the coming decade.

The current boom in office space development has been fueled by a series of events: On the east side of Midtown, where scores of sleek new office towers have risen in recent years, few sites remain that are large enough for buildings of substantial size.

Land prices per buildable square foot on the west side are lower — quite a bit lower a few years ago than today, but still low enough to enable developers to build office space at comparatively attractive rents.

Important and complex zoning law changes approved in 1983 reflect a conscious decision by the city government to reduce the quantity of construction on the east side of Manhattan and encourage it on the west side in the interests of better environmental balance.

Real estate tax incentives for new commercial construction (and major remodeling) have also been adjusted to increase the prospect for profits from office building construction on the west side.

For office building with zoning and tax inducements, the boundaries of Midtown West are not just locations west of Fifth Avenue. Thanks to the durable success of Rockefeller Center, which spread west in the 1960's from its original site between Fifth and Sixth Avenues to encompass the west side of Sixth Avenue as well, the city government has defined the east border of "Midtown West" as a line 150 feet west of Sixth Avenue. The new tax incentives and more generous zoning rules apply only to the west of that boundary in midtown, all the way to the Hudson River, north to 96th Street (from Central Park West) and below 34th Street across the entire island — except for an excluded sector in the financial district.

As a practical matter, however, the office development action is confined to the land between that mid-block eastern border, the Penn Station area, West 62nd Street, and Eighth Avenue (with an occasional outpost on Ninth Avenue).

Today, much of that large and diverse area—one of the nation's most valuable central locations—is cluttered with obsolete and dilapidated structures. Midtown West did not always suffer from such comparative neglect. Large and prestigious corporations including General Motors, U.S. Rubber, and Permanent Pictures once had major offices along Broadway or Seventh Avenue between Times Square and Columbus Circle. The Astor Hotel, at Broadway and 44th Street, The Metropolitan Opera House, and the Great White Way added glamour and vitality to the neighborhood.

It may seem curious to laymen that efforts to press Midtown West

---

VOLUME II · Gordon's · WINTER 1986

NEWYORK

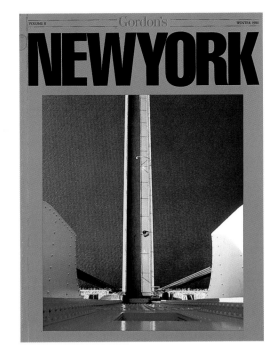

ART DIRECTOR:
Richard Hess/Lyle Metzdorf

DESIGNER:
Richard Hess

PHOTOGRAPHER:
Peter B. Kaplan

AGENCY:
Jonson Pirtle Pedersen Alcorn Metzdorf & Hess

PUBLISHER:
Edward S. Gordon

■387

Arbitrary, astronomical, or absurd? Our primer on the cost of constructing an office building in New York claims "none of the above." The volatility of interest rates in recent years has made it difficult to accurately forecast break-even rents. Three components of financing are construction, carrying charges, and permanent financing.

WHY ARE NEW YORK CON-STRUC-TION COSTS SO HIGH?

Land, construction costs, and financing: To a commercial real estate developer these words represent the keys to a successful project or land moves that can sabotage their dreams. Based on these three variables, developers calculate their costs of new construction and establish their "threshold" or break-even rents on new buildings. Considering that construction of an office tower can take up to five years from concept to completion—and that price swings in land, construction costs, and financing can be enormous—it becomes clear just how critical and complex those calculations really are. Ultimately, the prices paid by developers will affect the prices paid by tenants.

Land cost encompasses all the factors connected with readying a site for construction: demolition, site preparation, carrying charges, legal fees, and the buying out of leasehold estates. The island of Manhattan has strict boundaries; the prime area for commercial tenancy is also stringently defined. As demand for space in midtown expands, land prices can hit astronomical heights.

Since large parcels are scarce, assembling construction sites for buildings with large floors is becoming much more difficult than ever before. Tenants who require large blocks of contiguous space will pay a premium for it.

Quotes of land prices in midtown Manhattan range from $800 per square foot on the West Side to $3,000 on the East Side. What do they mean? The true value of land depends on what a developer can do with it. Developers refer to land prices in terms of buildable square feet. The number of square feet that a developer can build in relation to every square foot of land he buys is contingent upon the zoning rights that control a site's Floor to Area Ratio or FAR. For example, an FAR of 15 means a developer can build 30 square feet of building area for each one square

foot of land area. The higher the FAR, the greater a building's rentable space. On the West Side, the FAR average is 18; under certain circumstances it goes as high as 21.6. On the East Side, the FAR ranges from 10 to 18. Using the average of 15 FAR, land can rise up to $200 per buildable square foot.

Zoning is an extremely complex issue; many variables affect many different districts. What follows is an overview in broad strokes.

A developer has the choice of building "as of right," within zoning guidelines, or to go through the long, complicated and expensive procedures of trying to supersede the guidelines and build "not as of right." In so doing, the developer faces zoning district limitations regarding bulk, setbacks, and sky exposure planes. He must also consider the end use for which the area is zoned. Finally, a developer who wants to build in a special district has to weigh the effect of its particular stipulations on his plans.

In some districts the City of New York offers developers increased FAR and with that the ability to erect bigger, taller buildings on specific sites if the builder agrees to erect or upgrade public services or amenities as part of a project. For example, under certain circumstances a developer can increase his FAR by as much as 20% if he agrees to improve an adjacent subway station. (Case in point: developer Mortimer Zuckerman is required to plan their buildings around a design criteria and daylight diagram. An architect uses the formula which allows for light and air to the street and may restrict bulk as a guideline. The formula varies from the East to the West Side.

Design plays an increasingly important role in deciding the size of a building, and, in effect, its FAR. Since 1984 developers have been part of his deal (for the Coliseum site.)

ART DIRECTOR:
Richard Hess/Lyle Metzdorf

DESIGNER:
Richard Hess

ILLUSTRATOR:
Mark Hess

AGENCY:
Jonson Pirtle Pedersen Alcorn Metzdorf & Hess

PUBLISHER:
Edward S. Gordon

■388

The product of 20 years of planning, six years of construction, and a budget of $486 million, the new state-owned Jacob K. Javits Convention Center (facing page) stretches from Eleventh to Twelfth Avenues between 34th and 35th Streets. I.M. Pei & Partners designed the 18-story building which is attracting thousands of people to Midtown West.

Since the turn of the century Times Square has been the site of America's most joyful public celebrations. But besides its internationally known New Year's Eve "ball" and its great Broadway theaters, the blocks surrounding the Square (below) also have a reputation for their seediness. Clean-up has suffered many false starts and stalls before the current plans promised success.

development in recent years have been at best too scattered and sporadic to overcome the onslaught of urban blight. This area, which includes attractions such as the theater district and Carnegie Hall, offers the most extensive network of mass transportation facilities in the city. Four subways, the Sixth, Seventh and Eighth Avenue lines, and the Broadway BMT line, run north and south through the area, or near it, and the Number 7 crosstown subway runs across it east and west. The subways provide quick access to commuter and long-haul trains at both Penn Station and Grand Central Terminal, and to the Port Authority Bus Terminal at Eighth Avenue and 42nd Street. Despite these assets, even the transformation of the west side of Sixth Avenue in the 1960s and early 1970s—from a jumble of old, broken-down brick structures into a corridor of blockbuster office skyscrapers—failed to spread to the streets immediately to the west.

Despite the popular impression to the contrary, there was a considerable amount of office building in Midtown West during the late 1960s and early 1970s. A compilation by the New York Real Estate Board lists nineteen structures with a total of nearly 13 million square feet of office space built in the entire area between 1965 and 1972. It should be noted, however, that a quarter of that total was contained in two glass-sheathed skyscrapers near Penn Station, one of 57 stories and the other 51 stories high. Eleven of these nineteen buildings line Broadway between 51st and 67th Streets. Their architecture, though modern

in style, was not particularly distinguished. Most of it was monotonously similar: glass sheathing with narrow vertical mullions of thermolytic aluminum or stainless steel—the signature of the era. These buildings appealed to companies that were anxious to escape rising rents on the east side of Midtown. As the last of these structures went up, a glut of Manhattan office space halted new office construction for several years.

One of the most striking aspects of the renaissance in Midtown West office development is the wide use of architects who are regarded as among today's foremost designers. Names like Skidmore, Owings & Merrill, Edward Larrabee Barnes, Moshe Safdie, I.M. Pei, Philip Johnson and partner John Burgee are participants in many of the largest and most significant projects now taking shape. The quality of their work has already been demonstrated in the first of the "new generation" of office skyscrapers — Equitable Life Assurance Society's handsome 54-story office tower at 787 Seventh Avenue, which was designed by Edward Larrabee Barnes and covers the entire block between West 51st and 52nd Streets.

Equitable, the nation's third largest life insurance company, poured some $200 million into the edifice, including a huge budget for art and sculpture as well as lavish public amenities. The insurance company moved its headquarters into the top third of the 1.5 million square foot building but fell; it has been asking Park Avenue rents for the balance: $40 to $50 per square foot, compared with about $35 per square foot for other modern but less sensational buildings nearby.

ART DIRECTOR:
Amanda Tatham

DESIGNER:
Amanda Tatham/Gill Davies

ILLUSTRATOR:
Ian Hands/Allan Drummond

STUDIO:
Lambton Place Design

CLIENT:
Next plc

■ 390–395

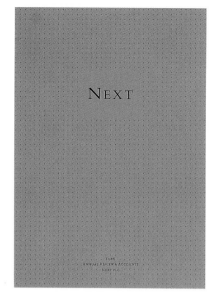

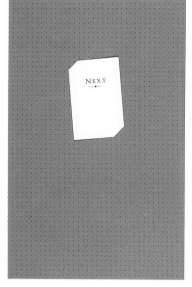

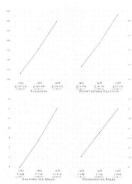

◼**390–395** Duskjacket, frontispiece spread (title inset on loose card) and four further spreads from the 1986 annual report of Next plc., a group manufacturing and retailing *Next* clothing (recently diversified also into mail order and property development). (GBR)

◼**396–398** Cover and spreads of the 1986 annual report of Micom Systems, Inc., a leading producer of data communications products. Quotes from the text that represent key elements of 1986 are interpreted in the lighthearted illustrations. Shown: "Choices" and "Back to Basic". (USA)

◼**390–395** Schutzumschlag, Frontispiz (Titel auf separater, in die Klappe eingesteckter Karte) und vier weitere Doppelseiten aus dem Jahresbericht 1986 für *Next* eine Gruppe, die Kleidung herstellt und vertreibt (und kürzlich unter anderem auch in den Versandhandel eingestiegen ist). (GBR)

◼**396–398** Umschlag und Doppelseiten aus dem 1986 Jahresbericht der Micom Systems, eines Herstellers auf dem Gebiet der elektronischen Datenvermittlung. Humorvolle Illustrationen interpretieren die wichtigsten Aussagen des Begleittextes, hier »Entscheidungen« und »Zurück zur Basis«. (USA)

◼**390–395** Jaquette, double page du frontispice (titre sur carte mobile encartée) et quatre doubles pages du rapport annuel 1986 de Next plc., groupe fabriquant et distribuant les vêtements *Next* qui s'est adjoint récemment un département de V.P.C. et de gestion immobilière. (GBR)

◼**396–398** Couverture et pages doubles du rapport annuel 1986 de Micom Systems, Inc., l'un des grands fabricants de systèmes de communication de données. Des illustrations humoristiques interprètent les faits marquants du rapport, ici: «les choix à faire», «retour aux sources». (USA)

ART DIRECTOR:
Robert Miles Runyan

DESIGNER:
Douglas Joseph

ILLUSTRATOR:
Guy Billout

AGENCY:
Robert Miles Runyan & Associates

CLIENT:
Micom Systems, Inc.

◼ **396–398**

MICOM *Systems, Inc.*

1986   Annual Report

Fiscal Year Ended March 31, 1986

ART DIRECTOR:
Kit Hinrichs

DESIGNER:
Kit Hinrichs/Karen Berndt

ILLUSTRATOR:
Doug Johnson

AGENCY:
Pentagram Design, Inc.

CLIENT:
MGM/UA Communications Company

■ 399–402

MGM/UA
COMMUNICATIONS CO.
ANNUAL REPORT
1986

"TWO PROUD
PASTS.
ONE GLORIOUS
FUTURE."

Note: MGM/UA owns some or all of the worldwide rights to a large number of films and TV programs including approximately 950 feature films and 87 TV series from the United Artists catalogue. In addition, MGM/UA has the worldwide home video distribution rights for 15 years and the worldwide theatrical distribution rights for ten years for all of the approximately 2,950 films in the MGM library (including much of the pre-1950 Warner Bros. catalogue). On the following pages, the films that are currently in the MGM/UA library are denoted by (•) and the MGM films, to which MGM/UA maintains worldwide home video and theatrical distribution rights, are denoted by (›). Films without a (•) or a (›) are no longer distributed by MGM/UA.

The film industry's evolution begins in 1895, with audiences witnessing for the first time phantom images moving across a silver screen. Since that time, films have left an indelible imprint on the imaginations and cultural identities of each succeeding generation. Movies continue to be a part of nearly everyone's life, with today's audiences—reached through theaters, television, cable TV, home video and other formats—numbering in the billions.

MGM and United Artists have played an integral part in the industry's development from the very start. The two companies' films have attracted, entertained and influenced audiences the world over, and, despite their distinct operating histories, both companies have been driven by the same goal from the very beginning: providing the very best in top-quality entertainment.

1919
THE MGM/UA STORY
1986

Just as World War II touches every person's life, so too does it influence films. And films influence the war effort, as well.

Hollywood masters its resources to back the war effort, motivating the audiences at home and the troops on the battle lines. Thousands of front line soldiers view the latest films from Hollywood at "Beach Head Bijous"—stark contrast from the movie palaces that had been built in the twenties and thirties.

The effect of the movies on the war is noted even by Winston Churchill, who credits the impact of Mrs. Miniver, as being worth "many battleships" in England's effort.

After the war's end, other factors begin to affect the film industry. In the United States, veterans are having children in unprecedented numbers, and the new families are spending money to buy consumer goods. One "appliance" in particular captures the family's interest, Television.

Between 1947 and 1951, the number of homes with TV sets in the U.S. grows from a handful to 10 million.

For the first time, a generation grows up with entertainment as an everyday event. It will soon become an everyday necessity. They are the Baby Boomers who, as they grow, will continue to be avid entertainment consumers.

But while TV searches for its audience, it is constrained by the limits of young technology and production techniques. Early on, it is essentially a visual version of radio.

Theatrical films continue their hold on worldwide audiences by stressing things TV cannot—the big screen, big stars, big directors.

Both MGM and United Artists release impressive hits capitalizing on these differences. Howard Hawks, one of the great independent producers and directors of the time, creates Red River for United Artists. It is a popular and critical success, reinforcing the heroic scope of the Western. MGM, celebrating its 25th anniversary in 1949, marks the occasion with two hits of its own: Adam's Rib and On the Town.

Red River, 1948

For MGM/UA Communications Co., today is the culmination of a history that began 67 years ago. It is also the start of a new history—one that will take the company into the years ahead.

MGM/UA Communications Co. has, as its base, the work and product of two distinct and glorious pasts—MGM's and United Artists'. Building on that base is an organization that is uniquely positioned for growth in several media in the years ahead—theatrical motion pictures, home video, pay and basic cable television, network television and TV syndication. In the next 12 to 18 months, many of the steps toward that future will become evident.

In addition to the near term releases (some of which are illustrated on the following pages), the company intends to broaden its base, through internal growth and acquisition of enterprises related to its core business—communications and entertainment.

The communications and entertainment industries will continue to merge into one global industry, and MGM/UA Communications Co. will have a fundamental role in it. But the legacy that has served MGM and United Artists since the very beginning will remain our guiding principle today and tomorrow: Providing the audience with top-quality entertainment.

ART DIRECTOR:
Michael Weymouth

DESIGNER:
Jose Lizardo

ILLUSTRATOR:
Jose Lizardo

PHOTOGRAPHER:
George Simian

STUDIO:
Weymouth Design, Inc.

CLIENT:
Art Directors Club Boston

■ **403–405**

■ **399–402** Cover and three double spreads from the 1986 annual report of MGM/UA Communications Co. The report is illustrated with stills from MGM/UA films (for which the corporation owns worldwide home video rights.) *401* shows a film still from *Red River* (1948). (USA)

■ **403–405** Double spreads and cover from the Art Directors Club of Boston 1986 Annual Review. Portrayed in the spreads are Dick Pantano and Geoff Currier. (USA)

■ **399–402** Umschlag und drei Doppelseiten aus dem Jahresbericht 1986 der MGM/UA Communications Co. Der Bericht ist mit Standphotos aus den Filmen illustriert, für die diese Gesellschaft die weltweiten Heimvideo-Rechte besitzt. *401* zeigt ein Standphoto aus dem Film *Red River* (1948). (USA)

■ **403–405** Doppelseiten und Umschlag des Jahresberichtes 1986 des Art Directors Club von Boston, hier mit Porträts der Art-Direktoren Dick Pantano und Geoff Currier. (USA)

■ **399–402** Couverture et trois doubles pages du rapport annuel de MGM/UA Communications pour 1986, rapport illustré de photos de travail des films MGM/UA pour lesquels la société possède les droits mondiaux de reproduction vidéo. La fig. *401* est une photo de travail du film *Red River* tourné en 1948. (USA)

■ **403–405** Doubles pages et couverture du rapport annuel 1986 de l'Art Directors Club de Boston. Doubles pages illustrées des portraits de Dick Pantano et Geoff Currier. (USA)

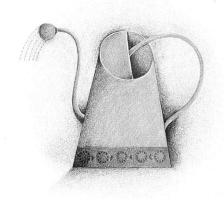

SUNBELT NURSERY GROUP, INC. ANNUAL REPORT 1986
For the year ended August 31, 1986

FINANCIAL STATEMENTS

SELECTED FINANCIAL DATA

(Dollars in thousands except per share data)

	Year ended August 31,				
	1986	1985	1984	1983	1982
SUMMARY OF OPERATIONS					
Revenues	$131,885	$126,570	$97,864	$78,241	$70,582
Gross profit	55,004	53,069	42,608	33,487	30,303
Income before income taxes	1,514	3,953	6,676	4,352	3,695
Income before extraordinary credit	782	2,071	3,476	2,267	1,936
Net income*	782	2,071	5,789	3,972	3,313
Net income per share*	.21	.55	.94	.61	.52
FINANCIAL POSITION					
Working capital	4,566	3,513	4,653	4,388	5,459
Inventories	15,692	15,722	13,925	10,553	8,947
Net property, plant and equipment	13,822	13,664	10,190	8,167	9,253
Total assets	45,378	44,350	39,797	25,439	23,134
Long-term debt and capital lease obligations	4,351	2,532	2,759	3,011	3,331
Shareholders' equity	25,958	26,788	24,717	15,448	12,507
OTHER INFORMATION					
Cash provided by operations	8,667	4,339	5,228	3,582	2,196
Depreciation and amortization	2,885	2,268	1,587	1,313	1,292
Capital expenditures	2,680	5,398	1,959	649	689
Weighted average shares outstanding**	3,751	3,783	3,783	3,785	3,783
Number of retail stores	114	103	98	80	81

Includes unaudited pro forma earnings for the three years ended August 31, 1984 adjusted to reflect income taxes on a separate company basis.

**Pro forma weighted average shares outstanding for August 31, 1985, 1984, 1983 and 1982.*

ART DIRECTOR:
Ron Sullivan

DESIGNER:
Ron Sullivan
Willie Baronet

ILLUSTRATOR:
Linda Helton/Gerry Kano

AGENCY:
Sullivan Perkins

CLIENT:
Sunbelt Nurseries, Inc.

■ 406–408

nies economies of scale by centralizing accounting and management systems and through increased purchasing power.

Aside from its stores, the Company operates warehouses and growing facilities, which produce a small portion of what it sells. But most of Sunbelt's products are acquired, increasing the Company's flexibility. Because Sunbelt purchases from a wide variety of suppliers, it is free of dependence upon a single source of supply.

A good place to grow. Customer-oriented, service-oriented, Sunbelt Nursery Group is well on its way to achieving its destiny: to be the premier professional retailer of garden center merchandise in the Sunbelt, a gardening resource for our customers, and a profitable investment for each of you, our shareholders. In the next fiscal year, we intend to increase earnings per share; to intensify our management training and development efforts in support of our plans for growth; to standardize the look of our stores, with signage and

N ourishing a root system is crucial to the flourishing of any plant; so, too, for the operating companies of Sunbelt Nursery Group, which have well-rooted relationships with customers and suppliers. In Texas and Oklahoma, the Company has been doing business nearly 70 years.

display; to enhance our marketing efforts; to continue our expansion program, adding stores to take advantage of the continuing growth of the nursery industry. Where opportunities exist, Sunbelt will also pursue the possibility of acquiring other garden centers and nursery chains.

We are grateful to our directors, officers, and the 2000 employees of Sunbelt Nursery Group and its operating companies for the successes of the past year. With their support and yours, we look forward to the year ahead, and we invite you to grow with us.

Travis W. Bain II
President and Chief Executive Officer

October 10, 1986

■ **406–408** Cover and spreads from the 1986 annual report of the Sunbelt Nursery Group, garden centers and retailers of nursery/garden products. Messages on illustration pages relate both to gardening and to Sunbelt's business procedure. (USA)

■ **409–413** Cover and spreads from the 1986 annual report of H.J. Heinz Company. "In 1886 the founder sailed for England . . ." and the report celebrates the centennial of that day with paintings, line drawings and a history of its 100 years of being a multi-national. The cover illustration was painted in 1878. (USA)

■ **406–408** Umschlag und Doppelseiten aus dem Jahresbericht 1986 der Sunbelt Nursery Group, Gartenzentren und Gärtnereiprodukte. Die Botschaften der illustrierten Seiten beziehen sich sowohl auf das Gärtnern wie auf die Geschäftspolitik. (USA)

■ **409–413** Umschlag und Doppelseiten aus dem Jahresbericht 1986 der H.J. Heinz Company. «1886 segelte der Gründer nach England . . .» Der Bericht feiert den hundertsten Jahrestag dieses Ereignisses, mit dem der Weg zu einem multinationalen Unternehmen begann, mit Bildern und Zeichnungen. (USA)

■ **406–408** Couverture et doubles pages du rapport annuel 1986 du Sunbelt Nursery Group, qui regroupe des centres de jardinage et des pépiniéristes. Les messages des illustrations concernent le jardinage et la politique commerciale de Sunbelt. (USA)

■ **409–413** Couverture et pages doubles du rapport annuel 1986 de la H.J. Heinz Co. «En 1886, le fondateur s'embarqua pour l'Angleterre...» Ce centenaire est célébré par des peintures, des dessins au trait et un historique de cette multinationale. L'illustration de couverture est une peinture de 1878. (USA)

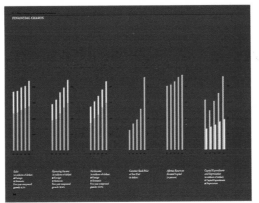

ART DIRECTOR:
Bennett Robinson

DESIGNER:
*Bennett Robinson/
Meera Singh*

ILLUSTRATOR:
*John Berkey 411
Kim ko Y Craft 412*

AGENCY:
Corporate Graphics, Inc.

CLIENT:
H.J. Heinz

■ 409–413

ART DIRECTOR:
Stephen Frykholm

DESIGNER:
Stephen Frykholm

PHOTOGRAPHER:
Nick Merrick

CLIENT:
Herman Miller, Inc.

■ **414–416**

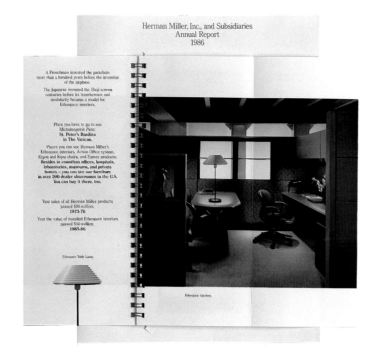

■ **414–416** Views of the Herman Miller, Inc. and Subsidiaries annual report for 1986 which also includes a tall spiral-bound brochure in its folder cover. The brochure has several double-width pages that fold out, for example in the lower illustration showing *Ethospace* interior and lamp. (USA)

■ **414–416** Ansichten aus dem Jahresbericht 1986 der Herman Miller Inc., einschliesslich Niederlassungen. Eine schmale, spiral-gebundene Broschüre ist in die Vorderseite des Berichtes einge-steckt. Sie enthält mehrere ausklappbare Seiten, hier ein Beispiel mit *Ethospace*-Möbeln und Lampe. (USA)

■ **414–416** Illustrations du rapport annuel de Herman Miller, Inc. et succursales pour 1986, dont la couverture comporte une brochure à reliure spirale. La brochure contient plusieurs pages qui se déplient au double de leur largeur, comme l'illustration du bas, qui montre des meubles et un éclairage *Ethospace*. (USA)

The first Survival System™ built to take you to hell and back.

Seems as though every knifemaker in the country has jumped onto the "survival" bandwagon, but only a few make survival knives tough enough to stake your life on.

You can bet the two Western® survival knives you see here will be around for a century of hard use. You have our 100-year full warranty behind it.

These knives are more than virtually indestructible. They have the features that a commando would want on his toughest mission. Like a broad, razor-sharp, saber-ground blade of the finest chrome-vanadium steel. Like a saw that's as tough as nails. And an end-knob that's able to drive 'em.

Some "survival knives" have hollow handles for accessories with a compass on the end knob; we think accessories belong in a sheath's pouch. Our 221 and new 221C knives give you the kind of storage room needed for a compass, matches – even hook, line, and sinkers.

A. The 221C "Camo Survival System" is our newest survival knife. Its reinforced handle is made of Valox®, one of the toughest composite materials made. It's specially scalloped for a better grip and shaped to fit even the biggest lumberjack's mitt. The 221C comes with a rugged fabric sheath with a plastic blade guard/sleeve, a camo-colored zippered front pouch with Velcro® closures, and an olive drab belt loop.

B. Our 221 survival knife got rave reviews wherever it was shown. We listened to the comments of knife experts from coast to coast to assure you that the production model is clearly today's premier survival knife. And now Western gives you a choice: the original Model 221 Survival System in basic black, and our 221C in today's favorite deepwoods color: camo. The 221 comes with the black sheath shown below.

The first lightweight knives that don't cut corners.

The finest lightweight knives yet – our Mighty Lights™ – have become an overnight success because they give sportsmen the feel, performance, and good looks of heavier, costlier knives – yet they don't weigh one gram more than they have to.

The scalloped, lightweight design of these knives lets them fit the hand better for incredibly easy handling. And, thanks to durable Valox® handles, they can really take a beating.

For 1986, our Mighty Lights are available in both black and hunter green. The 526 and 546 black knives come with gray ballistic cloth sheaths and Velcro® closures; their 526G and 546G green counterparts have camouflaged sheaths making them ideal for hunters, survivalists, campers. And you.

A. The new Model 516G Mighty Light, like all five of its brothers, features a 440A stainless steel blade that's warranted shaving sharp, right out of the box. Like all Western® blades, it has the proper heat treatment to make it really hold an edge, yet be easy to resharpen.

B. Our new mid-sized 526G Mighty Light has a 2½" stainless blade, ideal for most camping needs. Backpackers and climbers will like the way all our Mighty Lights deliver big knife performance – without a gram of excess weight.

C. The new 546G hunter green Mighty Light and the 546 (in black, right) are our longest and heftiest lightweights, yet they still only weigh 3½ ounces. Both knives have durable, versatile 3½" clip blades in stainless. On your hip or in your pack or pocket, you'll hardly know a Mighty Light knife is there. But you'll be glad it is.

For more on the weights and lengths of these and all our Cuts Above knives, see page 14.

Now available in black and hunter green.

ART DIRECTOR:
Linda Berg
ILLUSTRATOR:
Richard Wehrman
AGENCY:
Hutchins/Y&R
CLIENT:
Western Cutlery Co.
■**417, 418**

417, 418 With 75 years of knifemaking behind them, *Western Cutlery* celebrate their diamond anniversary with a catalog of their sports knives pictured in actual size. (USA)

419 Black-and-white photograph to illustrate a newspaper ad from a campaign for *Euroshell* to promote credit-card systems for goods vehicles – for tanking and servicing. (GER)

417, 418 Sportmesser in Originalgrösse aus einem Katalog der *Western Cutlery*, die damit auf eine 75jährige Tradition in der Herstellung von Messern aufmerksam macht. (USA)

419 Schwarzweissaufnahme aus einer Kampagne für das *Euroshell*-Kreditkartensystem für LKWs und Busse, die dadurch Kraftstoff- und Servicekosten sparen können. (GER)

417, 418 *Western Cutlery* a fêté ses 75 ans d'activité dans la coutellerie par la publication de ce catalogue où des couteaux de sport sont représentés en grandeur nature. (USA)

419 Photo noir et blanc pour une annonce de journal pleine page dans une campagne *Euroshell* visant à établir l'usage des cartes de crédit pour les véhicules utilitaires. (GER)

ART DIRECTOR:
MICHAEL GRAF HOCHBERG
ILLUSTRATOR:
PETER KRÄMER
AGENCY:
ART DIRECTION
CLIENT:
EURO SHELL GMBH
■**419**

DUGALD STERMER
1844 Union Street
San Francisco 94123

Joe

L O U I S

ART DIRECTOR:
Wendy Thomas
ILLUSTRATOR:
Dugald Stermer
PUBLISHER:
Monthly Detroit
■**420**

ART DIRECTOR:
Howard Koslow
DESIGNER:
Marvin Koenigsberg
ILLUSTRATOR:
Howard Koslow
CLIENT:
Howard Koslow
■**421–430**

■**420** Portrait of American heavyweight world champion Joe Louis as illustration in the *Monthly Detroit* magazine. (USA)

■**421–430** Portraits of American "Heroes" from a one-man exhibition of paintings by Howard Koslow at the Museum of American Illustration. Shown are, top left to right: Nathan B. Forrest, George Washington, General Custer, David D. Porter, Matthew Perry. Bottom row: Matthew Ridgway, George Patton Jr., Holland Smith, Edward V. Rickenbacker, Charles E. Yeager. (USA)

■**420** Porträt von Joe Louis, dem amerikanischen Boxweltmeister im Schwergewicht, aus *Monthly Detroit* (USA)

■**421–430** Porträts amerikanischer Militär-Helden für die Einladung zu einer Ausstellung von Howard Koslow im Museum of American Illustration. Oben v.l.n.r.: Nathan B. Forrest, George Washington, General Custer, David D. Porter, Matthew Perry. Unten v.l.n.r.: Matthew Ridgway, George Patton Jr., Holland Smith, Edward V. Rickenbacker, Charles E. Yeager. (USA)

■**420** Portrait de Joe Louis, champion du monde des poids lourds, en pleine page du magazine *Monthly Detroit* (USA)

■**421–430** Portraits de grands militaires américains dans une exposition individuelle du peintre Howard Koslow au Musée de l'illustration américaine. En haut, de g. à dr.: Nathan B. Forrest, George Washington, George Custer, David D. Porter, Matthew Perry. En bas, de g. à dr.: Matthew Ridgway, George Patton Jr., Holland Smith, Edward V. Rickenbacker, Charles E. Yeager. (USA)

ART DIRECTOR:
Michael Aron

DESIGNER:
Michael Aron

ILLUSTRATOR:
Terry Widener

AGENCY:
Michael Aron Design

CLIENT:
New York Magazine

■431

ART DIRECTOR:
Jeff Boudreau

DESIGNER:
Jeff Boudreau

ILLUSTRATOR:
Douglas Smith

AGENCY:
Robinson Assoc.

CLIENT:
GSX Corporation

■432

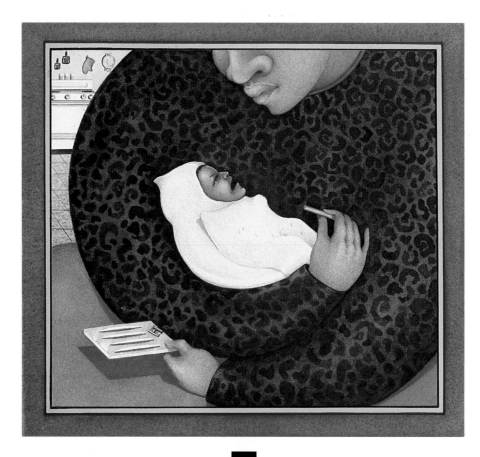

ART DIRECTOR:
Cheri Dorr

ILLUSTRATOR:
Cheri Dorr

■433

ART DIRECTOR:
*Uscho Carvalho/
Ricardo van Stean*
ILLUSTRATOR:
Braldt Bralds
AGENCY:
CUS Communications
CLIENT:
Pirelli
■434

■431 Full-page illustration for a special advertising section on the 1986 New York City Marathon. (USA)

■432 Full-page illustration for a trade advertisement offering the waste management services of GSX Corporation. (USA)

■433 Illustration, unpublished; personal work addressing the issue of drug addiction and abuse among mothers. (USA)

■434 Illustration for an institutional calendar published by *Pirelli*, Brazil. (BRA)

■431 Der New Yorker Marathon 1986 ist Gegenstand dieser Illustration aus einer Werbebeilage für diese Veranstaltung. (USA)

■432 Ganzseitige Illustration für ein Inserat der GSX Corp., ein Unternehmen für Abfallbeseitigung. (USA)

■433 Illustration (unveröffentlicht) zum Problem von Drogenabhängigkeit oder -missbrauch bei Müttern. (USA)

■434 Illustration aus einem Kalender, der von *Pirelli*, Brasilien, veröffentlicht wurde. (BRA)

■431 Illustration pleine page dans une section publicitaire spéciale à l'occasion du marathon de New York 1986. (USA)

■432 Illustration pleine page pour une annonce de revue professionnelle: les services de voirie de la GSX Corp. (USA)

■433 Illustration inédite sur le problème poignant des jeunes mères droguées. (USA)

■434 Illustration pour un calendrier de prestige publié par *Pirelli* au Brésil. (BRA)

ART DIRECTOR:
Lynne Spitalny

ILLUSTRATOR:
Roy Montibon

AGENCY:
Schema

CLIENT:
*Lease Accounting
Software Systems*

■435

ART DIRECTOR:
Tom Staebler

DESIGNER:
Kerig Pope

ILLUSTRATOR:
Braldt Bralds

PUBLISHER:
Playboy Enterprises, Inc.

■436

ART DIRECTOR:
Jeff Laramore

DESIGNER:
Jeff Laramore

ILLUSTRATOR:
Jeff Laramore

AGENCY:
Young & Laramore

PUBLISHER:
Hilltop Press

■437

■435 Computer graphic illustration in a corporate brochure for Lease Accounting Software Systems. (USA)

■436 Illustration on double spread for a story in *Playboy* magazine entitled "The Professional Soldier". (USA)

■437 "Pointillism" – illustration for the Hilltop Press. (USA)

■435 Mit dem Computer hergestellte Illustration für eine Firmenbroschüre der *Lease Accounting Software Systems* (USA)

■436 Illustration für einen Beitrag im Magazin *Playboy* mit dem Titel «Der Berufssoldat». (USA)

■437 «Pointillismus» – Illustration für Hilltop Press. (USA)

■435 Illustration CAO pour une brochure de Lease Accounting Software Systems (logiciels de comptabilité en leasing). (USA)

■436 Illustration double page pour un récit du magazine *Playboy* intitulé «Le Soldat professionnel». (USA)

■437 «Pointillisme» – illustration pour Hilltop Press. (USA)

ART DIRECTOR:
John Cayea
ILLUSTRATOR:
Mirko Ilic
PUBLISHER:
New York Times
■438

■**438** Illustration for an article in the *New York Times* Week in Review: "The Supreme Court works at its Mandate." (USA)

■**439, 440** From an image brochure for *Unifor*, producers of office furnishing systems: far left for Chapter 1 "Office Projects", left for Chapter 7 "Design and Technology". (ITA)

■**441** Portrait of Samuel Beckett from *La Repubblica* (ITA)

■**438** Illustration für die Rubrik «Rückblick der Woche» in der *New York Times* «Das Bundesgericht erfüllt sein Mandat.» (USA)

■**439, 440** Aus einer Image-Broschüre für *Unifor*, Hersteller von Büromöbeln. *439* gehört zu dem Kapitel «Büro-Projekte», *440* zu «Design und Technologie». (ITA)

■**441** Samuel Beckett, aus der Zeitung *La Repubblica* (ITA)

■**438** Illustration d'un article du *New York Times* «La Cour suprême au travail», dans les Faits de la semaine. (USA)

■**439, 440** Brochure de prestige du fabricant de meubles de bureau *Unifor.* à l'extrême-gauche, pour le chap. 1 (Projets de bureaux), à g. pour le chap. 7 (Design et technologie). (ITA)

■**441** Samuel Beckett dans le journal *La Repubblica* (ITA)

ART DIRECTOR:
Pierluigi Cerri
ILLUSTRATOR:
Tullio Pericoli
AGENCY:
Gregotti & Associati
CLIENT:
Unifor
■**439, 440**

ILLUSTRATOR:
Tullio Pericoli
PUBLISHER:
La Repubblica
■**441**

ART DIRECTOR:
Kit Hinrichs

DESIGNER:
Kit Hinrichs/Karen Berndt

ILLUSTRATOR:
Doug Johnson

AGENCY:
Pentagram Design

PUBLISHER:
MGM/UA Communications Company

■442

■**442** For the cover of the 1986 annual report of MGM/UA Communications Co. referring to the merger of the two firms; "Two Proud Pasts. One Glorius Future." (USA)

■**443** Sample illustration from a company brochure entitled "DuPont and the Environment Today" issued by E.I. DuPont de Nemours & Co., diversified chemicals. (USA)

■**442** Illustration für den Umschlag des Jahresberichtes 1986 der MGM/UA Communications: «Zwei stolze Vergangenheiten. Eine ruhmreiche Zukunft.» (USA)

■**443** Beispiel der Illustrationen aus einer Firmenbroschüre mit dem Titel «DuPont und die Umwelt heute», herausgegeben von E.I. DuPont de Nemours & Co., Chemische Werke. (USA)

■**442** Illustration pour la couverture du rapport annuel de MGM/UA Communications pour 1986 avec allusion à la fusion des deux entreprises. (USA)

■**443** Illustration type pour la brochure «DuPont et l'environnement aujourd'hui» publiée par le groupe de produits chimiques diversifiés E.I. DuPont de Nemours & Co. (USA)

ART DIRECTOR:
James Jarratt
DESIGNER:
James Jarratt/Dale Parenti
ILLUSTRATOR:
Charles Santore
AGENCY:
The Creative Departement
CLIENT:
E.I. DuPont de Nemours
■**443**

■**445–448** A series of self-promotional cards for an illustrator/designer and a lithographer. (USA)

■**449** Illustration (enlarged) from the cover of a novel by Carole Maso entitled *Ghost Dance.* (USA)

■**445–448** Illustrationen als Gemeinschaftswerbung für einen Illustrator/Designer und einen Lithographen. (USA)

■**449** Illustration (vergrössert) für den Umschlag eines Romans von Carole Maso mit dem Titel «Geistertanz». (USA)

■**445–448** Série de cartes autopromotionnelles réalisées par un illustrateur-designer et un lithographe. (USA)

■**449** Illustration (agrandie) pour la couverture du roman *Ghost Dance* (Danse des fantômes) de Carole Maso. (USA)

ART DIRECTOR:
Michael David Brown
ILLUSTRATOR:
Michael David Brown
AGENCY:
Michael David Brown
CLIENT:
The Art Litho Company
◄ ■**445–448**

ART DIRECTOR:
Joseph Montebello
DESIGNER:
Gloria Adelson
ILLUSTRATOR:
John Jinks
PUBLISHER:
Harper & Row Publishers,
■**449**

450 Full-page illustration from the series "Western Art" appearing in *Texas Monthly* magazine. (USA)

451 Full-page illustration from the magazine *Air & Space* to accompany an article about the French aviation heroes François Coli and Charles Nungesser, who got lost with their biplane in an attempt to cross the Atlantic. (USA)

452 Illustration for a story entitled "An Element of Surprise" published in *Playboy* magazine. (USA)

450 Illustration mit dem Titel »Zephyr, Texas« für eine Kunstseite, die regelmässig in *Texas Monthly* erscheint. (USA)

451 Illustration aus der Zeitschrift *Air & Space* für einen Artikel über die französischen Flugpioniere François Coli und Charles Nungesser, die mit ihrem Doppeldecker bei dem Versuch, den Atlantik zu überqueren, verschollen sind. (USA)

452 Illustration für eine Geschichte mit dem Titel »Ein Überraschungsmoment«, veröffentlicht im *Playboy*. (USA)

450 Illustration pleine page dans la série «Western Art» publiée régulièrement dans le magazine *Texas Monthly*. (USA)

451 Illustration pleine page d'un article du magazine *Air & Space* relatant la tentative de traversée de l'Atlantique par Charles Nungesser et François Coli, les aviateurs français qui disparurent avec leur biplan. (USA)

452 Illustration d'un récit du magazine *Playboy* intitulé «Un elément de surprise». (USA)

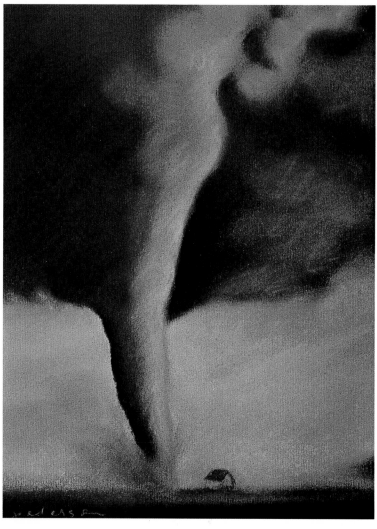

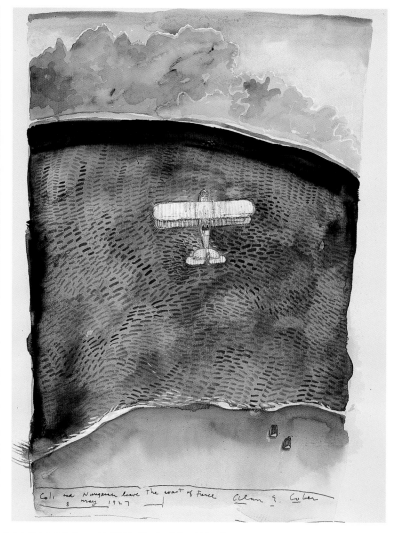

ART DIRECTOR:
Fred Woodward
DESIGNER:
Fred Woodward
ILLUSTRATOR:
Judy Pedersen
PUBLISHER:
Texas Monthly
450

ART DIRECTOR:
Lee Battaglia
DESIGNER:
Phil Jordan
ILLUSTRATOR:
Alan E. Cober
PUBLISHER:
Air & Space Magazine
451

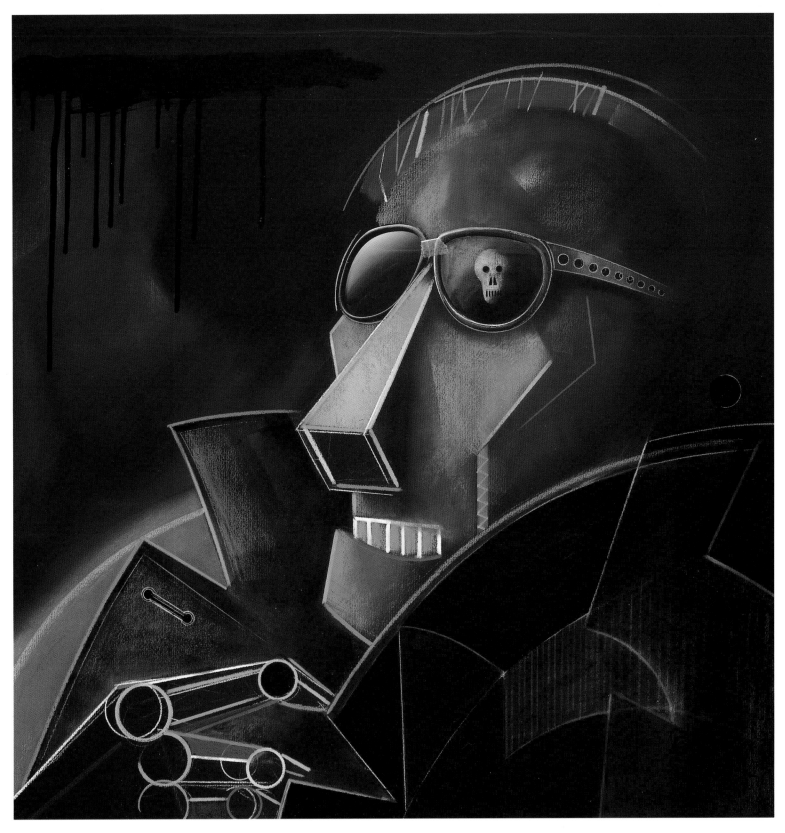

ART DIRECTOR:
Tom Staebler

DESIGNER:
Kerig Pope

ILLUSTRATOR:
Andrzej Dudzinski

PUBLISHER:
Playboy Enterprises, Inc.

■452

ART DIRECTOR:
Fred Woodward
DESIGNER:
Fred Woodward
ILLUSTRATOR:
Dugald Stermer
PUBLISHER:
Texas Monthly
■453

ART DIRECTOR:
Peter Good

ILLUSTRATOR:
Brad Holland

AGENCY:
Peter Good Design

PUBLISHER:
Hammermill Co.

■454

ILLUSTRATOR:
Brad Holland

PUBLISHER:
Legal Assistant Today

■455

■**453** "The Yellow Rose of Texas", slightly enlarged, from the series of full-page illustrations under the heading "Western Art" from *Texas Monthly* magazine. (USA)

■**454** Illustration for an article about the implications of social and political factors on the business development of the paper manufacturers *Hammermill*. (USA)

■**455** Cover illustration of the quarterly journal for the legal profession, *Legal Assistant Today*. (USA)

■**453** «Die gelbe Rose von Texas», leicht vergrössert, für eine in der Zeitschrift *Texas Monthly* regelmässig erscheinende Seite mit dem Titel «Kunst aus dem Westen». (USA)

■**454** Ganzseitige Illustration für einen Bericht über den Einfluss sozialer und politischer Faktoren auf die Geschäftsentwicklung des Papierherstellers *Hammermill*. (USA)

■**455** Umschlagillustration für *Legal Assistant Today*, eine Fachzeitschrift für Juristen. (USA)

■**453** «La Rose jaune du Texas», légèrement agrandie, figure dans la série «Western Art» d'illustrations pleine page publiées régulièrement dans le magazine *Texas Monthly*. (USA)

■**454** Illustration pleine page d'un article où sont examinées les implications de divers facteurs sociaux et politiques quant à la politique commerciale du papetier *Hammermill*. (USA)

■**455** Illustration de couverture de la revue juridique trimestrielle *Legal Assistant Today*. (USA)

ILLUSTRATOR:
MARCO J. VENTURA
CLIENT:
MARCO J. VENTURA
■456

ART DIRECTOR:
Nicolas Dusonchet

ILLUSTRATOR:
Nicolas Dusonchet

PUBLISHER:
Gallimard

■457

■**456** Illustration as self promotion for an Italian artist. (ITA)

■**457** Cover illustration for a book *A cœur perdu* ("With the Whole Heart") by Boileau-Narcejac. (FRA)

■**456** Eigenwerbung eines italienischen Illustrators. (ITA)

■**457** Umschlagillustration für ein Buch mit dem Titel *A cœur perdu* («Aus ganzem Herzen»). (FRA)

■**456** Illustration d'un artiste italien, pour sa pub. (ITA)

■**457** Illustration de couverture pour l'ouvrage de Boileau-Narcejac *A cœur perdu.* (FRA)

458 Double-spread illustration as advertisement for *British Leyland* trucks. (GBR)

459 Illustration from a brochure devoted to *DuPont's* commitment to the environment. (USA)

458 Doppelseitige Illustration aus einer Anzeige für *British-Leyland*-Lastwagen. (GBR)

459 Illustration aus einer Broschüre der chemischen Werke *DuPont* über ihr Engagement für die Umwelt. (USA)

458 Illustration double page pour une annonce en faveur des camions *British Leyland*. (GBR)

459 Page d'une brochure où le groupe chimique *DuPont* explique sa politique en faveur de l'environnement. (USA)

DESIGNER:
James Marsh

ILLUSTRATOR:
James Marsh

AGENCY:
Cogent Elliott

CLIENT:
British Leyland

458

ART DIRECTOR:
James Jarratt
DESIGNER:
James Jarratt/Dale Parenti
ILLUSTRATOR:
Charles Santore
AGENCY:
The Creative Department
CLIENT:
E.I. DuPont De Nemours
■459

ART DIRECTOR:
Judy Garlan

DESIGNER:
Judy Garlan

ILLUSTRATOR:
Guy Billout

PUBLISHER:
The Atlantic Monthly

■ **460–464**

■ **460–464** From a regular series in *The Atlantic* full-page illustrations in which the artist is given total freedom. Opposite: "The Filling of the Mediterranean Sea"; "Light"; "Ballistics"; "Prop". Above: (in actual size) "Umbra". (USA)

■ **460–464** Freie Illustrationen für eine regelmässig in *The Atlantic* erscheinende Seite. Die Titel: «Auffüllen des Mittelmeers»; «Licht», «Ballistik», «Stütze». Oben, in Originalgrösse, «Umbra». (USA)

■ **460–464** Illustrations pleine page dans une série régulière du magazine *The Atlantic* qui donne carte blanche aux artistes. Ci-contre: «Remplissage de la Méditerranée»; «Lumière»; «Balistique»; «Soutien». Ci-dessus: «Ombre», format original. (USA)

■ **465, 466** Two illustrations from a Christmas card for the new National Interbanking Credit Card. Portrayed: left, Christopher Columbus; right: Dante Alighieri. (ITA)

■ **465, 466** Zwei Illustrationen für eine Weihnachtskarte von der Bankenvereinigung Servizi Interbancari. Porträtiert sind Christoph Kolumbus und Dante Alighieri – mit Kreditkarten. (ITA)

■ **465, 466** Deux illustrations pour la carte de fin d'année de la nouvelle carte de crédit interbancaire italienne. A g., Christophe Colomb; à dr., Dante Alighieri. (ITA)

ART DIRECTOR:
Piero Ventura
DESIGNER:
Rossella Rabuffi/
Marco J. Ventura
ILLUSTRATOR:
Marco J. Ventura
AGENCY:
Immagine Design
CLIENT:
Servizi Interbancari
■ **465, 466**

CORPORATE IDENTITY

Stationery

Trademarks

PACKAGING

CORPORATE IDENTITY

Briefpapier

Schutzmarken

PACKUNGEN

CORPORATE IDENTITY

Papier à lettres

Marques et emblèmes

EMBALLAGES

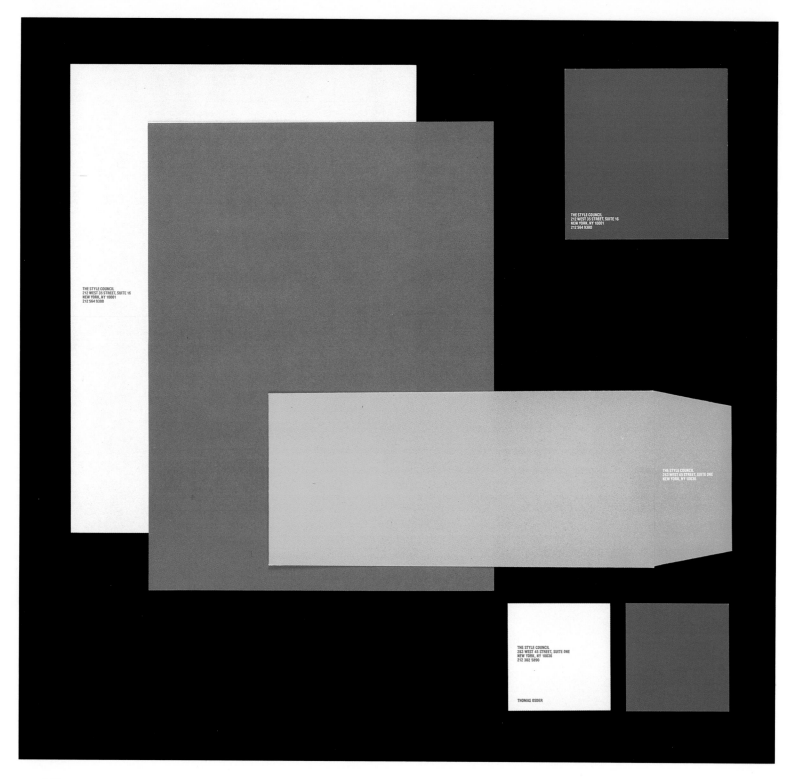

ART DIRECTOR:
Susan Slover

DESIGNER:
Susan Slover

AGENCY:
Susan Slover Design

CLIENT:
The Style Council

■**467**

ART DIRECTOR:
Arthur Niemi
DESIGNER:
Arthur Niemi/Mark Koudys
ILLUSTRATOR:
Robert Lear
AGENCY:
Atlanta Art and Design
CLIENT:
IDI Design Contractors
■468

ART DIRECTOR:
Harumasa Misaki
DESIGNER:
Harumasa Misaki
CLIENT:
R & H Suzuki
■469

ART DIRECTOR:
Brian Collins
DESIGNER:
Brian Collins
CLIENT:
*Art Directors Club
of Boston*
■470

ART DIRECTOR:
Sue Crolick
DESIGNER:
Sue Crolick
PHOTOGRAPHER:
Mark LaFavor
CLIENT:
Sandra Heinen, Inc.
■471

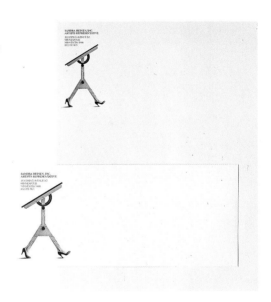

■467 Letterhead (front and back), sticker, envelope and both sides of a visiting card for the Style Council New York. (USA)

■468 Stationery for IDI Design Contractors Ltd. (CAN)

■469 Letterhead and envelope for a design office. (JPN)

■470 Letterhead, envelope and visiting card for the Art Directors Club of Boston. (USA)

■471 Stationery for an artists representative. (USA)

■467 Briefbogen (Vorder- und Rückseite), Aufkleber, Umschlag und Visitenkarte für Style Council. (USA)

■468 Briefpapier für IDI Design Contractors Ltd. (CAN)

■469 Briefpapier für ein japanisches Design-Studio. (JPN)

■470 Briefbogen, Umschlag und Visitenkarten für den Art Directors Club, Boston. (USA)

■471 Briefpapier für eine Künstler-Agentur. (USA)

■467 En-tête (recto, verso), autocollant, enveloppe et carte de visite recto-verso du Style Council New York. (USA)

■468 Papier à lettres d'IDI Design Contractors, Toronto. (CAN)

■469 En-tête et enveloppe d'un bureau de design. (JPN)

■470 En-tête, enveloppe, carte de visite pour l'Art Directors Club de Boston. (USA)

■471 Papier à lettres d'un représentant d'artistes. (USA)

ART DIRECTOR:
Guido Gribl

DESIGNER:
Guido Gribl

AGENCY:
Guido Gribl

CLIENT:
Guido Gribl

■**472**

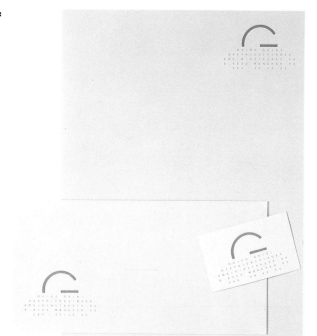

DESIGNER:
Kathleen Wilmes Herring

ILLUSTRATOR:
Barry Zaid

AGENCY:
Yankee Doodles

■**473**

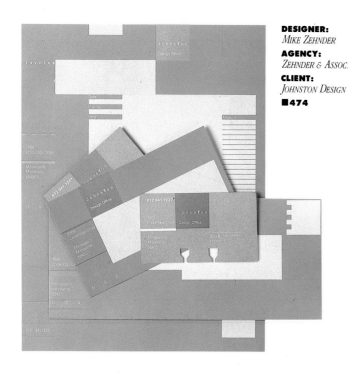

DESIGNER:
Mike Zehnder

AGENCY:
Zehnder & Assoc.

CLIENT:
Johnston Design

■**474**

ART DIRECTOR:
Charles Hively

DESIGNER:
Charles Hively

AGENCY:
The Hively Agency

CLIENT:
The Hively Agency

■**475**

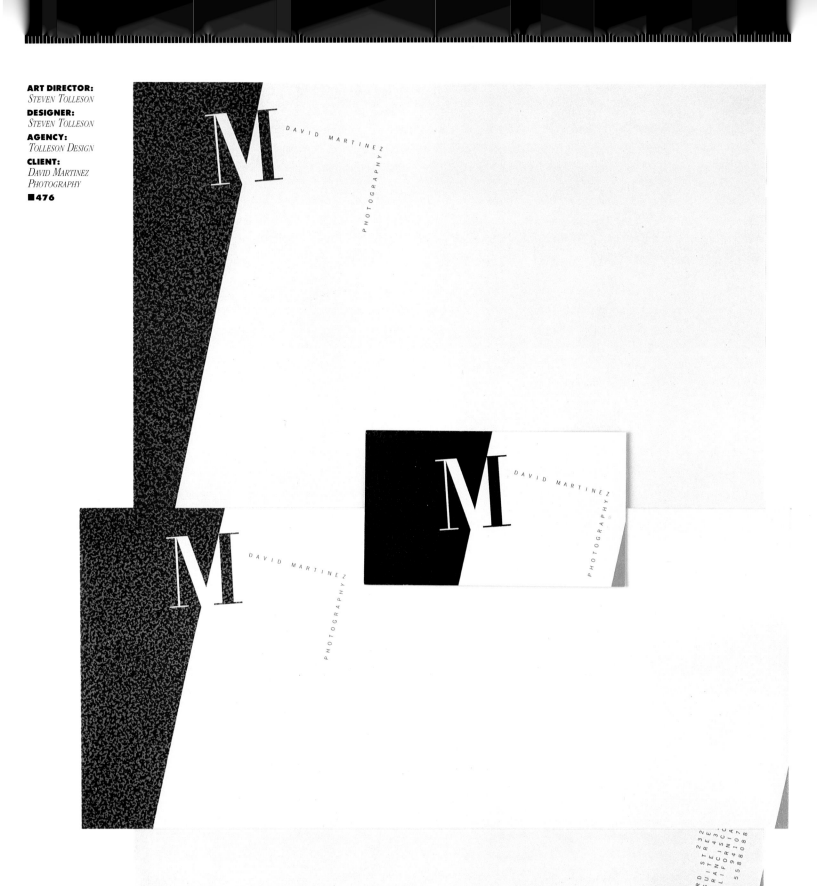

ART DIRECTOR:
Steven Tolleson
DESIGNER:
Steven Tolleson
AGENCY:
Tolleson Design
CLIENT:
David Martinez Photography
■476

■**472** Letterhead, envelope and visiting card for a graphic designer. (GER)

■**473** Stationery for *Yankee Doodles* (design) on which the logo "stamp" can be positioned as desired. (USA)

■**474** Stationery for Johnston Design Office – a graphic design firm in Minneapolis. (USA)

■**475** For the Hively Agency of Texas (advertising agency) – a bee straight from the hive(ly) on the stationery. (USA)

■**476** Set of stationery for a photographer. (USA)

■**472** Briefbogen, Umschlag und Visitenkarte für den Graphik-Designer Guido Gribl. (GER)

■**473** Briefpapier für *Yankee Doodles* (Design-Studio). Das Logo kann wie eine Briefmarke überall aufgeklebt werden. (USA)

■**474** Briefpapier für das Johnston Design Office – ein Graphik-Design Studio in Minneapolis. (USA)

■**475** Eine Biene als passendes «Wappentier» auf dem Brief-papier für die Hively-Werbeagentur (hive = Bienenstock). (USA)

■**476** Briefpapier für einen Photographen. (USA)

■**472** En-tête, enveloppe et carte de visite d'un designer graphique. (GER)

■**473** Papier à lettres du studio de design *Yankee Doodles*. Le logo autocollant peut être positionné à l'endroit voulu. (USA)

■**474** Papier à lettres pour Johnston Design Office, une société de design graphique établie à Minneapolis. (USA)

■**475** Pour l'agence de publicité Hively Agency of Texas: une abeille sortie tout droit de la ruche («hive», cf. Hively). (USA)

■**476** Jeu de papier à lettres pour un photographe. (USA)

ART DIRECTOR:
Clyde Winters

DESIGNER:
Jana Anderson

AGENCY:
Clyde Winters Design

CLIENT:
Kunst +Leben

■**477**

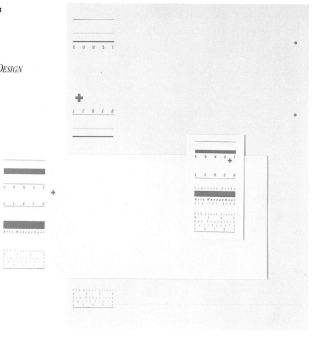

DESIGNER:
Milton Glaser

AGENCY:
Milton Glaser Inc.

CLIENT:
Astoria Greenhouse

■**478**

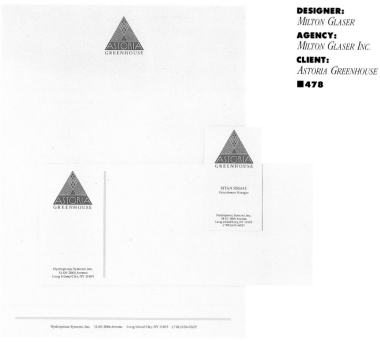

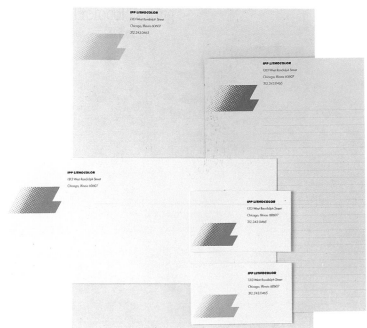

ART DIRECTOR:
Greg Samata/Jim Hardy

DESIGNER:
Greg Samata/Jim Hardy

AGENCY:
Samata Associates

CLIENT:
IPP LithoColor

■**479**

■477 Stationery set for an artists representative firm called "Kunst + Leben". (USA)

■478 Letterhead, envelope, visiting card for Hydroponic Systems Inc. (Astoria Greenhouse). (USA)

■479 Stationery system for IPP Lithocolor of Chicago. (USA)

■480 Notepad stationery for a management convention of IVECO with the logotype "Europe in a Company". (ITA)

■477 Briefpapier und Visitenkarte für eine Künstleragentur in San Francisco, die sich «Kunst + Leben» nennt. (USA)

■478 Für Astoria Greenhouse, Pflanzen-Hydrokulturen, entworfenes Briefpapier und Visitenkarte. (USA)

■479 Briefpapier für einen Lithographen in Chicago. (USA)

■480 Notizblock für eine Management-Konferenz von IVECO mit dem Logo «Europa in einem Unternehmen». (ITA)

■477 Jeu de papier à lettres pour la société «Kunst + Leben» spécialisée dans la représentation d'artistes. (USA)

■478 En-tête, enveloppe, carte de visite pour Hydroponic Systems Inc. (les serres dites Astoria Greenhouse). (USA)

■479 Papier à lettres pour IPP Lithocolor à Chicago. (USA)

■480 Bloc-notes pour une conférence de management d'Iveco, orné du logo «l'Europe dans une entreprise». (ITA)

DESIGNER:
Giorgio Tramontini
AGENCY:
F.T.G.
CLIENT:
Iveco
■480

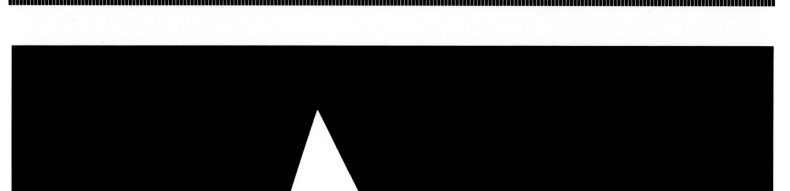

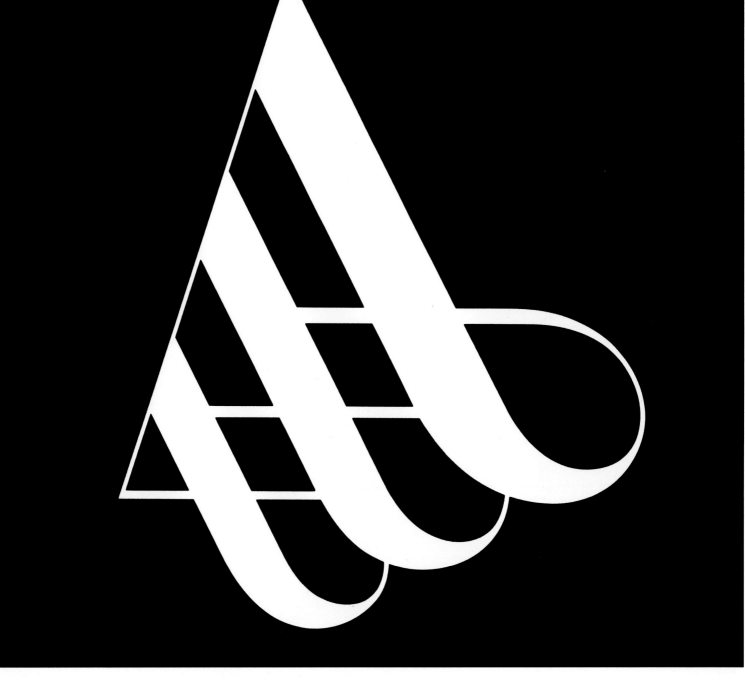

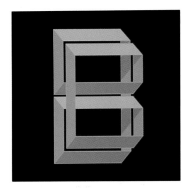

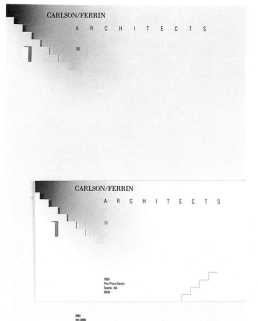

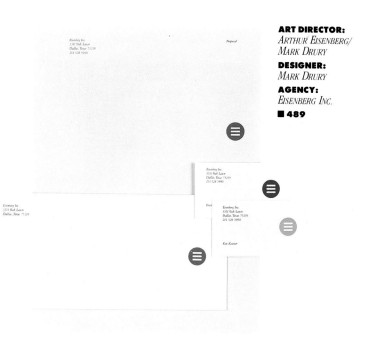

DESIGNER:
Jack Anderson
PHOTOGRAPHER:
Greg Krogstad
AGENCY:
*Hornall Anderson
Design Works*
CLIENT:
Carlson/Ferrin Architects
■ **487**

ART DIRECTOR:
Scott Nash
DESIGNER:
Joanna Bodenweber
AGENCY:
Corey & Company
CLIENT:
Enterprise Media Inc.
■ **488**

ART DIRECTOR:
*Arthur Eisenberg/
Mark Drury*
DESIGNER:
Mark Drury
AGENCY:
Eisenberg Inc.
■ **489**

■ **487** Stationery for a new architectural firm in Seattle. (USA)

■ **488** Letterhead and envelope for Enterprise Media Inc. (USA)

■ **489** Letterhead, envelope and visiting cards for Eisenberg Inc. of Dallas. (USA)

■ **490** Stationery system for *Esprit/Kids* (children's clothes) of California. (USA)

■ **487** Briefbogen für ein Architekturbüro in Seattle. (USA)

■ **488** Briefbogen und Umschlag für Enterprise Media Inc. (USA)

■ **489** Briefbogen, Umschlag und Visitenkarten für das Design-Studio Eisenberg Inc., Dallas. (USA)

■ **490** Briefpapier für *Esprit/Kids*, Kinderbekleidung der Marke *Esprit* in Kalifornien. (USA)

■ **487** Papier à lettres d'un bureau d'architectes. (USA)

■ **488** En-tête et enveloppe d'Entreprise Media à Boston. (USA)

■ **489** En-tête, enveloppe, cartes de visite pour la société Eisenberg Inc. de Dallas. (USA)

■ **490** Système intégré de papier à lettres pour les fabricants de vêtements pour enfants *Esprit/Kids* de Californie. (USA)

DESIGNER:
Tamotsu Yagi
AGENCY:
Esprit Graphic Design
CLIENT:
Esprit De Corp.
■ 490

ESPRIT

ESPRIT/KIDS
THE VILLAGE AT CORTE MADERA
1738 REDWOOD HIGHWAY
CORTE MADERA, CA 94925

ESPRIT

ESPRIT/KIDS
THE VILLAGE AT CORTE MADERA
1738 REDWOOD HIGHWAY
CORTE MADERA, CA 94925

ESPRIT

ESPRIT/KIDS
THE VILLAGE AT CORTE MADERA
1738 REDWOOD HIGHWAY
CORTE MADERA, CA 94925

ART DIRECTOR:
Tamotsu Yagi
DESIGNER:
Tamotsu Yagi
PHOTOGRAPHER:
Oliviero Toscani
AGENCY:
*Esprit Graphic
Design Studio*
CLIENT:
Esprit De Corp
■ 491, 492

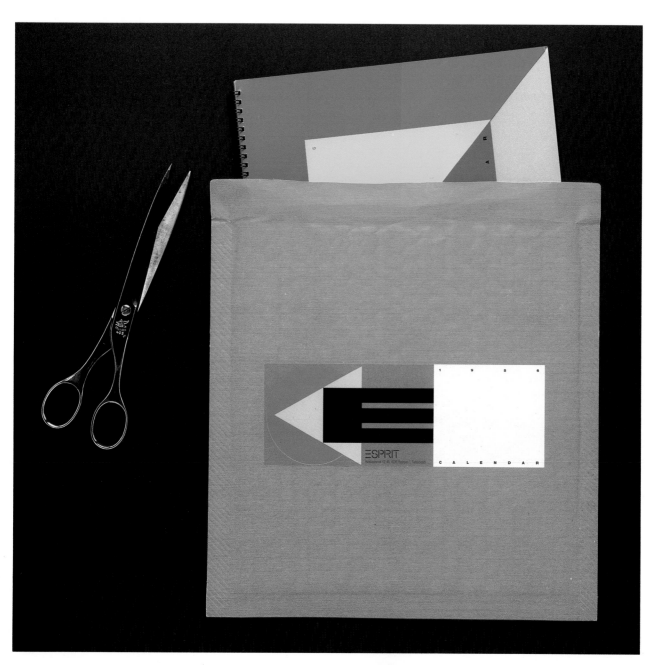

ART DIRECTOR:
Tamotsu Yagi
DESIGNER:
Tamotsu Yagi
PHOTOGRAPHER:
Oliviero Toscani
AGENCY:
*Esprit Graphic
Design Studio*
CLIENT:
Esprit De Corp.
■ 493—495

■ **491, 492** Cover and spread from a corporate-identity book (200 pages, richly illustrated, with plastic slipcase) for *Esprit* (international fashion) entitled *Esprit, The Making of an Image.* Purporting to be "authored" by the 4-year-old son of *Esprit*'s chief photographer, Oliviero Toscani, it tells a whimsical tale of the people of *Esprit* and their work and it amplifies the slogan: "*Esprit* is an attitude not an age." (USA)

■ **493–495** Puffer envelope with the 1986 spiral-bound, die-cut 1986 calendar for *Esprit* and (below) calendar covering-card opened and the calendarium/illustration sheets for May. (USA)

■ **491, 492** Umschlag und Doppelseite aus einem Buch für *Esprit* (internationale Mode) mit dem Titel «*Esprit*, die Entstehung eines Firmen-Image». Es enthält 200 reich illustrierte Seiten und hat einen Plastikschuber. Hier wird aus der Sicht des vierjährigen Sohnes des Chef-Photographen Oliviero Toscani die Geschichte der Leute von *Esprit* und ihrer Arbeit erzählt. Das Motto: «*Esprit* ist eine Haltung, nicht ein Alter». (USA)

■ **493–495** Farbenfroher, wattierter Umschlag für den spiralgebundenen Kalender 1986 für *Esprit*. Hier eine Ansicht des aufgeklappten Deckblatts und des Monatsblattes für Mai. (USA)

■ **491, 492** Couverture et double page d'un ouvrage de présentation réalisé pour *Esprit* (modes internationales) sous le titre de *Esprit, The Making of an Image*. Prétendument écrit par le fils du photographe en chef d'*Esprit*, Oliviero Toscani, il présente sur 200 pp. richement illustrées (sous emboîtage plastique) l'histoire de l'entreprise vue à travers des yeux d'enfant sous cette devise: «*Esprit* – une attitude, pas un âge». (USA)

■ **493–495** Enveloppe ouatée haute en couleur pour le calendrier d'*Esprit* 1986 à reliure spirale; en bas, feuillet de couverture rabattu et feuillets pour le mois de mai. (USA)

ART DIRECTOR:
Tamotsu Yagi

DESIGNER:
Tamotsu Yagi/
Hiroshi Serizawa

PHOTOGRAPHER:
Roberto Carra

AGENCY:
Esprit Graphic
Design Studio

CLIENT:
Esprit De Corp.

■ 496

ART DIRECTOR:
Tamotsu Yagi

DESIGNER:
Tamotsu Yagi

AGENCY:
Esprit Graphic
Design Studio

CLIENT:
Esprit De Corp.

■ 499, 500 ▶

ART DIRECTOR:
Tamotsu Yagi

DESIGNER:
Tamotsu Yagi

AGENCY:
Esprit Graphic
Design Studio

CLIENT:
Esprit De Corp.

■ 497

ART DIRECTOR:
Leslie Barnett

DESIGNER:
Birgit Nottelmann

AGENCY:
Esprit Design Studio

CLIENT:
Esprit De Corp.

■ 498

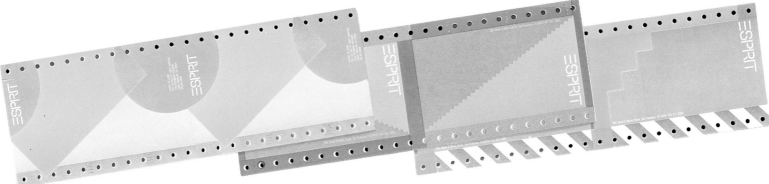

■ **496** Continuing the *Esprit* corporate identity theme, a party was held for the firm's employees from all over the world, after which the book *Some Party* was produced. Shown here: the corrugated plasticized case, the cover and a sample spread showing party guests "on the night". Also shown here: an invitation card to a Dallas *Esprit* store-opening party and a Caffe *Esprit* opening announcement card containing loose die-cut tokens. (USA)

■ **497, 498** Two examples of the firm's announcements using silkscreen printing on plastic: for *Esprit* shoes at the Chicago Apparel Mart, and for a cocktail party invitation to the spring collection in Düsseldorf. (USA, GER)

■ **499, 500** Plastic portfolios, plastic shopping bags and a corrugated plastic *Esprit/Kids* shoe box (with woven strap) and samples of *Esprit* stores cash-register slips, size 15 x 10 cm each – all an integral part of *Esprit's* corporate image program. (USA)

■ **496** Fortsetzung (s. *485–490*) des Corporate Identity Programms von *Esprit*. Es entstand ein Buch nach einer Feier mit Mitarbeitern des Unternehmens aus aller Welt. Hier der Umschlag dafür aus plastifiziertem Wellkarton, die Vorderseite des Buches und eine Doppelseite mit den Partygästen sowie die Einladungskarte zur Eröffnung eines *Esprit*-Ladens und die Speisekarte des neu eröffneten Café *Esprit* mit losen Elementen. (USA)

■ **497, 498** Zwei Beispiele für Bekanntmachungen von *Esprit* (Siebdruck auf Plastik) für *Esprit*-Schuhe in Chicago und für eine Cocktail Party anlässlich der Präsentation der Frühjahrskollektion in Düsseldorf. (USA/GER)

■ **499, 500** *Esprit*-Plastikmappen, -Plastiktragtaschen und eine Wellplastik-Schuhschachtel für *Esprit/Kids* sowie drei Beispiele von Kassenquittungen im Format 15x10 cm, alles Bestandteile des Corporate Image Programms für *Esprit*. (USA)

■ **496** Sur le thème de l'image globale de marque d'*Esprit*, une fête a réuni les collaborateurs de l'entreprise venus du monde entier, ce qui a donné l'ouvrage *Some Party*. On en voit ici l'emboîtage plastifié ondulé, la couverture, une double page type regroupant les invités de la soirée folle, ainsi que deux cartes d'invitation à une inauguration de magasin *Esprit* à Dallas et à celle d'un Café *Esprit* (renfermant des éléments mobiles). (USA)

■ **497, 498** Deux exemples d'avis publicitaires *Esprit* (sérigraphie sur plastique): pour les chaussures *Esprit* à la foire Apparel Mart de Chicago, pour un cocktail accompagnant un défilé de mode printanier à Düsseldorf. (USA/GER)

■ **499, 500** Pochettes en plastique, cabas en plastique, carton à chaussures *Esprit/Kids* en plastique ondulé (cordelette tressée), trois types de tickets de caisse de 15 x 10 cm, – dans le programme d'identité globale de marque d'*Esprit*. (USA)

ART DIRECTOR:
Kazumi Akutagawa
DESIGNER:
Kazumi Akutagawa
■ 501, 502

ART DIRECTOR:
CHIE GOTO

DESIGNER:
CHIE GOTO

■ **503, 504**

ART DIRECTOR:
CHARLES SPENCER ANDERSON

DESIGNER:
CHARLES SPENCER ANDERSON

ILLUSTRATOR:
CHARLES SPENCER ANDERSON

AGENCY:
DUFFY DESIGN GROUP

CLIENT:
AVANT HAIR SALON

■ **505**

■ **503, 504** Sleek boxes to package and present the Japanese speciality "Yokan" – a sweet bean jelly. (JPN)

■ **505** Packaging for hair conditioner, shampoo and hair-spray for *Avant* Hair Salon. (USA)

■ **506** Black on silver stainless steel flask and glazed board pack for *Joseph* perfume. This design won a silver award at the 1986 British D&AD Show. (GBR)

■ **503, 504** Geschlossene und geöffnete Schachtel mit Inhalt, einer japanischen Spezialität aus süssen Bohnen. (JPN)

■ **505** Packungslinie für Haarpflegeprodukte (Conditioner, Shampoo und Haarspray) für das *Avant*-Haarstudio. (USA)

■ **506** Schwarz bedruckter Flacon aus rostfreiem Stahl und schwarze, laminierte Kartonschachtel für *Joseph*-Parfum. Diese Packung wurde 1986 vom britischen D&AD ausgezeichnet. (GBR)

■ **503,504** Boîtes élégantes pour le conditionnement de la spécialité japonaise «Yokan» – une gelée de fèves sucrées. (JPN)

■ **505** Conditionnements pour les produits de capilliculture (conditionneur, shampooing, spray) du salon *Avant.* (USA)

■ **506** Flacon en acier inox, noir sur argent et emballage en carton glacé pour le parfum *Joseph* – une conception qui a remporté une médaille d'argent à la D&AD Show (G.-B.) 1986. (GBR)

ART DIRECTOR:
Madeleine Bennett

DESIGNER:
Madeleine Bennett

AGENCY:
Michael Peters & Partners

CLIENT:
Penhaligon's Ltd.

■506

SAY "ZAY-LAY" **ZÉLÉ**

THE BEER REFRESHER OF FRANCE

PANACHÉ

ART DIRECTOR:
Michael Mabry/
Noreen Fukumori

ILLUSTRATOR:
Michael Mabry

STUDIO:
Michael Mabry Design

CLIENT:
SEH Importers Ltd.

■ **507**

ART DIRECTOR:
Gail Sharp

DESIGNER:
Tony Blurton

ILLUSTRATOR:
Anthony Sidwell/
Frances Barrett/
Colin Frewin

AGENCY:
Michael Peters & Partners

CLIENT:
Fine Fare

■ **508**

ART DIRECTOR:
Hal Riney/Jerry Andelin

DESIGNER:
Primo Angeli/Mark Jones

AGENCY:
Hal Riney & Partners

STUDIO:
Primo Angeli Inc.

CLIENT:
Blitz-Weinhard Co.

■ **509**

ART DIRECTOR:
Barrie Tucker

DESIGNER:
Barrie Tucker/
Elizabeth Schlooz

ILLUSTRATOR:
Robert Marshall

STUDIO:
Barrie Tucker Design

CLIENT:
SA Brewing company

■ **510**

■ **507** Bottle styling for a French beer refresher, *Zélé* imported to the USA by SEH Importers Ltd. (USA)

■ **508** Range of canned beverages designed for the *Fine Fare* chain of retailers. (GBR)

■ **509** Bottle livery for *Weinhard's* premium light beer. (USA)

■ **510** For an Australian brewery, a design for the sale of a new product: *Old Southwark Stout.* (AUS)

■ **507** Flaschenausstattung für ein französisches Bier, das für den amerikanischen Markt bestimmt ist. (USA)

■ **508** Dosengestaltung für verschiedene Getränke, die von der *Fine-Fare*-Lebensmittelkette vertrieben werden. (GBR)

■ **509** Flaschenausstattung für *Henry-Weinhard's*-Bier. (USA)

■ **510** Für die Einführung eines neuen Produktes einer australischen Bierbrauerei gestaltete Flasche. (AUS)

■ **507** Etude de bouteille pour la bière française *Zélé* importée aux Etats-Unis par SEH Importers Ltd. (USA)

■ **508** Gamme de boissons en boîte commercialisées par la chaîne de détaillants *Fine Fare.* (GBR)

■ **509** Conception de bouteille pour la bière *Weinhard.* (USA)

■ **510** Bouteille réalisée pour une brasserie australienne qui lance un nouveau produit, l'*Old Southwark Stout.* (AUS)

ART DIRECTOR:
Barrie Tucker
DESIGNER:
*Barrie Tucker/
Elizabeth Schlooz*
ILLUSTRATOR:
Robert Marshall
STUDIO:
Barrie Tucker Design
CLIENT:
S. Smith & Son Pty Ltd.
■511

ART DIRECTOR:
Josh Freeman
DESIGNER:
Vickie Sawyer
ILLUSTRATOR:
Karen Mercedes McDonald
AGENCY:
Josh Freeman/Associates
CLIENT:
The Christiana Companies
■512

■**511** Classic label design for an Australian wine: Yalumba Carte d'or Rhine Riesling. (AUS)

■**512** Packaging for bottles of wine as presentation gift to new occupants of a housing colony. (USA)

■**513** For a white wine from *Hanna* Winery. (USA)

■**511** Ein klassisches Etikett für die Verpackungsgestaltung von «Australiens klassischem Rheinwein». (AUS)

■**512** Flaschenausstattung als Geschenk an die neuen Bewohner einer Wohnkolonie. (USA)

■**513** Flaschengestaltung für einen Weisswein. (USA)

■**511** Etiquette classique pour un vin australien, le riesling Yalumba Carte d'or tiré de ceps rhénans. (AUS)

■**512** Etude de bouteilles de vin offertes en cadeau aux occupants d'un nouveau logissement. (USA)

■**513** Pour un vin blanc produit par la *Hanna* Winery. (USA)

ART DIRECTOR:
Michael Manwaring

DESIGNER:
Michael Manwaring

AGENCY:
The Office of
Michael Manwaring

CLIENT:
Hanna Winery

■513

ART DIRECTOR:
Michael Peters

DESIGNER:
Frances Lovell

ILLUSTRATOR:
Janet Wheeler/
Frances Lovell

AGENCY:
Michael Peters & Partners

CLIENT:
Seagram

■514

ART DIRECTOR:
Glenn Tutsell
DESIGNER:
Glenn Tutsell
ILLUSTRATOR:
Rory Kee
AGENCY:
Michael Peters & Partners
CLIENT:
Fine Fare
■515

ART DIRECTOR:
Glenn Tutsell
DESIGNER:
Mark Pearce
ILLUSTRATOR:
Harry Willock
AGENCY:
Michael Peters & Partners
CLIENT:
Fine Fare
■516

■**514** For *Coladina* Pineapple and Coconut Liqueur. (GBR)

■**515, 516** Products of Guyana, specially bottled and designed for the *Fine Fare* chain – Dark Rum and White Rum. (GBR)

■**514** Flaschenausstattung für Ananas-Kokosnuss-Likör. (GBR)

■**515, 516** Speziell für die *Fine-Fare*-Lebensmittelkette gestaltete Flaschen für dunklen und weissen Rum aus Guyana. (GBR)

■**514** Bouteille pour une liqueur à l'ananas-noix de coco. (GBR)

■**515, 516** Bouteilles pour deux variétés de rhum guyanais commercialisées par la chaîne de détaillants *Fine Fare*. (GBR)

ART DIRECTOR:
Sara Giovanitti

DESIGNER:
Sara Giovanitti

ILLUSTRATOR:
Russell Patterson

AGENCY:
Sara Giovanitti Design

CLIENT:
21 Club

■ 517

ART DIRECTOR:
R.P. DeVito/Kathy Keating

DESIGNER:
Lisa Brussell

AGENCY:
Axion Design Inc.

CLIENT:
S & W Fine Foods

■ 518

■**517** Elegance on a pretzel tin for *The 21 Club.* (USA)

■**518** Packaging for Espresso coffee *Il Classico.* (USA)

■**519** A range of cans for soups, sauces and stews for the brand *Hotel new Hankyu* of Osaka. (JPN)

■**517** Ausstattung einer Blechdose für *Club-21-*Bretzel. (USA)

■**518** Packungsgestaltung für den Espresso *Il Classico.* (USA)

■**519** Ausstattung für eine Reihe von Dosen für Suppen, Saucen und Fertiggerichte eines neuen Hotels in Osaka. (JPN)

■**517** Boîte à bretzels élégante pour *The 21 Club.* (USA)

■**518** Emballage du café expresso *Il Classico.* (USA)

■**519** Gamme de boîtes de soupes, sauces et ragoûts pour la marque *Hotel new Hankyu* d'Osaka. (JPN)

DESIGNER:
Shinnosuke Sugisaki

AGENCY:
Dentsu Inc.

CLIENT:
Hotel New Hankyu

■**519**

ART DIRECTOR:
PRIMO ANGELI
DESIGNER:
PRIMO ANGELI/VICKI CERO/
RAY HONDA/MARK JONES
AGENCY:
PRIMO ANGELI INC.
CLIENT:
TREESWEET PRODUCTS CO.
■ **520, 521**

■ **520, 521** Range of cans for fruit-juices and fruit cocktails marketed under the *TreeSweet* label. (USA)

■ **522** Box containing four screwtop mustard jars – with one mustard variety for each season of the year; for *Victorian Pantry* brand. (USA)

■ **520, 21** Dosenausstattung für eine Reihe von Fruchtsäften und Fruchtcocktails der Marke *TreeSweet*. (USA)

■ **522** Töpfchen mit Schraubverschluss für vier verschiedene Senfsorten (eine für jede Jahreszeit) der Marke *Victorian Pantry* und die dazugehörige Kartonschachtel. (USA)

■ **520, 521** Gamme de boîtes pour des jus de fruits et cocktails de fruits commercialisés sous la marque *TreeSweet*. (USA)

■ **522** Boîte pour quatre bocaux de moutarde (bouchonnage à pas de vis), une variété pour chaque saison, distribués sous la marque *Victorian* Pantry (Garde-manger victorien). (USA)

ART DIRECTOR:
Gerald Reis

DESIGNER:
Gerald Reis

ILLUSTRATOR:
Gerald Reis/
Wilson Ong

AGENCY:
Gerald Reis & Co.

CLIENT:
Victorian Pantry

■ **522**

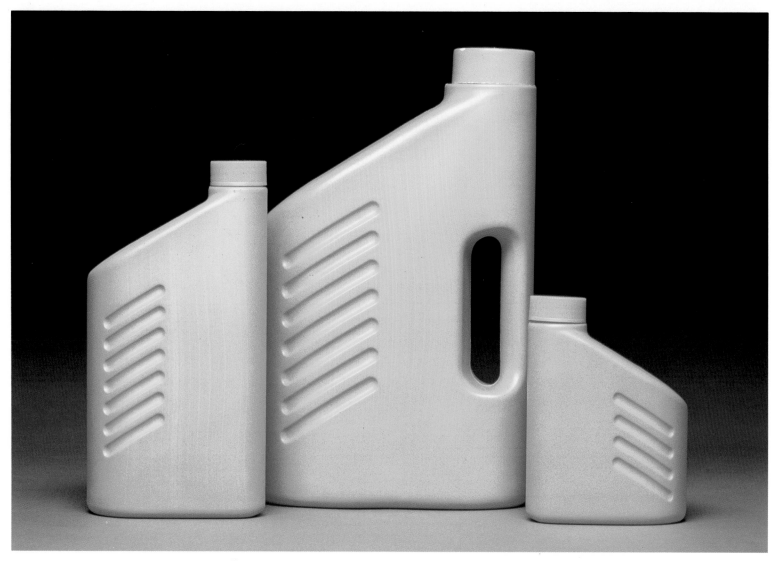

DESIGNER:
Glenn Tutssel/
Graham Thomson

AGENCY:
Michael Peters & Partners

CLIENT:
Shell

■ **523**

■ **523** Structural design for containers of *Shell* oil. (GBR)

■ **524** Series of labelled tins for a wax balm to protect and enrich the color of leatherware. (GER)

■ **525** Packaging for a line of van ladders and roof racks. (USA)

■ **526** Packages designed for a line of *Mesa* dinnerware by Dansk International Designs Ltd. Each pack contains four place settings and reflects the American Southwest influence on the product line. (USA)

■ **523** Strukturierte Kunststoffbehälter für *Shell*-Öl. (GBR)

■ **524** Eine Reihe von Dosen mit Papieretiketten für Lederbalsam zur Pflege und Farbauffrischung von Lederprodukten. (GER)

■ **525** Verpackung für Alu-Leitern und Gepäckträger. (USA)

■ **526** Kartongestaltung für eine neue Linie des *Mesa*-Geschirrs der Dansk International Design Ltd. Die Schachteln enthalten je vier Gedecke und sollen den Einfluss des amerikanischen Südwestens auf die Produktgestaltung sichtbar machen. (USA)

■ **523** Bidons en plastique structuré pour l'huile *Shell*. (GBR)

■ **524** Série de boîtes à étiquettes papier pour un cirage balsamique soignant le cuir et ravivant les coloris. (GER)

■ **525** Emballages d'échelles alu et de porte-bagages. (USA)

■ **526** Emballages carton d'une gamme de vaisselle *Mesa* conçus par Dansk International Designs Ltd. Chaque carton contient quatre couverts qui trahissent une influence de design venue du Sud-Est des Etats-Unis. (USA)

ART DIRECTOR:
Tim Buktu

DESIGNER:
Tim Buktu

AGENCY:
Tim Buktu

CLIENT:
Tapir Wachswaren

■ 524

ART DIRECTOR:
Ron Zimmerman

DESIGNER:
*Ron Zimmerman/
Jaimie Alexander/
Chris Prater*

PHOTOGRAPHER:
Larry Frier

STUDIO:
Richardson Smith

CLIENT:
Christianson Industries, Inc.

■ 525

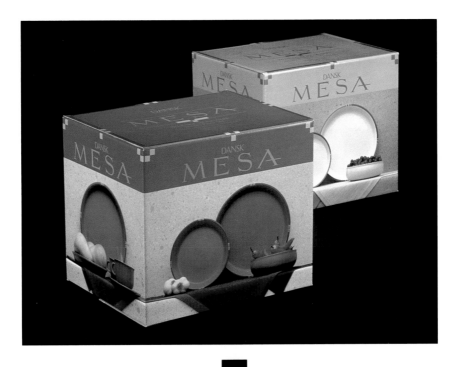

ART DIRECTOR:
John Emery

DESIGNER:
John Emery

STUDIO:
Vie Design Studios, Inc.

CLIENT:
*Dansk International
Designs Ltd.*

■ 526

■**527** "Potted Puzzles" – a series of jig-saw puzzles designed as upmarket souvenirs, each featuring an animal from "down under". (AUS)

■**528** Design for a series of video cassette cartons for *Vestron Video*. (USA)

■**527** »Puzzles in Dosen«, Verpackung für eine Reihe von Puzzles als anspruchsvolle Souvenirs aus Australien, die den einheimischen Tieren gewidmet ist. (AUS)

■**528** Gestaltung der Kartonverpackung für eine Reihe von Video-Kassetten von *Vestron Video*. (USA)

■**527** »Puzzles en boîtes« – série de puzzles haut de gamme pour l'industrie touristique australienne. Chaque puzzle est consacré à un animal des antipodes. (AUS)

■**528** Design d'une gamme de cartons à cassettes vidéo pour *Vestron Video*. (USA)

ART DIRECTOR:
Barrie Tucker

DESIGNER:
Barrie Tucker

ILLUSTRATOR:
Robert Marshall

STUDIO:
Barrie Tucker Design

CLIENT:
The Finger Print Co.

■**527**

ART DIRECTOR:
Scott A. Mednick

DESIGNER:
Scott A. Mednick/
Cheryl Rehman/
Tom LeClerc

AGENCY:
Scott Mednick & Associates

CLIENT:
Vestron Video

■ 528

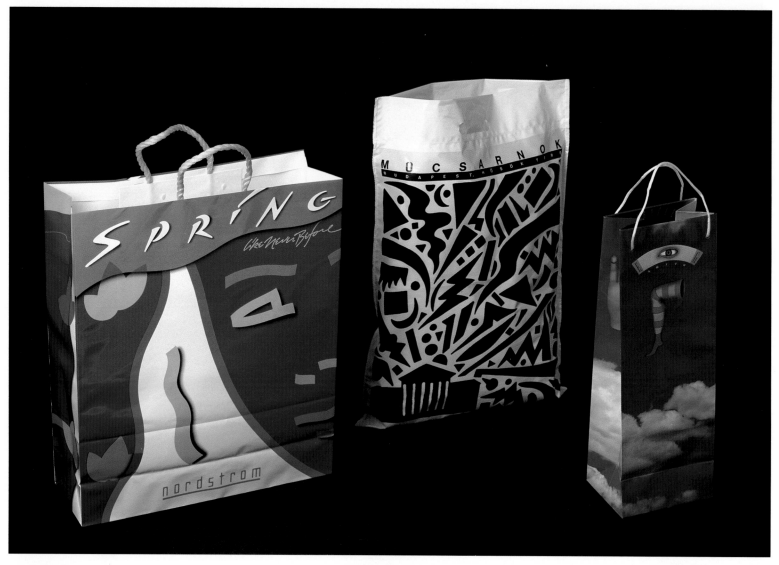

ART DIRECTOR:
Cheryl Fujii
DESIGNER:
Anton Kimball
ILLUSTRATOR:
Anton Kimball
AGENCY:
Anton Kimball Design
CLIENT:
Nordstrom Inc.
■ **529**

ART DIRECTOR:
Katalin Neray
DESIGNER:
György Kemeny
ILLUSTRATOR:
György Kemeny
CLIENT:
Mücsarnok
■ **530**

ART DIRECTOR:
Seth Jaben
DESIGNER:
Seth Jaben
ILLUSTRATOR:
Seth Jaben
STUDIO:
Seth Jaben
CLIENT:
E.G. Smith Inc.
■ **531**

■ **529** The brief for this was "to design a striking and seasonal image for a major fashion retailer" – spring carrier bag for *Nordstrom.* (USA)

■ **530** Vinyl carrier bag for catalogs, posters etc. for Mücsarnok (Palace of Art) in Budapest. (HUN)

■ **531** Tall carrier bag (with cord handle) for socks by *E.G. Smith.* (USA)

■ **529** «Frühjahr wie nie zuvor.» Laminierte Papiertragtasche für *Nordstrom*, ein führendes Modegeschäft. Die Elemente wurden auch für verschiedene Drucksachen verwendet. (USA)

■ **530** Plastik-Tragtasche für Kataloge, Plakate usw. des Kunsthauses Mücsarnok in Budapest. (HUN)

■ **531** Schmale, hohe Tragtasche mit Kordel für Socken der Marke *E.G. Smith.* (USA)

■ **529** Il s'agissait ici de «créer une image frappante, adaptée à la saison, pour un grand magasin de mode». Il en est résulté ce cabas printanier pour *Nordstrom.* (USA)

■ **530** Cabas en plastique pour les catalogues, affiches, etc. du Mücsarnok (Palais de l'art) de Budapest. (HUN)

■ **531** Grand cabas doté d'une cordelette de transport, pour les chaussettes *E.G. Smith.* (USA)

CALENDARS
RECORD COVERS
BOOKS

KALENDER
SCHALLPLATTENHÜLLEN
BÜCHER

CALENDRIERS
POCHETTES DE DISQUES
LIVRES

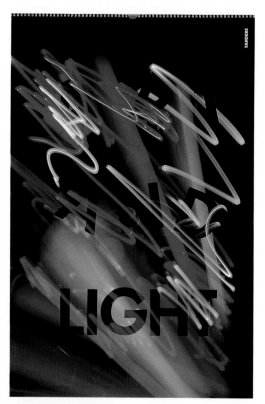

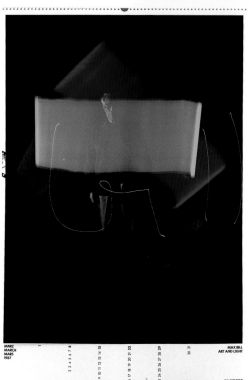

ARTIST:
MAX BILL
■ **534**

ARTIST:
DAVID HOCKNEY
■ **535**

ARTIST:
ROY LICHTENSTEIN
■ **536**

■ **532-537** The *Zanders* "Art and Light" Calendar 1987; an international project with major artists who "painted" or "wrote" spontaneous pictures using artificial light. The monthly "light paintings" are loose and held in place by the die-cut calendarium (see opposite for full January sheet). Each artist's biography is printed trilingually above calendarium (hidden by illustration). Shown this page: Cover (embossed); second translucent cover over information sheet; and monthly illustrations by Max Bill, David Hockney, and Roy Lichtenstein and Arakawa. (GER)

■ **532–537** Der *Zanders* «Art and Light» Kalender 1987, für den internationale Künstler mit Lichtquellen - Glühbirnen, Neonröhren und Taschenlampen - spontane Bilder in den Raum «gemalt» oder «geschrieben» haben. Die Monatsblätter sind lose, nur vom Kalendarium gehalten, wie anhand des Januarblattes (537) gezeigt. Die Biographien der Künstler oberhalb des Kalendariums werden von den Illustrationen verdeckt. Hier der geprägte Umschlag, ein transparentes Blatt über den Informationen und Monatsblätter von Max Bill, David Hockney, Roy Lichtenstein und Arakawa. (GER)

■ **532–537** Calendrier «Art et Lumière» de *Zanders* pour 1987. Ce projet international a réuni de grands artists qui ont «peint» ou «écrit» des compositions de lumière artificielle. Les feuillets mensuels volants ne sont tenus en place que par le calendrier proprement dit (voir ci-contre le feuillet complet de janvier). La biographie trilingue de chaque artiste figure au haut du calendrier (masquée par l'illustration). Ici, couverture gaufrée, titre transparent, illustrations de Max Bill (mars), David Hockney (juin), Roy Lichtenstein (juillet) et Arakawa (janvier). (GER)

ART DIRECTOR:
Harald Schlüter

DESIGNER:
Harald Schlüter

PHOTOGRAPHER:
Harald Schlüter/
Roland Tintrup

AGENCY:
Zanders Feinpapiere

■ 532–537

JANUAR
JANUARY
JANVIER
1987

ARAKAWA
ART AND LIGHT

1 2 3 **4**

5 6 7 8 9 10 **11**

12 13 14 15 16 17 **18**

19 20 21 22 23 24 **25**

26 27 28 29 30 31

ZANDERS

ART DIRECTOR:
CONNY WINTER
DESIGNER:
CONNY WINTER
PHOTOGRAPHER:
CONNY WINTER
AGENCY:
BERTSCH/DOMBERGER/WINTER
CLIENT:
BERTSCH/DOMBERGER/WINTER
■ **538–540c**

■ **538–540c** Sheets from a co-production calendar entitled "Sport 87" and published as joint promotion for Domberger/Bertsch/Winter (lithographer/printer/photographer). Each monthly sheet portrays a seasonal figure and sports articles over the days of the month. Shown are the cover and sheets for December, March, April, July and November. (GER)

■ **538–540c** Aus einem Kalender mit dem Titel »Sport 87«, einer Gemeinschaftswerbung für Domberger/Bertsch/Winter (Lithographen/Drucker/Photograph). Jedes Monatsblatt zeigt eine der Saison entsprechende Figur/Sportart, wobei die Tage mit Zubehör illustriert sind. Hier der Umschlag und die Monatsblätter für Dezember, März, April, Juli und November. (GER)

■ **538–540c** »Sport 87«, calendrier autopromotionnel d'un lithographe, Domberger, d'un imprimeur, Bertsch et d'un photographe, Winter. Chaque feuillet est illustré dans le style du mois, avec un sport assorti et des équipements sportifs pour les jours. Ici la couverture et les feuillets de décembre, mars, avril, juillet et novembre. (GER)

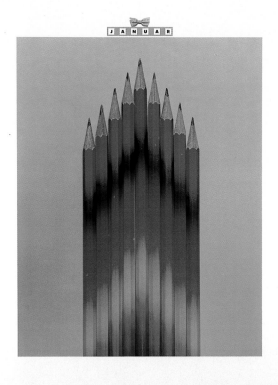

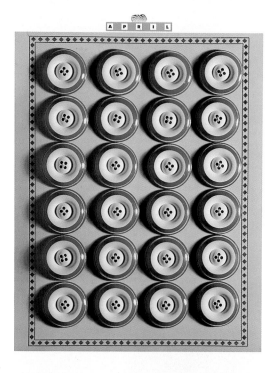

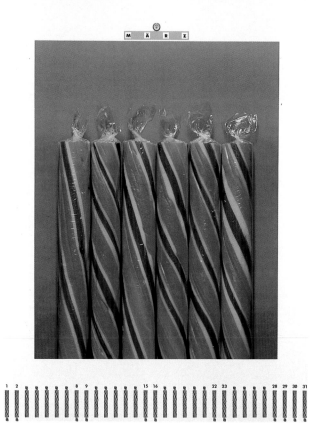

ART DIRECTOR:
Conny Winter

DESIGNER:
Conny Winter

PHOTOGRAPHER:
Conny Winter

CLIENT:
Bertsch KG

■ 541–546

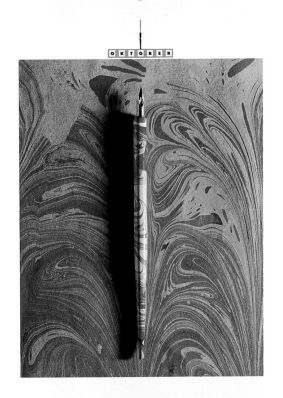

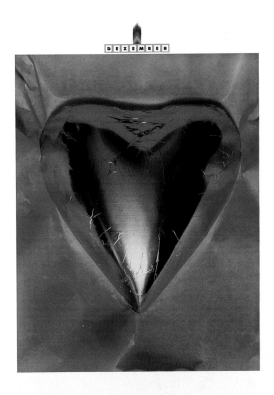

■ **541–546** Spiral-bound 1986 calendar called "Dinge" (Things) a co-production piece as self-promotion for a photographer and a printer. Shown opposite are sheets for January, April and March. Above: October, August and December. (GER)

■ **541–546** Spiralgebundener Kalender 1986 mit dem Titel »Dinge«, für die Druckerei Bertsch und den Photographen Conny Winter. Gegenüber die Blätter für Januar, April und März, auf dieser Seite für Oktober, August und Dezember. (GER)

■ **541–546** »Dinge« (Choses), calendrier 1986, à reluire spirale, réalisé par un photographe et un imprimeur pour leur promotion. Ci-contre, les feuillets de janvier, avril, mars; ci-dessus, ceux d'octobre, août, décembre. (GER)

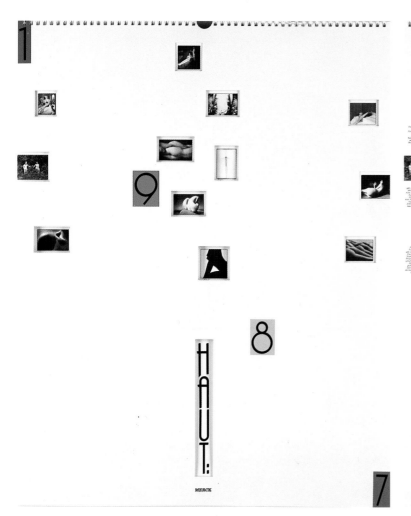

ART DIRECTOR:
Hans Buschfeld

DESIGNER:
Dietmar Brombach/Hans Buschfeld

PHOTOGRAPHER:
Kishin Shinoyama 549
Eiko Hosoe 550
Peter Basch 551
Josef Snobl 552

AGENCY:
Buschfeld Concept & Design

CLIENT:
E. Merck

■ **547–552**

■**547–552** Calendar for 1987 issued by *E. Merck* (pharmaceuticals) presented to doctors to promote a therapeutic skin cream. Above: The title "Haut" (Skin) is printed on the under-cover and is visible through the die-cut top cover – as are the miniatures of the nude figures that are photographed enlarged on the monthly sheets. Opposite: The January, April, December and November sheets, showing the slanting advertising interleaves. (GER)

■**547–552** Vom Pharmaunternehmen *E. Merck* herausgegebener Kalender für 1987, als Werbung für eine therapeutische Hautsalbe. Durch Ausstanzungen im Deckblatt werden der Titel «Haut» und die verkleinerten Reproduktionen der Aktaufnahmen sichtbar, die auf den Monatsblättern gezeigt werden. Gegenüber die Blätter für Januar, April, Dezember und November mit den Werbeinformationen auf schräg geschnittenen Extrablättern. (GER)

■**547–552** Calendrier pour 1987 que la société pharmaceutique *E. Merck* destine au corps médical pour lancer une pommade médicinale. Le titre «Haut» (Peau) et les reproductions miniatures des photos de nus ornant les feuillets mensuels sont visibles à travers les découpes de la couverture. Ci-contre: les feuillets de janvier, avril, décembre et novembre et les feuillets d'information publicitaire intercalaires coupées en biais. (GER)

Was macht Decoderm trivalent Creme in
ihrem Indikationsbereich zu einem der
besten Hauttherapeutika?

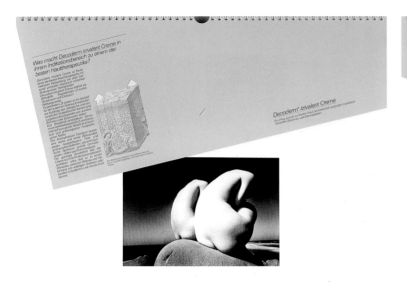

Decoderm®-trivalent Creme
Ein Weg zurück zur heilen Haut bei bakteriell und/oder mykotisch
infizierten Ekzemen und Dermatitiden.

87–96%
ERFOLGSQUOTE

79%
ERFOLGSQUOTE

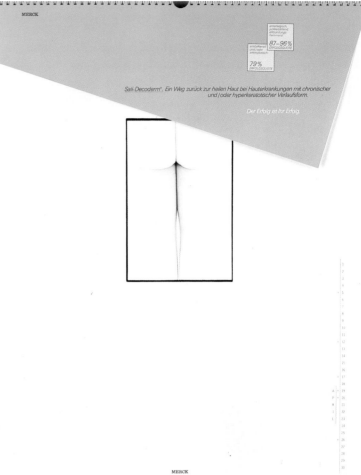

Sali-Decoderm®. Ein Weg zurück zur heilen Haut bei Hauterkrankungen mit chronischer
und/oder hyperkeratotischer Verlaufsform.

Der Erfolg ist Ihr Erfolg.

JANUAR

Weshalb gehören Decoderm-Präparate
zu den besten Hauttherapeutika?

Decoderm® Creme/Salbe/Lotio
Wege zurück zur heilen Haut bei symptomatischen Hauterkrankungen.

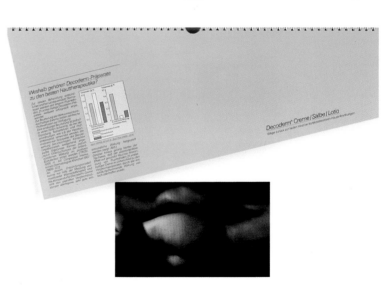

NOVEMBER

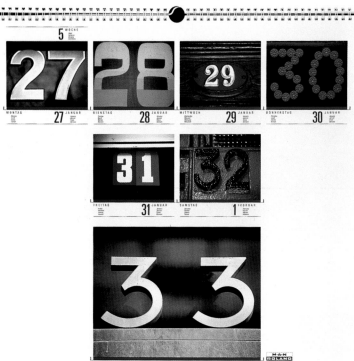

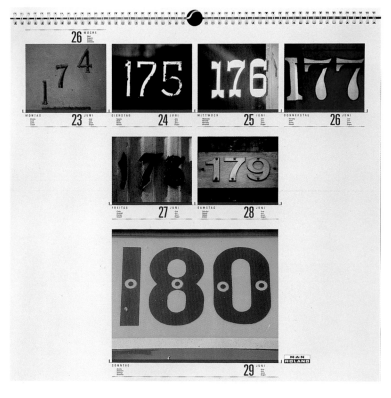

ART DIRECTOR:
Olaf Leu

DESIGNER:
Olaf Leu

PHOTOGRAPHER:
Minori Morita

AGENCY:
Olaf Leu Design & Partner

CLIENT:
M.A.N.-Roland Druckmaschinen AG

■ 553–557

34 WOCHE
Week
Semaine
Semana
Settimana

MONTAG 18 **AUGUST**
Monday *August*
Lundi *Août*
Lunes *Agosto*
Lunedì *Agosto*

DIENSTAG 19 **AUGUST**
Tuesday *August*
Mardi *Août*
Martes *Agosto*
Martedì *Agosto*

MITTWOCH 20 **AUGUST**
Wednesday *August*
Mercredi *Août*
Miércoles *Agosto*
Mercoledì *Agosto*

DONNERSTAG 21 **AUGUST**
Thursday *August*
Jeudi *Août*
Jueves *Agosto*
Giovedì *Agosto*

FREITAG 22 **AUGUST**
Friday *August*
Vendredi *Août*
Viernes *Agosto*
Venerdì *Agosto*

SAMSTAG 23 **AUGUST**
Saturday *August*
Samedi *Août*
Sábado *Agosto*
Sabato *Agosto*

SONNTAG 24 **AUGUST**
Sunday *August*
Dimanche *Août*
Domingo *Agosto*
Domenica *Agosto*

M·A·N ROLAND

■ **553–557** A five-language calendar inspired by numbers in all their manifestations, issued by M.A.N. Roland (printing machinery) of Germany. Entitled "The 365 Days of the Year" house numbers, car number plates, price tag numbers etc. have been photographed by Minori Morita in New York to represent the days. Shown is the cover and sample (weekly) sheets for January, February, June and August. (GER)

■ **553–557** Zahlen, allgemeinstes Verständigungsmittel aller Kulturen, sind in ihrer vielfältigen Ausprägung und Gestaltung Gegenstand dieses Kalenders von M.A.N. Roland (Druckmaschinen). Hier das Deckblatt und Beispiele der Wochenblätter, wobei die Zahlen jeweils den Tag des Jahres bezeichnen. Die aus ihrem Umfeld herausgelösten Zahlen sind Hausnummern, Ziffern auf Autoschildern, Preisschildern usw. (GER)

■ **553–557** Calendrier en 5 langues sur le thème de l'universalité des nombres publié par le fabricant allemand de machines à imprimer M.A.N. Roland sous le titre de «Les 365 Jours de l'année». Couverture et divers feuillets hebdomadaires pour les mois de janvier, février, juin, août où les jours sont représentés par des numéros d'immeubles, des plaques minéralogiques, des étiquettes commerciales, etc. (GER)

The theme of this year's APL calendar is global trade and how the economic and cultural interdependence it creates has made our world grow smaller. Commerce has always mixed the economies and cultures of trading partners. When you see a new, white baseball or a colorful dragon kite, you may imagine the places and people that inspired them. Over the years, international travel and trade have allowed us to transport these symbols, and exchange, adapt, and absorb them according to our own needs. Baseball and sushi–although each is identified with a different culture–now enjoy international favor. However, the details of exporting these cultural and culinary elements can be complex. When we see how many nations contribute their products to the manufacture of a baseball, or the far-flung efforts required to produce a string of cultured pearls, we realize how much these cross-pollinations depend on trade. Trade enriches us economically and cultur- ally, and we invite you to enjoy our celebration of that fact in words and images throughout the year.

American President Lines
1987 Calendar

ART DIRECTOR:
KIT HINRICHS

DESIGNER:
KIT HINRICHS/BELLE HOW

PHOTOGRAPHER:
TERRY HEFFERNAN

AGENCY:
PENTAGRAM DESIGN, INC.

CLIENT:
AMERICAN PRESIDENT LINES

■ **558–563**

■ **558–563** The *American President Lines* (cargo shipping/ transportation) Calendar for 1987 has the theme: global trade and how it has enriched us economically and culturally. Shown above is the top translucent cover (printed black) with title sheet visible, and complete sheet for December. Opposite: January sheet with "sushi"; March sheet with Japanese sci-fi figures; May sheet with oyster and natural pearl, and inside back cover which gives international information to world travellers. (USA)

■ **558–563** Thema dieses Kalenders der *American President Lines* (Frachter und Passagierschiffe) ist der Welthandel und seine Auswirkungen auf unsere Wirtschaft und Kultur. Hier das Deckblatt mit transparentem, schwarz bedrucktem Überblatt und das voll- ständige Dezemberblatt. Rechts das Januarblatt mit Sushi, das Märzblatt mit japanischem Roboterspielzeug, das Maiblatt zur Geschichte der Perle und das letzte Blatt mit internationalen Infor- mationen für Weltreisende. (USA)

■ **558–563** Calendrier 1987 de la compagnie de navigation (car- gos et paquebots) *American President Lines* sur le thème du com- merce mondial et de ses répercussions bénéfiques sur l'économie et la culture. Ci-dessus: couverture transparente (impression en noir), titre, feuillet de décembre. Ci-contre: feuillet de janvier (sushi), de mars (robots de SF japonais), de mai (huître et perle fine); troisième page de couverture où figurent des renseignements destinés aux globe-trotters. (USA)

January

December 1986 · February

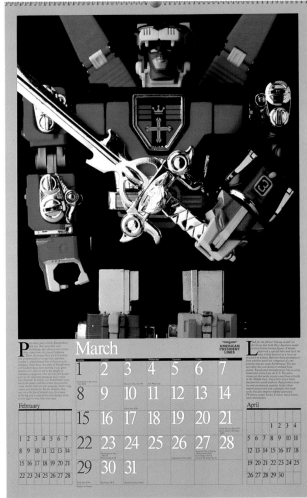

March

February · April

May

April · June

International Information Guide 1987

International trade creates economic interdependence. Likewise, it promotes a world of opportunities, encouraging an exchange of ideas, manufacturing techniques, products, and of course, information. With the charts on this page, American President Lines contributes a selection of international information — useful to world travelers, nautical enthusiasts or businesses that need to know how their products can be delivered to a destination securely and on time.

1987

American President Companies

We live in a world of interdependent nations and, it is said the glue of that interdependency is commerce. The British, for example, wouldn't be quite British without their afternoon tea. Yet that beverage might have been imported from Sri Lanka or China. Western fashions from Paris, New York, and California are popular in Asia, creating an exotic blend of the chic and the traditional. The world is indeed one big marketplace, and this is made possible by efficient transportation networks which can carry goods to consumers everywhere.

Our 1987 American President Companies Executive Desk Calendar salutes this global interdependency. The images convey not only the products of international commerce, but also a bit of history about how we got to this stage, and finally some background on APC's leading role in the business of transporting products on time, over land and sea.

ART DIRECTOR:
Kit Henrichs

DESIGNER:
Kit Hinrichs/Belle How

PHOTOGRAPHER:
Terry Heffernan

AGENCY:
Pentagram Design, Inc.

CLIENT:
American President Lines

■ 564–569

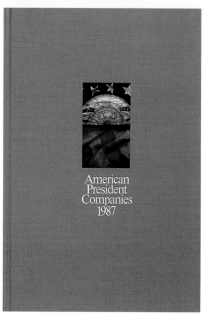

American President Companies 1987

■ **564–569** The 1987 *American President Companies* Executive Desk Diary, richly illustrated to present some of the products of international commerce. Shown top left is the introductory spread; bottom, the cover. This page, various spreads, left to right: "Pachinko" – a Janpanese pinball game; a ship's figurehead; baseball necessities; an interbox connector (ships'/trains' containers locking device). (USA)

■ **564–569** Agenda der Reederei *American President Companies* für 1987, reich illustriert mit Gegenständen des internationalen Handels. Oben links die einführende Doppelseite, unten der Umschlag. Auf dieser Seite Beispiele der Doppelseiten, v.l.n.r.: »Pachinko«, ein japanisches Flipper-Spiel, eine Gallionsfigur, Baseball-Zubehör und Verbindungsstücke für das Befestigen von Containern. (USA)

■ **564–569** Agenda de bureau 1987 pour managers publié par *American President Companies* avec une abondante illustration (produits transportés dans le cadre du commerce international). En haut, à gauche: double page initiale; en bas: la couverture. Sur cette page: diverses doubles pages; de g. à dr.: le pachinko (flipper japonais), figure de proue, accessoires de base-ball, raccord pour conteneurs (trains, bateaux). (USA)

DESIGNER:
Michael Mabry/Noreen Fukumori

PHOTOGRAPHER:
Michele Clement 571
Kathryn Kleinman 572
Randy Green 573
John McDermott 574

STUDIO:
Michael Mabry Design

PUBLISHER:
Hal Belmont

■ **570–575**

■ **570–575** Cover and sample double spreads from a spiral-bound desk diary with glossy photographs between the daily entry pages. Issued by a design studio. (USA)

■ **576** Perspex stand calendar with sliding monthly cards, mailed in a black gloss tube, for Bitstream Inc., computer software. (USA)

■ **577–582** Cover and double spreads from Happy Birthdays, a hard-backed book to note down everyone's birthday. With water-colors on nature subjects corresponding to the season. (USA)

■ **570–575** Umschlag und Doppelseiten aus der spiralgebundenen Agenda eines Design-Studios. Laminierte Photoseiten kontrastieren mit dem stark holzhaltigen Papier. (USA)

■ **576** Plexiglasständer für die losen Blätter eines Kalenders des Computer-Software-Herstellers Bitstream Inc. (USA)

■ **577–582** Umschlag und Doppelseiten aus einem «Geburtstagskalender» mit festem Einband; illustriert mit Aquarellen, die zu den jeweiligen Jahreszeiten passen. (USA)

■ **570–575** Couverture et pages doubles types d'un agenda de bureau à reliure spirale réalisé par un studio de design. Photos glacées intercalaires, papier à forte teneur en bois. (USA)

■ **576** Calendrier à support, en plexiglas, recevant des feuillets mensuels mobiles, pour la société de logiciels *Bitstream*. (USA)

■ **577–582** Couverture et doubles pages d'un calendrier d'anniversaires relié, «Happy Birthdays». Les aquarelles qui l'illustrent ont trait aux différentes saisons de la nature. (USA)

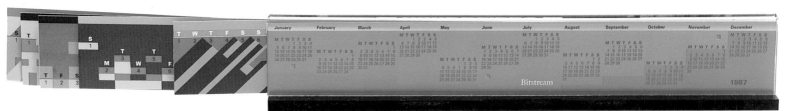

ART DIRECTOR:
Kathleen Forsythe

DESIGNER:
Julie Curtis Reed/
Kathleen Forsythe/
Julie Mott

AGENCY:
Forsythe Design

CLIENT:
Bitstream Inc.

■ 576

DESIGNER:
Rita Marshall

ARTIST:
Etienne Delessert

PUBLISHER:
Stewart, Tabori & Chang

■ 577–582

A NOTEBOOK FOR EVERYONE'S BIRTHDAY
ETIENNE DELESSERT & RITA MARSHALL

JANUARY
BIRTHDAYS

APRIL
BIRTHDAYS

DECEMBER
BIRTHDAYS

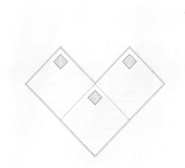

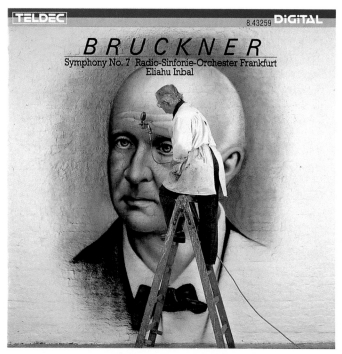

ART DIRECTOR:
Holger Matthies
DESIGNER:
Holger Matthies
ILLUSTRATOR:
Kurt Wendt
PHOTOGRAPHER:
Holger Matthies
PUBLISHER:
Teldec
■ 583

ART DIRECTOR:
*Tony Lane/
Nancy Donald*
PHOTOGRAPHER:
Dominick
PUBLISHER:
CBS Records
■ 584

ART DIRECTOR:
Mark Larson
DESIGNER:
Mark Larson
ILLUSTRATOR:
Brad Holland
PUBLISHER:
CBS Records
■ 585

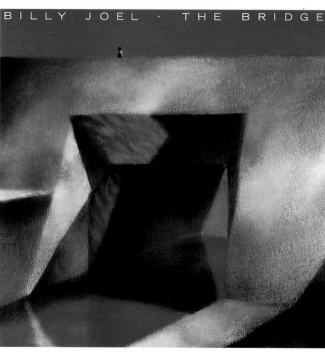

ART DIRECTOR:
Felipe Taborda
DESIGNER:
Felipe Taborda
PUBLISHER:
SIGLA Records
■ 586

■ **583** Cover of a booklet to accompany a Compact Disc with Bruckner's 7th Symphony played by the Radio Symphony Orchestra of Frankfurt. (GER)

■ **584** Album cover for a CBS record with music by Eleanor Academia. (USA)

■ **585** Cover of Billy Joel's album "The Bridge". (USA)

■ **586** Cover of an album issued by the *Sigla* Record Company with a compilation of rock music. (BRA)

■ **587** Portrait of vocalist/guitarist Digney Fignus on the cover of his new album. (USA)

■ **583** Umschlag einer kleinen Broschüre als Begleitinformation zu einer Compact Disc mit Bruckners 7. Symphonie, gespielt vom Radio-Sinfonie-Orchester Frankfurt. (GER)

■ **584** Hülle für eine CBS-Schallplattenaufnahme mit Musik von Eleanor Academia. (USA)

■ **585** Hülle für Billy Joels Platte «The Bridge». (USA)

■ **586** Schallplattenhülle für verschiedene Rock-Aufnahmen, erschienen bei *Sigla Records*. (BRA)

■ **587** Porträt des Sängers/Gitarristen Digney Fignus auf dem Umschlag seiner neuen Schallplatte. (USA)

■ **583** Couverture d'une brochure accompagnant un enregistrement sur compact de la 7e Symphonie de Bruckner jouée par l'Orchestre symphonique de la radio de Francfort. (GER)

■ **584** Couverture d'un disque CBS: prestations musicals de l'Eleanor Academia. (USA)

■ **585** Couverture d'un disque «The Bridge» de Billy Joel. (USA)

■ **586** Couverture d'un disque *Sigla* regroupant diverses formations de rock. (BRA)

■ **587** Portrait du chanteur et guitariste Digney Fignus illustrant la couverture de son nouvel album. (USA)

DIGNEY FIGNUS

ART DIRECTOR:
Allen Weinberg

DESIGNER:
Allen Weinberg

PHOTOGRAPHER:
Beverly Parker

PUBLISHER:
CBS Records

■ 587

DESIGNER:
Bernd Köhler
PHOTOGRAPHER:
Bernd Köhler
PUBLISHER:
Bernd Köhler
■ **588**

ART DIRECTOR:
Jeffrey Kent Ayeroff
DESIGNER:
Jeri McManus Heiden
PHOTOGRAPHER:
Matt Mahurin
PUBLISHER:
Warner Bros. Records, Inc.
■ **589**

■ **588** "Exemplary Answers" - cover of an album comprising a collection of songs dealing with topical occurrences, with text, music, guitar lead and vocals by Bernd Köhler. (GER)

■ **589** Cover of an album for a collection of music by Kitaro, including the title song "Tenku". (USA)

■ **590** In the *CBS Masterworks* series, an album cover for "Three Orchestral Pieces Opus 6 - To the Memory of an Angel" (Pinchas Zukerman/Pierre Boulez/Berg). (USA)

■ **591** In the *Columbia Jazz Masterpieces* series, an album (digitally reworked from the original recording) of Louis Armstrong playing W.C. Handy. (USA)

■ **592** Same series as above - an album with the Benny Goodman Sextet for CBS Records. (USA)

■ **593** Portrait of Rudolf Serkin who plays Bach and Haydn on this album in the *Artist Laureate Masterworks* series for CBS. (USA)

■ **588** Für eine im Eigenverlag herausgegebene Schallplatte mit kritischen Liedern von Bernd Köhler, der auch den Umschlag gestaltete. (GER)

■ **589** Schallplattenhülle für Aufnahmen von Kitaro. «Tenku» ist der Titel eines der Songs. (USA)

■ **590** Hülle für eine in der CBS-Reihe «Meisterwerke der klassischen Musik» erschienene Schallplatte mit dem Titel «Dem Andenken eines Engels». (USA)

■ **591** Schallplattenhülle für die Reihe *Columbia*-Jazz-Meisterwerke. Es handelt sich um eine Digitalüberspielung der Originalaufnahme von «Louis Armstrong spielt W.C. Handy». (USA)

■ **592** Für Aufnahmen vom Benny-Goodman-Sextet aus der Jazz-Meisterwerk-Reihe von *Columbia*. (USA)

■ **593** Porträt von Rudolf Serkin für eine Platte mit Stücken von Bach und Haydn, aus der Meisterwerk-Reihe von CBS. (USA)

■ **588** «Réponses exemplaires» - couverture d'un disque de chansons sur des thèmes d'actualité sociale. L'auteur-compositeur-parolier-guitariste Bernd Köhler l'a réalisée. (GER)

■ **589** Couverture d'un disque de Kitaro. La chanson qui y est illustrée s'intitule «Tenku». (USA)

■ **590** Couverture de l'album «Trois Œuvres orchestrales Opus 6 - A la mémoire d'un ange» (Pinchas Zukerman/Pierre Boulez/Berg) paru dans la série des *CBS Masterworks*. (USA)

■ **591** Album «Louis Armstrong joue W.C. Handy» dans la série *Columbia Jazz Masterpieces*. L'enregistrement original y a été converti en numérique. (USA)

■ **592** Dans la même série que précédemment, un disque du sextette Benny Goodman illustré pour CBS Records. (USA)

■ **593** Portrait de Rudolf Serkin jouant du Bach et du Haydn sur un disque de la série *Artist Laureate Masterworks* de CBS. (USA)

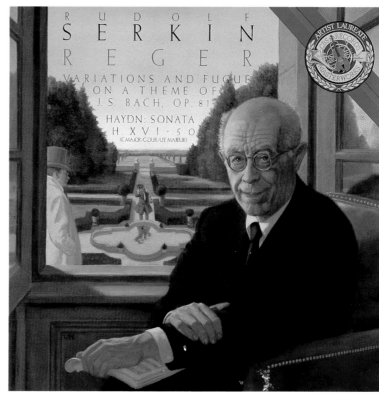

DESIGNER:
Allen Weinberg

LETTERING:
Georgina Lehner

PUBLISHER:
CBS Records

■ 590

ART DIRECTOR:
Allen Weinberg

DESIGNER:
Allen Weinberg

PUBLISHER:
CBS Records

■ 591

DESIGNER:
Allen Weinberg

ILLUSTRATOR:
Bill Nelson

PUBLISHER:
CBS Records

■ 592

DESIGNER:
Allen Weinberg

ILLUSTRATOR:
Robert Van Nutt

PUBLISHER:
CBS Records

■ 593

■ **594—596** Cover and double spreads from the book *Katzengeschichten* (Cats' Tales) – and the cat is the main protagonist in all the stories. Cover illustration relates to an excerpt from an old German tale "Tomcat Murr Learns to Read". Top: illustration to Kipling's *The Cat Goes Her Own Way*. Bottom: illustration for "When the Cat Wasn't at Home". (GER)

■ **597—600** Dustjacket and spreads from the *Banana Republic Guide to Travel & Safari Clothing*. The authors are founders of a mail-order/retail clothes stores called *Banana Republic*. This book (not a catalog) offers anecdotes and historical facts and quotations about "tough" clothing. (USA)

■ **594—596** Umschlag und Doppelseiten aus dem Buch *Katzengeschichten* mit Beiträgen von berühmten Autoren. Die Umschlagillustration bezieht sich auf einen Auszug («Kater Murr lernt lesen») aus E.T.A. Hoffmanns Erzählung, die anderen Abbildungen gehören zu Kiplings *Die Katze geht ihre eigenen Wege* und zu der Erzählung *Als die Katze nicht zu Hause war*. (GER)

■ **597—600** Schutzumschlag und Seiten aus einem *Bananen-Republic*-«Führer für Reise- und Safari-Kleidung». Die Autoren sind Gründer der Versand/Ladenkette für Bekleidung der Marke *Banana Republic*. Dieses Buch enthält Anekdoten, historische Tatsachen und Zitate über strapazierfähige Kleidung. (USA)

■ **594—596** Couverture et doubles pages du livre *Katzengeschichten*, un recueil d'histoires de chats d'auteurs célèbres. L'illustration de couverture se réfère à un extrait de conte («Le Chat Murr apprend à lire») d'E.T.A. Hoffmann. Les deux autres illustrations concernent (en haut) «Le Chat suit son propre chemin», de Kipling, (en bas) «Quand le chat se fut absenté». (GER)

■ **597-600** Jaquette et doubles pages du «Guide des tenues de voyage et de safari» *Banana Republic*, dont les auteurs sont les fondateurs de la chaîne de magasins et de V.P.C. *Banana Republic*. On trouve dans ce guide des anecdotes, des faits d'histoire et des citations relatifs aux vêtements solides. (USA)

ART DIRECTOR:
Hartmut Brückner

DESIGNER:
Hartmut Brückner

ILLUSTRATOR:
Peter Fischer

AGENCY:
Petra Much, art consultant

PUBLISHER:
Ellert & Richter Verlag

■ **594-596**

ART DIRECTOR:
Stephen McNabb/Alex Jay

DIRECTOR OF PRODUCTION:
Fred Dodnick

DESIGNER:
Alex Jay/Studio J/
James R. Harris

PHOTOGRAPHER:
Carl Mydans/Time/
Life Picture Archive

PUBLISHER:
Ballantine Books

■ **597-600**

ART DIRECTOR:
Jackie Merri Meyer/
Barbara Buck
DESIGNER:
Irv Freeman
ILLUSTRATOR:
Nancy Stahl
PUBLISHER:
Warner Books
■ 601

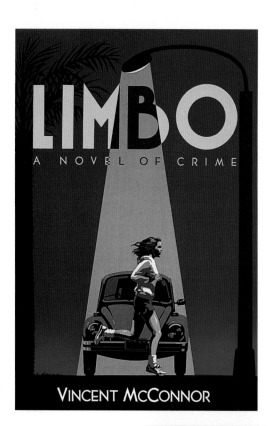

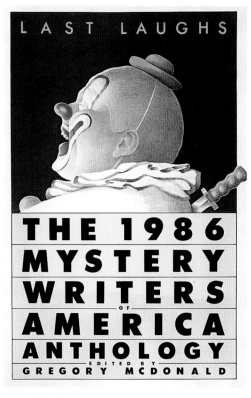

ART DIRECTOR:
Jackie Merri Meyer
DESIGNER:
Fred Mercellino
ILLUSTRATOR:
Fred Mercellino
PUBLISHER:
Warner Books
■ 602

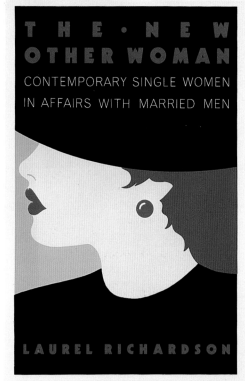

ART DIRECTOR:
Jackie Merri Meyer
DESIGNER:
Scot Carouge
ILLUSTRATOR:
Scot Carouge
PUBLISHER:
The Free Press/MacMillan
■ 603

■**601** Cover of a crime novel entitled *Limbo* published by the *Mysterious Press, Warner Books.* (USA)

■**602** Cover of an anthology of mystery stories by American authors published by *Mysterious Press, Warner Books.* (USA)

■**603** Cover of a book published by *Free Press.* (USA)

■**604-611** Dustjacket and spreads from *Ideas on Design*, a 160-page book about the international design partnership Pentagram. The illustrations, mostly colored, are neatly captioned with purpose of design, briefing and method. First published by *Faber & Faber Ltd.* (GBR)

■**601** Umschlag eines Kriminalromans in Taschenbuchform, erschienen in einer Krimi-Reihe von *Warner Books.* (USA)

■**602** «Letztes Lachen» ist der Titel dieses Buches mit einer Sammlung von Kriminalgeschichten. *Warner Books.* (USA)

■**603** Buchumschlag für «Die neue andere Frau». (USA)

■**604–611** Schutzumschlag und Doppelseiten aus «Ideen zum Thema Design», ein Buch über Aufträge und Design-Lösungen des internationalen Design-Studios Pentagram. Die Illustrationen, mehrheitlich in Farbe, sind von Angaben über Zweck, Aufgabe und Methode begleitet. Erstausgabe bei *Faber & Faber.* (GBR)

■**601** Couverture du roman policier *Limbo* paru en poche aux Editions *Mysterious Press, Warner Books.* (USA)

■**602** Couverture d'un recueil d'histoires mystérieuses d'auteurs américains. *Mysterious Press, Warner Books.* (USA)

■**603** Couverture d'un livre de *Free Press (MacMillan).* (USA)

■**604–611** Jaquette et doubles pages d'*Ideas on Design*, un ouvrage de 160 pages consacré au studio international de design Pentagram. Les illustrations, pour la plupart en couleurs, sont accompagnées de références complètes – objectif, mission, méthode. 1re édition chez *Faber & Faber Ltd.* (GBR)

ART DIRECTOR:
Alan Fletcher

DESIGNER:
Alan Fletcher/
Debbie Martindale

AGENCY:
Pentagram

PUBLISHER:
Pentagram

■ 604-611

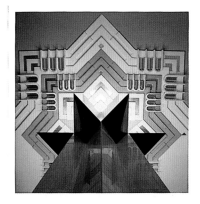

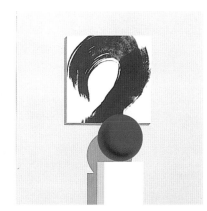

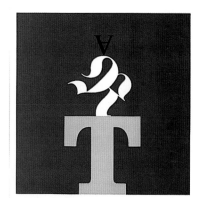

ART DIRECTOR:
Judith Loeser

DESIGNER:
Carin Goldberg

ILLUSTRATOR:
Gene Greif

AGENCY:
Carin Goldberg Design

PUBLISHER:
*Random House/
Vintage Books*

■ **612**

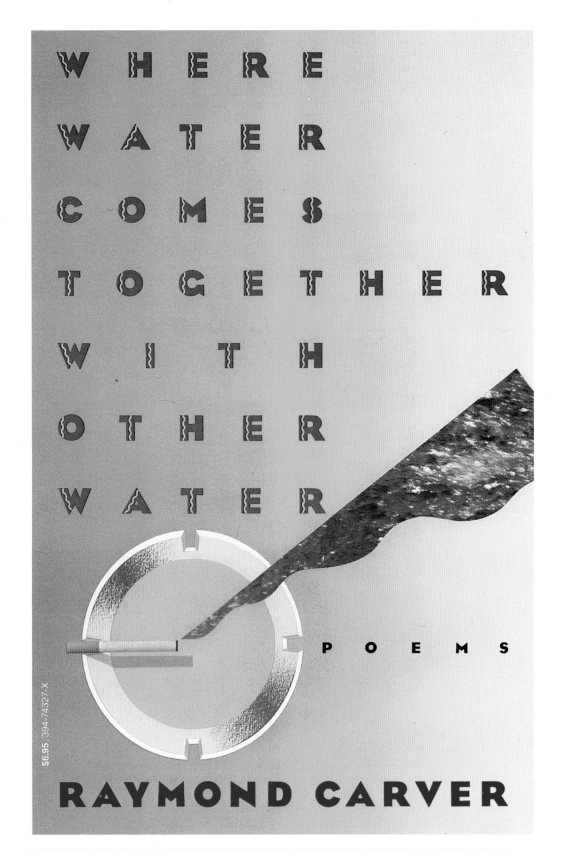

■ **612** Cover of a book containing poems by Raymond Carver, published by *Vintage Books*. (USA)

■ **613** Cover of a paperback of the comedy play "A Filling Station" which premièred on 10 January 87 in Amsterdam. (NLD)

■ **614** Cover of *Inside the Cold War* by John Sharnik, published by Arbor House Publishing Co. (USA)

■ **615** Paperback cover of the Spanish edition of a novel by Italian writer Italo Calvino. (SPA)

■ **616** Cover of a paperback novel entitled "Anarchists Thank Goodness", published by *Alianza Editorial*. (SPA)

■ **612** Umschlag für ein Buch mit Gedichten von Raymond Carver, «Wo Wasser mit anderem Wasser zusammentrifft». (USA)

■ **613** Umschlag für ein Taschenbuch mit der Komödie «Eine Tankstelle», die in Amsterdam aufgeführt wurde. (NLD)

■ **614** Der kalte Krieg zwischen Osten und Westen ist Gegenstand des Buches, zu dem dieser Umschlag gehört. (USA)

■ **615** Umschlag für eine spanische Taschenbuchausgabe eines Romans von Italo Calvino. (SPA)

■ **616** Umschlag eines Taschenbuches mit dem Titel «Anarchisten, Gott sei Dank», Verlag *Alianza Editorial*. (SPA)

■ **612** Couvertures d'un recueil de poésies de Raymond Carver, «Où les eaux se mêlent à d'autres eaux». (USA)

■ **613** Couverture du poche «Une Station-Service». Il s'agit d'une comédie créée le 10 janvier 1987 à Amsterdam. (NLD)

■ **614** Couverture d'*Inside the Cold War* (A l'intérieur de la Guerre froide) par John Sharnik, aux Ed. *Arbor House*. (USA)

■ **615** Couverture d'un roman de l'Italien Italo Calvino paru en poche en traduction espagnole. (SPA)

■ **616** Couverture du roman «Anarchistes, Dieu merci» paru en poche aux Editions *Alianza Editorial*. (SPA)

ART DIRECTOR:
Paul Koeleman
DESIGNER:
Paul Koeleman
ILLUSTRATOR:
Paul Koeleman
AGENCY:
Paul Koeleman
PUBLISHER:
Het Publiekstheater
■ 613

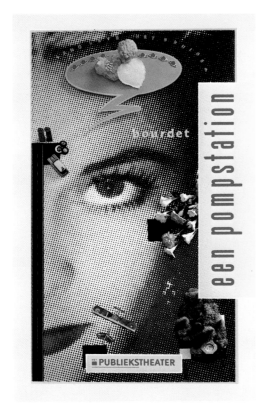

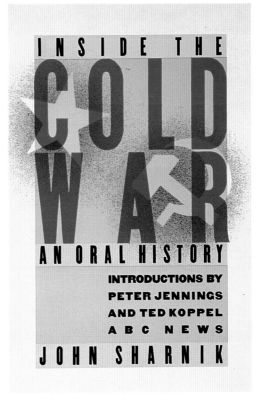

ART DIRECTOR:
Dorothy Wachtenheim
DESIGNER:
Carin Goldberg
PUBLISHER:
Arbor House Publishing Co.
■ 614

DESIGNER:
Daniel Gil
PHOTOGRAPHER:
Daniel Gil
PUBLISHER:
Alianza Editorial, S.A.
■ 615

DESIGNER:
Daniel Gil
PHOTOGRAPHER:
Daniel Gil
PUBLISHER:
Alianza Editorial, S.A.
■ 616

ART DIRECTOR:
Louise Fili
DESIGNER:
Dugald Stermer
ILLUSTRATOR:
Dugald Stermer
PUBLISHER:
Pantheon Books
■ 617

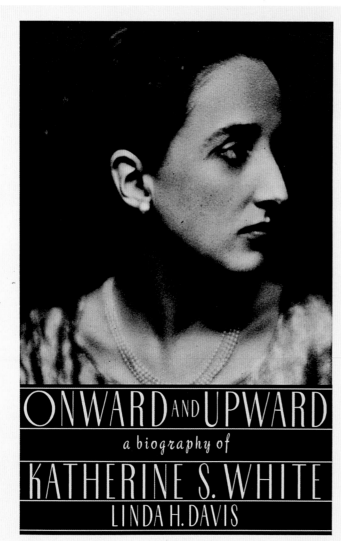

ART DIRECTOR:
Joseph Montebello
DESIGNER:
Julie Metz
PUBLISHER:
Harper & Row
■ 618

ART DIRECTOR:
Joseph Montebello
DESIGNER:
Carin Goldberg
PUBLISHER:
Harper & Row
■ 619

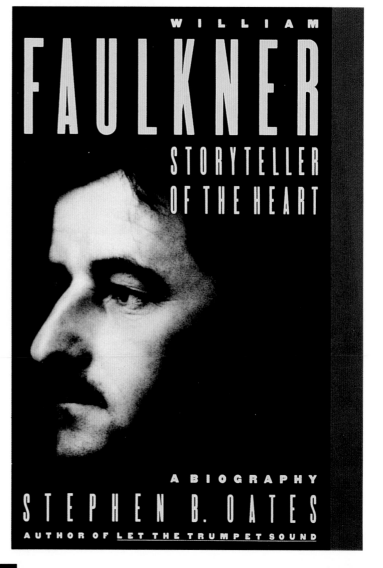

■ **617** Cover for a book of short stories published by *Pantheon Books* on the subject of European peasantry overcoming advancing industrialization. (USA)

■ **618** *Onward and Upward* - cover of a biography of Katherine S. White, published by *Harper & Row*. (USA)

■ **619** Cover for a biography of William Faulkner published by *Harper & Row*. (USA)

■ **620** Cover for Ionesco's *Rhinoceros*. (IRN)

■ **617** Umschlag für ein Buch mit Kurzgeschichten über den Kampf der Bauern Europas gegen die Industrialisierung, erschienen bei *Pantheon Books*. (USA)

■ **618** Umschlag mit einem Schwarzweissporträt für eine Biographie, erschienen bei *Harper & Row*. (USA)

■ **619** Umschlag für eine Biographie von William Faulkner, erschienen bei *Harper & Row*. (USA)

■ **620** Umschlag für Ionescos *Die Nashörner*. (IRN)

■ **617** Couverture d'un recueil de nouvelles paru dans *Pantheon Books*, sur le thème de la résistance paysanne contre l'industrialisation croissante en Europe. (USA)

■ **618** Couverture d'une biographie de Katherine S. White, *Onward and Upward*, illustrée d'une photo noir-blanc. (USA)

■ **619** Couverture d'une biographie de William Faulkner publiée par *Harper & Row*. (USA)

■ **620** Couverture pour *Rhioncéros* d'Ionesco. (IRN)

DESIGNER:
Ardeshir Mohasses
ILLUSTRATOR:
Ardeshir Mohasses
PUBLISHER:
Javaneh Publications
■ **620**

ART DIRECTOR:
Judith Loeser
DESIGNER:
Carin Goldberg
AGENCY:
Carin Goldberg
PUBLISHER:
*Random House/
Vintage Books*

■ **621**

ART DIRECTOR:
D. Wachtenheim
DESIGNER:
Karen Katz
PUBLISHER:
Arbor House Publishing Co.
■ 622

COMRADE CHAIRMAN

SOVIET
SUCCESSION
AND
THE RISE OF
GORBACHOV

RICHARD OWEN

■ **621** Cover (in original size) of James Joyce's masterpiece *Ulysses*, an edition published by *Random House*. (USA)

■ **622** Cover (in original size) of *Comrade Chairman* by Richard Owen, published by Arbor House Publishing Co. (USA)

■ **621** Umschlag in Originalgrösse für eine bei *Random House* erschienene Ausgabe von James Joyce' *Ulysses*. (USA)

■ **622** «Genosse Vorsitzender», Umschlag in Originalgrösse für ein Buch über den Aufstieg Gorbatschows. (USA)

■ **621** Couverture au format original d'une édition d'*Ulysses* par James Joyce publiée par *Random House*. (USA)

■ **622** Couverture grandeur nature de *Comrade Chairman* (Camarade Président) de Richard Owen. (USA)

Kleine
Boote

KLEIN·BILD·BAND 7
JÜRG ANDERMATT

W O L K E N

KLEIN·BILD·BAND 8
JÜRG ANDERMATT

ART DIRECTOR:
Ingo Wulff
DESIGNER:
Ingo Wulff
PHOTOGRAPHER:
Jürg Andermatt
PUBLISHER:
Nieswand Verlag
■ **623, 624**

■ **623, 624** Covers in actual size for "Small Picture Books", a series published by Nieswand Verlag, Kiel. Left, the title is "Small Boats" and right, the title is "Clouds". (GER)

■ **625–628** Paperback covers in the series of stories created by Stuart Palmer in which a female sleuth, Miss Hildegarde Withers, is faced with solving the mystery. (USA)

■ **623, 624** Umschläge in Originalgrösse für zwei «Klein-Bild-Bände», eine Buchreihe des Nieswand Verlags, Kiel, mit Aufnahmen von Jürg Andermatt. (GER)

■ **625–628** Umschläge für eine Taschenbuchreihe mit Kriminalgeschichten von Stuart Palmer, in welchen ein weiblicher Detektiv, Hildegard Withers, die Fälle löst. (USA)

■ **623, 624** Couverture grandeur nature pour la collection des «Petits Albums Photo» des Editions Nieswand de Kiel, à g. «Petits bateaux», à dr. «Nuages». Photos Jürg Andermatt. (GER)

■ **625–628** Couvertures d'une série de policiers par Stuart Palmer où une femme détective, Miss Hildegarde Withers, élucide toutes sortes de mystères. Collection de poche. (USA)

ART DIRECTOR:
Krystyna Skalski

DESIGNER:
Krystyna Skalski

ILLUSTRATOR:
John Jinks

PUBLISHER:
Bantam Books

■ 625–628

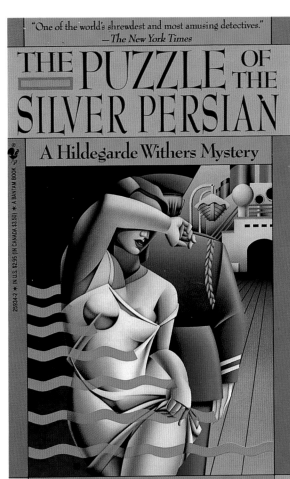

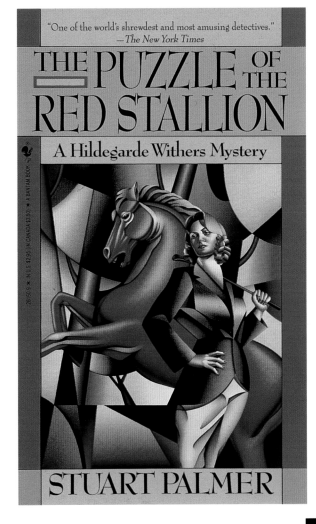

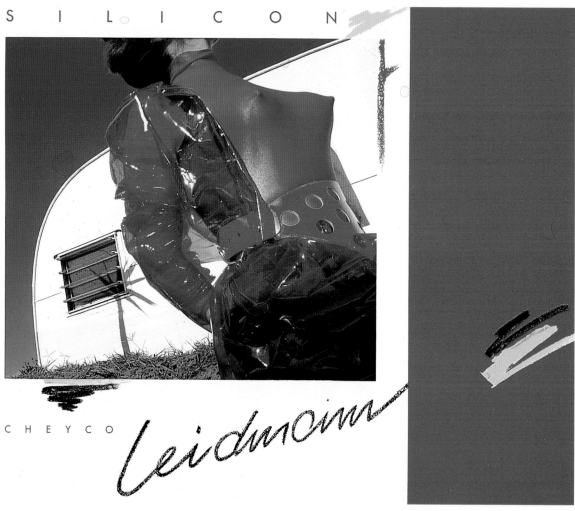

S I L I C O N

CHEYCO *Leidmann*

DESIGNER:
Cheyco Leidmann
PHOTOGRAPHER:
Cheyco Leidmann
PUBLISHER:
Octobus Creative Medium
■ 629

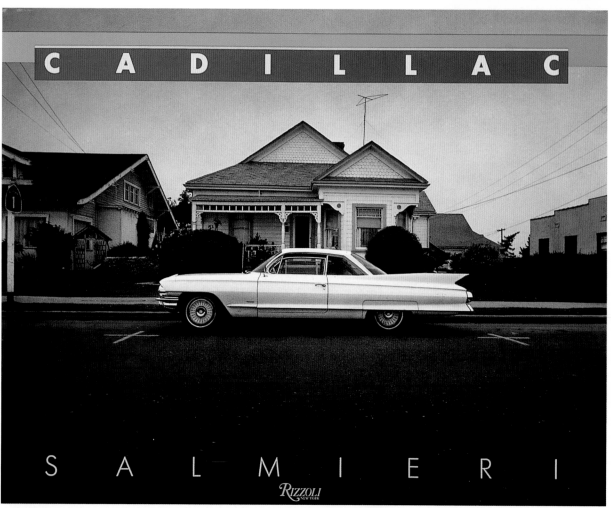

C A D I L L A C

S A L M I E R I

RIZZOLI
NEW YORK

ART DIRECTOR:
*Walter Bernard/
Milton Glaser*
DESIGNER:
*Walter Bernard/
Milton Glaser*
PHOTOGRAPHER:
Stephen Salmieri
AGENCY:
WBMG, Inc.
PUBLISHER:
Rizzoli
■ 630

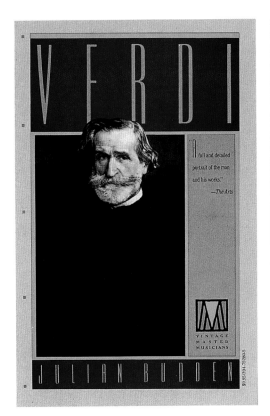

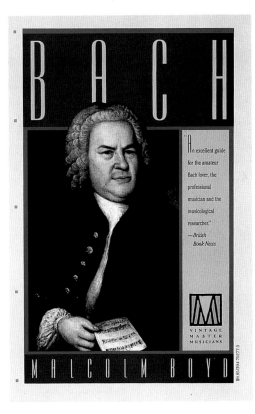

ART DIRECTOR:
Judith Loeser

DESIGNER:
Carin Goldberg

AGENCY:
Carin Goldberg Design

PUBLISHER:
*Random House/
Vintage Books*

■ **631–633**

■ **629** Cover of a book by Paris-domiciled photographer/designer Cheyco Leidman entitled *Silicon*, published by the *Octobus Creative Medium*. (USA)

■ **630** Dustjacket of a book with over 80 handcolered black-and-white photographs devoted to the Cadillac. (USA)

■ **631–633** Three covers for books in the *Master Musicians* series published by *Vintage*: Verdi, Wagner and Bach. (USA)

■ **629** Umschlag für ein Buch des in Paris lebenden Photographen Cheyco Leidmann, mit dem Titel *Silicon*, erschienen bei *Octobus Creative Medium*. (FRA)

■ **630** Schutzumschlag mit handkolorierter Schwarzweissaufnahme für ein Buch mit dem Titel *Cadillac*. (USA)

■ **631–633** Drei Umschläge aus der Buchreihe «Meister der Musik», hier Verdi, Wagner und Bach. (USA)

■ **629** Couverture d'un ouvrage du photographe et designer Cheyco Leidmann, qui vit à Paris. Intitulé *Silicon*, il a paru aux Editions *Octobus Creative Medium*. (FRA)

■ **630** Jaquette de *Cadillac*, un ouvrage illustré de 80 photos noir et blanc coloriées à la main: les modèles *Cadillac*. (USA)

■ **631–633** Trois couvertures pour la série *Master Musicians* des Editions *Vintage*: Verdi, Wagner et Bach. (USA)

ART DIRECTOR:
Jack Woody
DESIGNER:
Jack Woody
PHOTOGRAPHER:
Alice Springs
PUBLISHER:
Twelvetrees Press
■634

FRANK THIESS
TSUSHIMA
IL ROMANZO DI UNA
GUERRA NAVALE

JULIEN GREEN

LEVIATAN

ART DIRECTOR:
Lidia Guibert Ferrera
DESIGNER:
Lidia Guibert Ferrera
AGENCY:
Lidia Guibert Ferrera
PUBLISHER:
C.D.E., Gruppo Mondadori
■635

ART DIRECTOR:
Lidia Guibert Ferrera
DESIGNER:
Lidia Guibert Ferrera
DESIGNER:
Tamara De Lempitzki
AGENCY:
Lidia Guibert Ferrera
PUBLISHER:
C.D.E., Gruppo Mondadori
■636

■**634** Dustjacket (portrait of Anjelica Huston, Los Angeles 1983) and various spreads from the book *Alice Springs: Portraits*, a limited edition of 3000 casebound copies; full-page black-and-white portraits of famous people, issued by *Twelvetrees Press*. (USA)

■**635** Dustjucket of a novel by Frank Thiess "Tsushima: The Story of a Naval War", describing the tragic battle of the Russian fleet at Tsushima (Korean Straits) against the Japanese. (ITA)

■**636** Book cover of a novel entitled *Leviathan*, published by *C.D.E. Gruppo Mondadori*. (ITA)

■**634** Schutzumschlag und verschiedene Doppelseiten aus einem Buch mit schwarzweissen Porträtaufnahmen der Photographin Alice Springs. Auf dem Umschlag Anjelica Huston, Los Angeles 1983. Limitierte Auflage von 3000 Exemplaren, erschienen bei *Twelvetrees Press*. (USA)

■**635** Schutzumschlag eines Buches von Frank Thiess über die tragische Seeschlacht zwischen der russischen und der japanischen Flotte im Jahre 1905 bei Tsushima. (ITA)

■**636** Umschlag für ein Buch mit dem Titel *Leviatan*, erschienen bei *C.D.E. Gruppo Mondadori*. (ITA)

■**634** Jaquette ornée d'un portrait d'Anjelica Huston (Los Angeles 1983) et diverses doubles pages du livre *Alice Springs: Portraits*: portraits noir et blanc, pleine page, de célébrités. Tirage limité à 3000 exemplaires, publié par les Editions *Twelvetrees Press*. (USA)

■**635** Jaquette d'un roman de Frank Thiess, «Tsushima: histoire d'une guerre navale», à propos de la défaite d'une escadre russe par les Japonais dans les eaux coréennes. (ITA)

■**636** Couverture du roman *Leviathan* publié par le groupe d'édition *C.D.E. Gruppo Mondadori*. (ITA)

No! Contemporary American DADA

2. By "Modernism," unless noted, I mean the aesthetic rebellion which appeared in the late 19th century, and ranged from the Romantics through Symbolism.

3. Courbet, for example, attacked the French government to its Salt of the Messias, 1848–9. A government cannot treat them as it did though it should not have been, and it had floundered with considerable ideas at times. The revolt within a political action did. David was executed by his caricatures of the bourgeois King as a Gargantua. Courbet was held responsible for the destruction of the Vendôme column, imprisoned, and was then freed, lived in exile; he fled to exile.

4. As quoted in Malcolm Bradbury and James McFarlane, Modernism (Harmondsworth: Penguin Books, 1976), p. 33.

5. As quoted in ibid., p. 20.

6. As quoted in ibid.

7. By "Modernism" I mean the art movement in which emerged during the first I.d as years of this century. It includes a continuation and a reaction to modern 19th century "Art." As for both Modernism counted Cubism, Futurism, German Expressionism, Dada and Surrealism among its manifestations.

8. Dada's relations to Futurism were antithetic. Of all Modern "isms Futurism had been the only one to be militant, but it had stopped short of an actual revolt to, and though this militancy was also its un-Dada part and the culture, Futurism had worshipped war and technology. Dada was the very opposite. It even rejected the expressionist milieu from which it arose; Dada had emerged as a reaction against the prevailing aesthetic. George Grosz said an expressionist style in his brutal attacks on society and the political games it plays. The approach has survived today under the Neo-Expressionist label.

9. Stephen Spender, "Moderns and Contemporaries," in The Struggle of the Modern (London: Hamish Hamilton Ltd., 1963), p. 46.

10. Ibid.

then art for life's sake.² But a minority, Goya, Géricault, Daumier, Courbet and to a lesser extent Millet, also referred to contemporary political and social issues, and even suffered when they translated these views into action, e.g., Daumier and Courbet.³ Such involved artistic rebellion meant a direct confrontation with the authorities, as the rebellious artist expanded his arena of action from art to life.

But by the outbreak of World War I a new change in sensibility had taken place, and one which set the tone for our present way of life and thoughts. It came into being when artists and writers alike realized that their world was not quite like that of the past, even though there was not agreement as to exactly when this change had occurred. Virginia Woolf, for example, considered that "on or about December 1910 human nature changed . . . All human relations shifted . . . And when human relations change there is at the same time a change in religion, conduct, politics and literature."⁴

In 1930 Herbert Read remarked that "the contemporary revolution . . . is not so much a revolution, which implies a turning over, even a turning-back, but a break-up, a devolution, some would say a dissolution. Its character is catastrophic."⁵ And as late as 1954 C. S. Lewis wrote: "I do not think that any previous age produced work which was, in its own time, as shatteringly and bewilderingly new as that of the Cubists, the Dadaists, the Surrealists, and Picasso has been in ours."⁶ This pinpoints the new aesthetics that developed from these changes: Modernism.

Modernism was a mushrooming of different movements which in more or less modified form have continued to the present. They appeared in response to the emergence of our modern world and its life-style, a world dominated by technology and depersonalization and by an ever increasing multiplicity of world problems of international dimensions, yet a world that continues to stress nationalism, as it did during World War I. Of these Modern rebellions the most extreme was Dada: it not only rejected tradition but the Modern "isms" as well, and in its confrontation with them, set the modern spirit in action.⁷

Describing the modern artists' responses to their world, Stephen Spender wrote: "The faith of the moderns is that by allowing their sensibility to be acted upon by the modern experience of suffering, they will produce, partly as the result of unconscious processes, and partly through the exercise of critical consciousness, the idioms and forms of a new art. The modern is the realized consciousness of suffering, sensibility and awareness of the past."⁸

Following Spender's terminology, I am inclined to consider Dada as a variation (or travesty) of the "Voltairean 'I'" rather than place it completely within the modern spirit. Like the "Voltairean 'I'," the

11. The political character of Dada was mostly manifested in Berlin, with George Gross, John Heartfield and others. For an excellent account of the political aspects of Dada, see Christopher Middleton, Dada-ism in Art and Other Paintings Writings (Manchester: Carcanet New Press, 1976), pp. 36-51.

12. Spender, "Moderns," p. 44.

13. As quoted in Gerd Kessel, Letters from Bohemia (Garden City, New York: Doubleday & Company, 1955), pp. 136-39.

14. Tristan Tzara, "Dada Manifesto on Feeble Love and Bitter Love," Seven Dada Manifestos and Lampisteries (New York: Riverrun Press, 1981), p. 14. Emphasis added.

15. A few earlier artists had been almost dada in character, before Dada began as a movement - Goya, Daumier and Courbet for example. But Goya for one walked the fine line between revolt and subordination to the Spanish court. The more outspoken Daumier clashed to adopt himself to the wishes of governmental policies, even though he had suffered by his satirical cartoons. And while Courbet may be considered the first scandalous painter of modern times, he was so in the anti-social character but he did not venture to question them. Besides, Courbet aimed for the public's understanding of his work — for a body that understanding is immaterial. For him, the public merely ceases to be of concern, as he paid little heed. The notorious Théophile Gautier and the Decadents cannot be considered as true dadas, even if they did develop shock as a fine art. Extravagantly dressed, smoking hashish and giving odd parties, they hit hard to confront the public with its own faddies. They publicized the idea of "art for art's sake" and did not arrive at "art for life's sake." Furthermore, most of these poseurs adhered to a number of principles. The pre-World War I independent spirit arose being, by its own volition, amoral forces at times, or purely destructive as others, it was not subordinate to any particular political, religious, social or philosophical ideology, even though it may have been called upon by political means. Dada did not cater to permission, duty and morality. Dada annihilated the concept of nationalism, and thereby the notion of duty that it implies.

Dadas for the most part were activists. In the widest sense of the term. But in contrast to the "nationalist, sociological, political and responsible,"¹¹ writing of the "Voltairean 'I'," the Dada's writing is irrational, antisocial, "irresponsible" and for the most part apolitical. And yet the Dadas shared with the "Voltairean 'I'" the capacity of being "clear sighted social prophets in a world of confusion."¹²

In contrast to the Modern, Dada was existential in character; it encompassed all facets of behavioral and intellectual negation. It even rebelled against itself. George Gross, a prime figure in Berlin Dada, stated:

*We are, I shall say, revolutionists; whatever is more important than one human being we are prepared to revolt against. Our final battle cry will be, "down with the Dadaists." Also "down with Dadaism." At that time . . . I will be proud to fight as a traitor, which is the secret of progress.*¹³

In his own manner Gross had echoed Tzara's manifesto: "the real dadas are against DADA."¹⁴

In its penchant for the negative, Dada carried negation to the very limits of meaning: it created a topsy-turvy world in which rationality was replaced by the irrational, art became anti-art, aesthetics were replaced by anti-aesthetics and banality was exalted as art. As a critique of the Modern, Dada introduced an alternative; as a critique of itself it proposed no alternatives.

Dada, however, was more than another critique in the evolution of modernist criticality, for Dada arose from the gathering of rebels sharing an unusual attitude to life, one independent of individual backgrounds, nationalities and ideas. This state of mind I call dada.¹⁵ What is dada?

Whenever there is an independent spirit accountable only to himself, questioning all traditions yet giving rise to no rules, respecting all individual rights and self-expression, we find a dada. And when dadas coalesce, we find a movement: Dada. But Dada is more than a particular aggregate of extremist individuals (which can exist in an ivory tower); Dada is direct confrontation with society in which individual anarchism is acquiescent to group activities. As dadas can exist independently of any given Dada movement, what I will call DADA is the sum total of individual dadas and the diverse manifestations of Dada. Distilling from each their rebellious essence, DADA is the most complex and most radical form of negation.

ART DIRECTOR:
Douglas Wadden
DESIGNER:
Douglas Wadden
AGENCY:
Design Collaborative
PUBLISHER:
Henry Art Gallery
◀ ■637-639

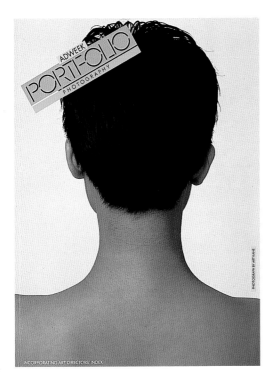

ART DIRECTOR:
Walter Bernard/
Milton Glaser
DESIGNER:
Walter Bernard/
Milton Glaser
PHOTOGRAPHER:
Matthew Klein
AGENCY:
WBMG, Inc.
PUBLISHER:
A/S/M Communications, Inc.
■640

ART DIRECTOR:
Walter Bernard/
Milton Glaser
DESIGNER:
Walter Bernard/
Milton Glaser
PHOTOGRAPHER:
Art Kane
AGENCY:
WBMG, Inc.
PUBLISHER:
A/S/M Communications, Inc.
■641

ART DIRECTOR:
Walter Bernard/
Milton Glaser
DESIGNER:
Walter Bernard/
Milton Glaser
PHOTOGRAPHER:
Matthew Klein
AGENCY:
WBMG, Inc.
PUBLISHER:
A/S/M Communications, Inc.
■642

■**637–639** *No: Contemporary American Dada* – a case-bound two-volume catalog of an exhibition of the same name at the Henry Art Gallery. Shown opposite, top: covers of Part 1, Part 2, and the case; below: two spreads. (USA)

■**640–642** Covers of three examples from a series of *Adweek Portfolios.* Here a complete listing guide to creative services - from actors to typographers; a guide listing American photographers and samples of their work and a guide featuring the work of designers and listing design services, professional organizations and contests. (USA)

■**637–639** «Nein: die zeitgenössische amerikanische Dada-Bewegung.» Zwei Kataloge im Schuber für eine Ausstellung in der Henry Art Gallery. Gegenüber, oben: Umschläge von Teil 1 und 2 und der Schuber; darunter zwei Doppelseiten. (USA)

■**640–642** Umschläge für drei Führer aus einer Reihe von *Adweek.* Hier ein Band über kreative Dienstleistungen, ein Spektrum, das von Schauspielern bis zu Typographen reicht; ein Band mit Adressen und Arbeitsbeispielen amerikanischer Photographen und ein Band mit Arbeitsbeispielen von Designern und Adressen von Studios, Berufsverbänden und Wettbewerben. (USA)

■**637–639** *No: Contemporary American Dada* (Non: le dadaïsme contemporain en Amérique), catalogue d'exposition de la Henry Art Gallery. Ci-contre: en haut, les couvertures des 2 volumes et l'emboîtage; en bas, deux doubles pages. (USA)

■**640–642** Couvertures de trois guides de la série *Adweek Portfolios*, annuaire des services créatifs, des comédiens aux typographes; annuaire des photographes américains illustré d'exemples de travaux; annuaire des designers, services de design, associations professionnelles et councours-expositions offrant également des échantillons de travaux représentatifs. (USA)

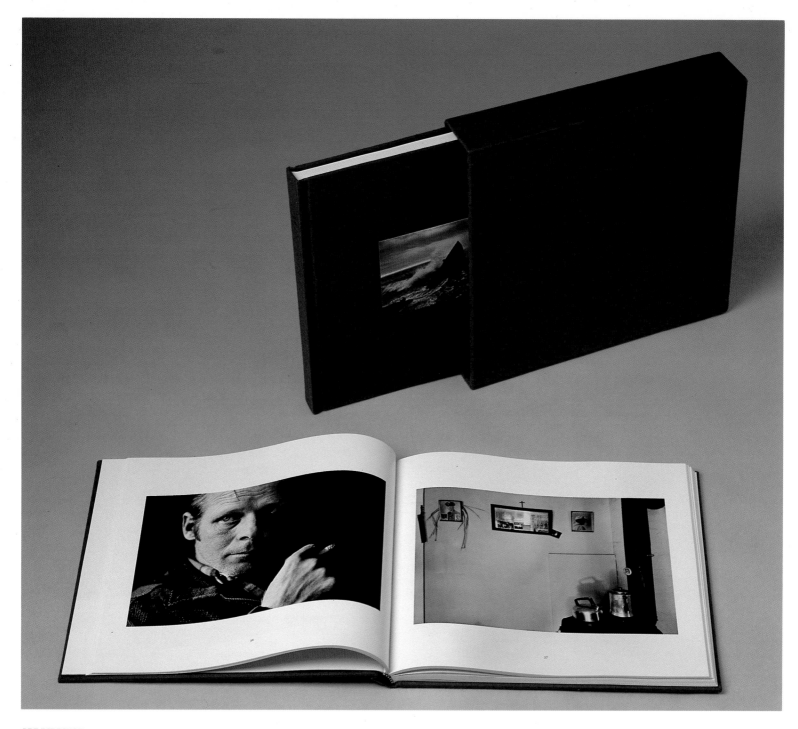

ART DIRECTOR:
Adelaide De Menil
DESIGNER:
Helen Buttfield
PHOTOGRAPHER:
Dan Budnik (Cover)
Lynn Johnson
PUBLISHER:
Random House, Inc.
■**643**

■**643** Views of two richly-produced linen-bound volumes (in matching slipcase) entitled *Men's Lives - The Surfmen and Baymen of the South Fork.* The books are part of the Long Island Fisherman Project. They contain black-and-white photos and drawings depicting a community of fishermen. (USA)

■**643** Ansichten von zwei Bänden (Leinenband, mit Schuber) mit dem Titel *Men's Lives,* die im Rahmen eines Projektes zugunsten der Fischer eines bestimmten Küstenstreifens entstanden sind. Die Bücher enthalten Schwarzweissaufnahmen und Zeichnungen, die das Leben dieser Fischer zeigen. (USA)

■**643** Ces deux volumes à la présentation luxueuse, reliés pleine toile sous emboîtage idoine, font l'inventaire d'un projet d'aide aux pêcheurs de Long Island sous le titre de *Men's Lives* (Vies d'hommes). On y trouve des photos noir et blanc et des dessins de la communauté de pêcherie. (USA)

INDEX

VERZEICHNIS